FORD FLATHEAD V-8
Builder's Handbook

By Frank Oddo

FISHER
er
BOOKS™

Publishers:	Bill Fisher	
	Howard Fisher	
Editor:	Bill Fisher	
Assistant:	Alison Fisher	
Technical Editorial Assistance:	Bill Herbert	
	Bill Ewing	
	Gene Scott	
Reprints of Early Ford Service Bulletins:	Dan Post Publications	
Cover Design:	Gary Smith, Performance Design	
Book production:	Randy Schultz	
Front cover photo:	Brendan Tucker	
Photography:	Frank Oddo	

Published by Fisher Books
4239 W. Ina Road, Suite 101
Tucson, AZ 85741
(520) 744-6110

© 1997 Fisher Books

Printed in U.S.A.

Printing 10 9 8 7 6 5 4 3 2 1

**Library of Congress
Cataloging-in-Publication Data**

Oddo, Frank.
    Ford Flathead V-8 builder's handbook / Frank Oddo.
       p.   cm.
    ISBN 1-55561-119-2
    1. Ford automobile—Motors—Maintenance and repair.
    2. Ford automobile—Motors—Modification.   I. Title.
    TL215.F7033 1997
    629.25'04—dc21   96-47929
                                     CIP

Front cover:
    My three sons: Frank is at top left, Angelo on the right and Tony is kneeling. Born into the world of hands-on hot rodding, all learned to drive in my '40. Angelo came home from the birthing hospital in the '40.

Inside Front cover:
    God Bless the Flatheads plaque on Al Drake's roadster. Photo by Al Drake.

Back cover:
    Flatheadder's dream garage scene at Williams Garage in Canfield, Ohio. Ron Williams, a true flathead enthusiast and collector, provided the photo.

Notice: The information in this book is true and complete to the best of our knowledge. It is offered without guarantees on the part of the author or Fisher Books. The author and publisher disclaim all liability in connection with the use of this book.

Table of Contents

Introduction iii

1.   The Origin & Evolution of the Ford Flathead V-8 1

2.   Buying & Disassembling a Flathead 13

3.   Inspecting & Derusting the Cylinder Block 23

4.   Reconditioning the Cylinder Block & Selecting Critical Components 29

5.   Flathead Breathing and Selecting Valve-Train Components 45

6.   Building the Bottom End: Installing the Crank & Cam 59

7.   Finishing the Valve-Train Installation 71

8.   Installing the Piston/Rod Assembly 77

9.   The Fluids, Modern Oil Filtering & Traditional Cooling 87

10. Capping Off the Block: Selecting & Installing Cylinder Heads 97

11. The Induction System: Carburetors & Manifolds 107

12. Supercharging: Forced Induction for the Flathead 117

13. Modern Flathead Ignitions & the Rest of the Electrical Story 125

14   Installation & Fire-up 131

15   The Flathead Buyers Guide 139

Dedication

Twenty-five years ago we were "walking the course" one Saturday afternoon on El Mirage Dry Lake. This is a ritual held the day preceding SCTA Time Trials. Its purpose is safety. A human drag net visually sweeps the course looking for debris that might cut a tire or otherwise endanger a hot rod at speed. The participants search for anything non-biodegradable—nails, glass, etc.

The most frequent offenders, however, are the bits and pieces of scattered engines, transmissions and rear ends—the shrapnel of racers past. The trash may have been deposited the preceding month, the preceding season, or two decades earlier. Who's to say? Pieces can lay buried under the hard alkali soil for many years only to be churned up during the rainy season when dirt bikers and 4WD enthusiasts crisscross a muddy lake bed hell-bent for mischief.

A triangular bit of rusty metal caught my attention, and I picked it up. It was only when I noticed the cast-in "5" that I realized what it was: the top of a 59AB bellhousing casting.

I do not know when the clutch or flywheel explosion occurred. Perhaps it was the year previous, 1971 . . . or 1951. I dropped the scrap iron into my pocket as a memento. A memento of what, I was never quite sure until recently.

* * *

This book is dedicated to all those who have spent countless hours squeezing the flathead in a never-ending search for better performance.

Foreword

In mid-1995 Bill Fisher at Fisher Books asked me to write a book on rebuilding the Ford flathead V-8. I eagerly accepted the assignment. What better subject could a member of the performance automotive press ask for than traditional street rodding's most-beloved engine? I was concerned about one thing: What could I possibly add to a saga that had been chronicled for nearly 50 years? I had written no less than 26 magazine articles on this one engine.

The first series I wrote for *Street Rodder Magazine* called "How To Build The Really Right Flathead" appeared in 1984. A second series appeared in 1994. Respectively, they provided the most up-to-date flathead-rebuild information I could find at the time. Judging by requests for reprints over the ensuing years, both were eagerly accepted by the magazine's readers.

As I continued to think over the project, I realized that what had always concerned me was the editorial space-allotment requirement that limits a magazine article to a very few pages. That always meant either reducing the size or number of photographs—or the detail in the body copy—or all three.

The length of a magazine series also falls prey to the editor's red pencil. Ten or 12 installments are always considered more than enough. A magazine by its very nature is meant to appeal to a variety of tastes, albeit within a specialized genre.

On the other hand, a book not only frees the writer to put in as much detail as he would like, it also frees the reader from worrying lest he miss an installment. The whole story is right there before him. He can pick a particular subject if he wishes, reading it and savoring it thoroughly. He can save the remainder of the book for more leisurely reading at another time. Or, he can read the book from first to last page at his own leisurely pace.

I updated and brought together all the procedures, products, resources and services uncovered in my original sojourns into the world of the flathead. I also took full advantage of the opportunity to build an engine for the roadster that is only a twinkle in my eye at this time.

Building my own engine alongside the comments and endeavors of my resource colleagues has proved a great advantage. There are details that I would have surely overlooked otherwise. Therefore, even though the Ford flathead story is an old one, I remain hopeful that by the time the last page of this most current work is turned, at least a few readers who fired up their first Ford flathead V-8 in the 1930s, 40s or 50s will have learned a thing or two.

Acknowledgments

For sharing their knowledge of the Ford flathead V-8 with me, I'd like to express my immense gratitude to Mark Kirby of Motor City Flathead, Allen Hail of Hail's Automotive Machine Shop and street rodder Jim Bremner of Forties Limited. I also thank Tom Vogele and his editorial predecessors at *Street Rodder Magazine* for suggesting a number of flathead-related topics and then publishing my efforts through the years. Many other people were generous with their time and assistance, and for that I am very grateful. I have attempted to identify them and their services throughout the book.

Frank Oddo
Brea, California
June 1997

Author Frank Oddo

Frank Oddo in his favorite "easy chair" behind the wheel of his 1940 Ford coupe, Desire.

* * * *

Frank Oddo is no stranger to hot rodding having been immersed in the subject since he first leafed through a *Hot Rod* magazine in 1951. He was 14 at the time, and only old enough to envy the young men of his New Orleans neighborhood all of whom seemed to drive flathead-powered, black 1939 and '40 Ford coupes!

The premier local street rod of the day belonged to Knot Farrington, who also operated a speed shop in the city. (For those who have a *Hot Rod* Magazine collection, Knot's '39 was featured in the April 1954 issue.) His shop was the locus of Crescent City street rodding, and Oddo was one of many teenage hangers-on soaking up flathead and hot rod lore on Saturday mornings. By 1955, Oddo was driving his own black '40 coupe, first with flathead, then eventually Cadillac power.

Oddo moved to Southern California in 1960 for no reason other than the region was the Mecca of hot rodding. A second '40 coupe was acquired, and in 1968, a third. It, now owned and driven for nearly 30 years, is his most treasured material possession. Inasmuch as his street rod photojournalism career commenced at the same time, the

coupe has earned the undisputed title as the World's Most Photographed 1940 Ford, having appeared in a significant percentage of his hundreds of "how to" magazine articles and "advice columns."

Oddo is best known for his 25-year contribution to *Street Rodder* Magazine and *Truckin'* Magazine. He has also written for the Ford Motor Company's *Ford Times, Rod & Custom* Magazine, *Hot Rod* Magazine and the British publication *Street Machine* as well as non-automotive periodicals. His *Street Rodders Handbook*, published by HPBooks, has been in print for 11 years and is still a brisk seller.

Today, Oddo divides his professional time between automotive photojournalism and Vintage Auto Body & Paint, the street rod and classic car restoration facility in Brea, California he co-owns with Bonneville/Dry Lakes racing partner John Hesford. In their spare time, Oddo and Hesford campaign their Ford 429-powered '40 Ford Comp Coupe and Boss 302-powered belly tank lakester. Oddo set the 225 MPH D/Gas Blown Lakester record at the 1996 Bonneville National Speed Trials.

1

The Origin & Evolution of the Ford Flathead V-8

*Our single object . . . is making motors
and putting them on wheels." - Henry Ford*

In terms of an efficient, modern transportation power plant, the Ford 90-degree, side-valve, L-Head V-8 is an engine that should have had the good sense to slip quietly into the pages of automotive history in 1954. However, it hasn't and probably never will. The flathead has assumed an undeniable mystique among many in the hot rodding fraternity, and in so doing has become one of the most famous internal-combustion engines of all time.

It is an engine that has been buried more than once, only to be resurrected by an enthusiast certain that he has found some new and innovative way of squeezing out yet another horsepower. Since its inception, the Ford flathead V-8 has always been more than just an engine, a device for doing work. First it was the centerpiece of the Depression-Era Ford Motor Company. Then it became the mainstay of the American hot-rod sport from the late 1930s until the mid-1950s. Today, it is the Prima Donna of the street rodding hobby. It has had a glorious past and a still promising future. It always has been, and always will be center-stage when hoods are lifted.

If today's amateur engine builder doesn't know where he's coming from, however, it's more difficult to know where he's going. Therefore, I'll kick off this "how-to book" with a brief look at the only part of the story that hasn't changed since 1932, the origin of the beloved Ford flathead V-8.

* * * * *

As far as can be determined with accuracy, Henry Ford's dream of a ground-breaking engine for his automobiles began in late 1929 when he gave engineers in the Company's experimental division the task of designing an engine larger and more powerful than his ubiquitous Model A four-banger. Ford was known to dislike inline six-cylinder engines because "the crank is too long and will wind up." Obviously then, an inline *eight* was out, and that left only one realistic design option—the V-8.

The V-8 configuration had been more-or-less proven, but only up to a point. Cadillac, Cunningham, LaSalle and Henry's own newly acquired Lincoln Motor Car Division had all produced successful V-8 engines, but their manufacturing design was such that the cylinder block and the crankcase were *bolted* together. Henry didn't like that, but what intrigued him about the Cadillac overhead-valve (OHV) engine was the exhaust manifolds bolted to the cylinder heads. Nevertheless, he felt OHV engines were too complicated for economical manufacture because they were composed of so many parts. There was another consideration as well—with an OHV, he could not recycle previous Ford engine development.

What Henry wanted was a bit unusual for a Vee engine configuration in those days—a one-piece casting,

1

The very first production flathead V-8 reposes almost unheralded in the cluttered aisles of the Henry Ford Museum in Dearborn, Michigan. It may be a mere afterthought in the minds of busy curators, but it is the unquestioned impetus that nurtured and developed today's far-reaching world of amateur, hands-on motorsports, a world we know as *hot rodding.*

sometimes called the *monobloc design.* Only two contemporary American V-8s were built that way, the 1929 Oldsmobile Viking and the 1930 Oakland Pontiac. Unfortunately, monobloc or *en bloc casting* as it was also called, required expensive tooling and manufacturing procedures. The engineering department doubted that a monobloc V-8 could be justified in a low-priced car.

Ah, but the low-priced car was Henry's forte; a 30-year achievement that had greatly benefited the American motoring public. He wasn't about to give up that crown. The engineers continued to argue against Henry's V-8 aspirations, pointing out that it put the company between a rock and a hard place: two-piece V-8 castings were complicated and expensive; one-piece V-8 castings were expensive and complicated. Characteristically, Ford sloughed off their pessimism saying, "Anything that can be drawn up can be cast." He wanted an economically produced monobloc V-8, and that was it.

The experimental engine group acquiesced and went to work in the secretive "Blue Room" of the Engineering Laboratory in early 1930. The Blue Room was staffed with the best and brightest automotive brain power, and state-of-the-art technology was at their disposal. When badgered by industry reporters during the incubation period of the V-8, Ford snapped, "In our engineering laboratory we are equipped to do almost anything we care to do, but our method is the Edison method of trial and error."

To many, however, the effort smacked more of capriciousness than Edisonism. After all, the company was still functioning under a virtual, and not always benevolent dictatorship. Only Henry had access to the entire operation, often assigning specific projects to individuals unbeknownst to their colleagues.

The most critical project, though, was the one-piece cylinder block. Ford was sure he already had a man on the payroll capable of handling that assignment: "Cast-Iron Charlie" Sorensen, the production-line wizard who had developed the proven method of pouring the one-piece Model T block.

Ford instructed Sorensen that he wanted the simplicity of outside exhausts and the economy of the L-head (side-valve) design. Sorensen, well aware that this had not been achieved previously (certainly not on the grand scale that Ford envisioned) nevertheless set to work. Of course, he had the vast resources of the Ford Motor Company at his disposal, resources that included the world's largest foundry—the massive 30-acre Rouge River plant . . . and $750 million of investment capital if needed!

With that kind of financial horsepower, Henry's brainchild moved quickly, if sometimes unsteadily, from the drawing board through the foundry and on to the machine shop. The year 1930 was a busy one indeed.

In early 1931, the first V-8 was installed on a wooden stand and fired up by a steam engine bolted to the back of it. More work ensued, and by mid-year self-starting prototype motors were fitted to dynamometers in the

Engineering Building. They were still experimental models, however, and had such ungainly features as front and rear exhaust ports exiting high up on the ends of the cylinder block.

The original port configuration was eventually redesigned, even though the final design has long been identified as the primary reason for overheating problems. An insight into Ford's acquiescence to the ultimate layout was suggested by Emil Zoerlein, the designer of the flathead ignition system. Ford lived in Detroit, a city noted for below-zero winters, and he believed his customers would appreciate an engine that warmed up quickly in cold weather!

Other Ford dictates, such as offsetting the crankshaft relative to the centerline of the cylinder block 0.265-inch, and full-floating big-end rod bearings remained in force even though they created headaches for the engineers. Economical designs were difficult, and the benefits were questionable.

The practice of offsetting the crankshaft in the direction of piston side thrust was called the *DeSaxe principle* after a French engineer. It was believed to offer smoother running and less piston slap. Several earlier automobile manufacturers subscribed to the principle, and a few modern engines have their piston pins offset for the same reason.

Ford also liked over-square engines, that is, those where the bore diameter is greater than the length of the stroke as in modern engines. He also favored lightweight crankshafts. He believed the combination of these two features meant less cylinder wear and less stress on the crankshaft that in turn contributed to greater reliability. These too, were not to be.

The flathead would forever and always remain an under-square engine with an uncommonly heavy crank— even as bore diameters grew. In fact, these particular features were not significantly achieved until the arrival of the thin-wall OHV V-8 (of the same displacement) 30 years later.

Although secrecy continued to rule the roost at the Blue Room, in mid-December 1931 *Automotive Industries Magazine* scooped the rest of the trade papers with the article "Make an Eight

Unquestionably, two of the most advanced hot rods of the immediate pre- and post-war years was Stu Hilborn's 1929 A/V-8 street and lakes roadster, and his all-out dry- lakes streamliner. The engine that powered the roadster (and later transferred to the streamliner) was a 1934 21-stud 239 cubic inch *carbureted* flathead. But don't let the fact that it was carbureted fool you. Hilborn, who later developed racing's most successful fuel injection, was obviously not content with a conventional induction system even in the early years. Eddie Miller, a former Indy 500 driver, designed and built the manifold for three Stromberg "E" carbs and one Stromberg "EE" carb. This set-up assisted Hilborn in reaching 124 MPH in the roadster and later, 139 MPH in the streamliner. The carbs were fed by a Miller-designed dual-fuel-pump system. Miller also ground the camshaft by hand! Photos courtesy Stu Hilborn.

One of the finest examples of pre- and post-war street rods existent today is John Athans 1929 Model A roadster atop Deuce (1932) rails. Originally built by Athans in 1937 and upgraded following World War II (hence the milled 59AB heads on the 24-studder) it lays claim not only to being a "living" monument to the way things were in the golden days of hot rodding, but was also driven by Elvis Presley in the 1957 movie *Loving You.* The imposing headers were built by Athans out of "a bunch of Model A manifold goosenecks."

Nearly every belly tank built with the exception of Bill Burke's very first and this subsequent Burke creation piloted by Jack Avakian, were balanced, efficient mid-engine designs. A few, however, had more conventional front-engine layouts and an almost streetable flathead with only two carburetors. Photo courtesy Bill Burke.

says Ford!" True, it was only speculation, but on December 7, 1931 Henry stopped four-cylinder-engine production to concentrate on the changeover to the V-8.

New production equipment had to be designed to deal with the complexity of the V-8. But in three months, as chief engineer Laurence Sheldrick recalled, ". . . this thing was whipped into shape." Readying the production line of the Ford flathead was indeed a 90-day wonder. Ultimately, it took but one hour for the metal to go from smelting pot to solid cylinder block.

On February 11, 1932 the *Detroit* *News* hit the streets with front-page headlines announcing, not that a major war had erupted or that President Hoover had miraculously taken the country out of the Depression, but that the Ford Motor Company would soon introduce its long-awaited new engine!

The *News* considered this event worthy of a place on the front page, and in headline type to boot.

Everybody "in the know" assumed that the lower-priced cars the middle class could afford would always be powered by undernourished inline four- and six-cylinder engines. V-8s would always be exclusively reserved for expensive prestige cars. The newspaper obviously had an interest in the virility of the predominant segment of its industrial community. It was apparent that the new engine would be good for Ford's business. That, in turn, would be good for southeastern Michigan, perhaps even the whole country!

It must have touched a national nerve as well, for within 24 hours most of the major newspapers in the United States had reprinted the story on their own front pages. It was more than simply good business news. The American motoring public *had* long hungered for a moderately priced automobile with a more powerful engine. The appetite for horsepower, then as now, is never appeased for long. Seizing the moment, Ford bought full-page advertisements in nearly 2,000 American and Canadian newspapers a few weeks later.

Nevertheless, for all the intense activity, production V-8s didn't come off the assembly line until March 9, 1932. On that day, a beaming Henry Ford personally stamped the serial number on the engine now residing in the Ford Museum: 18-1. That number wasn't meant to read "Eighteen Dash One," however. The digits "one" and "eight" designated the *first* Ford *eight* cylinder engine and the second "one" heralded the *first* of the breed. Nevertheless, as momentous as that event was, it was equally modest; only 38 complete engines were produced on the initial run.

Finally, on March 31, the new engine and its handsome host car were publicly displayed in Ford showrooms around the country. If tickets had been sold, it would have been a sell-out. It was reported that more than 5,500,000 people came to see what Henry had built *this* time.

* * * * *

In the 1920s and '30s Henry Ford had become a bonafide American hero to the public at large, first with the Model T, then with the Model A. In 1932, the public put its money where its collective heart was, for within the next few days more than 200,000 orders were placed. Three-quarters of them were for the new V-8. Still, it is interesting that 25 percent of those orders were for the old, but improved, inline four-cylinder engine. Even so, that option was only to last only two more years.

As one even vaguely familiar with flatheads might expect, the early V-8 days were not exactly sweetness and light. Surprise! The 1932-33 engines had trouble with cracks in the cylinder blocks near the valve ports. Blocks also suffered from casting porosity.

There were some maintenance headaches as well. Henry had expressly wanted a distributor mounted on the front of engine driven directly off the camshaft, and in July 1930 he had assigned the task of a new ignition system to Emil Zoerlein. It was a job well done, even if the points couldn't be adjusted *in place*. The distributor had to be removed and put on a test bench for even a minor adjustment!

The original intake manifold also proved wanting, but in 1934 David Anderson of the Bohn Aluminum Company designed the over-and-under manifold. It is probably stretching a point to say that this was the first piece of speed equipment for the flathead, but later aftermarket multiple-carburetor manifolds did not significantly improve upon the design proper. Bohn also was the Original Equipment Manufacturer (OEM) of aluminum-alloy pistons, 1933 cylinder heads, oil pans and distributor housings.

Typical of Ford thinking, i.e., save money on development, tooling and production costs by using last year's inventory, Model A water pumps were

Contrast it with its contemporary, a Tattersfield-Baron 4-carb-equipped Deuce roadster. There may have been significant differences of opinion with regard to cams, cylinder heads and induction in the post World War II Lakes days, but not when it came to the basic racing engine. For all practical purposes, 4-bangers and OHV 6-cylinder engines were rare, and Henry's V-8 reigned supreme. Photo courtesy Tony Baron.

The first dragster, also called a *rail job* for obvious reasons was *The Bug* fielded by Dick Kraft and Marvin Webb of Orange County, California. "The car we ran at the Lakes was complete, but every week we just knocked a little more weight off. Finally, we jerked the body and put on a '27 T cowl. The whole thing weighed about 1200 pounds. By then it was so light it would spin the wheels, so we put a 500-pound barbell set across the back. Ha! Then it wouldn't get going! Later we tried double wheels which didn't work out. A 296-inch motor just spun the wheels more, so we went to a 268-inch motor." By October 15, 1950, Kraft was turning a shade under 114 MPH with the Potvin cam and triple-carbed engine on alcohol. "The last time I ran, we threw the jets away and just used the dump tubes!" Photo courtesy Dick Kraft.

incorporated into the engine. The result only added to the ongoing overheating problems until a new pump system was designed for the 1937 model year.

By then, most of the major engine problems were solved. And if not solved, were at least deemed inconsequential by owners pleased with a no-frills 85-HP, 20-MPG car with a

In the late 1960s and early 1970s the flathead was just barely hanging on in street rod circles. The cars that sported them often seemed to represent stragglers from a bygone era as witness these two with split, stock wishbone front suspension and generators. The perseverance of their owners paved the way for an updated approach to nostalgia rodding.

maximum speed of over 90 MPH! As such, the flathead V-8 engine would live on "almost unchanged and unchallenged" for 21 years . . . and Ford would sell 25 million of them.

The Flathead and Early Hot Rodding

The first time a flathead saw a race track was when Fred Frame took his 1932 Indy 500 Victory Lap in a Ford V-8 roadster. By 1933, however, both amateur and professional racers began

to recognize the competitive potential of the V-8. That year, the first recorded victory of a flathead in a motorsports event took place—believe it or not—in Viet Nam! 'Nam, of course, was known as French Indo-China at the time, and the trophy for the Hanoi "Ford Day" 10-Kilometer Race went to one Madame A. Dassier.

That was only the beginning. The first seven places in the Elgin Road Race went to Ford V-8 powered "Specials." From there on the pros reg-

ularly fielded modified V-8 powered cars. In 1935, ten front-wheel-drive Ford-powered Miller race cars were entered in the Indianapolis 500. All were equipped with Bosch ignition systems and Bohnalite aluminum cylinder heads. Three different intake manifolds were used, a Hexagon Tool Company of Dearborn dual and two different Miller four-carb manifolds.

What the professionals did is only of tangential interest to present day hot rodders. To them, no matter how well the professionals performed, what really counts is what their peers—shade-tree mechanics and amateur weekend racers—did with Henry's cast-iron maiden.

As can be expected, shortly after V-8 motors made their appearance in wrecking yards, they were dropped between the grille and firewall of Southern California hot rods. The "A/V-8" was born in the home garage of some unknown, but not forgotten West Coast hot rodder in the late 30s.

Of the 182 entries listed in the Southern California Timing Association (SCTA) Dry Lakes program for May 28, 1939, 55 (or 30 percent) were powered by stock or mildly modified V-8s. At first, milled heads and a two-carb manifold were the most common modifications. High-lift cams came later. The Ford Model T and Model A engines were highly refined by that time, however, and they continued to set the lion's share of dry lakes records. It is not hard to understand why.

Hot rodders were familiar with the basic four-cylinder engine and its readily available aftermarket performance components. Speed equipment had been available for Ford four-cylinder engines since the 1920s. Add to the mix a couple of non-mechanical, but oh-so-human characteristics—loyalty to a known entity and just plain resistance to change—and you have the reason. No matter, it wasn't long before the "suped" V-8 would take over. (The word is "suped" not "souped." It was originally coined from "super," meaning a highly modified engine or car.)

A few manufacturers of four-cylinder equipment, most notably George Riley and Col. Alexander, made OHV conversions for the flathead. And Art

Sparks (later of Forged-True Piston fame) made a few conventional high-performance heads. But little bolt-on speed equipment was available for the flathead until the late 1930s. Before the decade ended, however, Southern California hot rodders had finally realized that the "bent eight" could produce more power with more reliability than the best four-banger, and speed-equipment experimentation began in earnest.

Karl Orr was modifying carburetors, Tom Spalding, Jim Kurten, Chuck Potvin and others were building dual-coil ignitions using Lincoln-Zephyr coils on a Ford distributor, Pierre "Pete" Bertrand and Ed Winfield were grinding cams, and Wayne Morrison cast an aluminum intake manifold for two carburetors in 1938. Unfortunately, the carburetors were placed side by side. That, and the fact that Morrison only advertised in the limited circulation *SCTA Racing News* prevented his manifold from gaining any widespread popularity.

It wasn't until Eddie Meyer started casting high-compression aluminum cylinder heads for both the early 21-stud Ford blocks and the "late-model" 24-stud engines that things really got moving. By 1939 Meyer, Jack McAfee, and Tommy Thickstun were offering inline dual-carburetor manifolds, and because the standard generator could be used, they were suitable for the street. Vic Edelbrock built his first dual intake manifold in 1939 and by 1941 Phil Weiand, Mal Ord and Dave Burns had joined the manifold wars. There were lots of others, so don't fault me for leaving out the long list that would be required to name all of the makers and brands.

Then there was a four-year intermission until the real War was over.

* * * * *

By the time the last World War II GIs were mustered out of military service, most of the serious hot-rod competition was built around the V-8. Best of all, the flathead (although it still wouldn't be called that until the overheads appeared in 1949) was just as

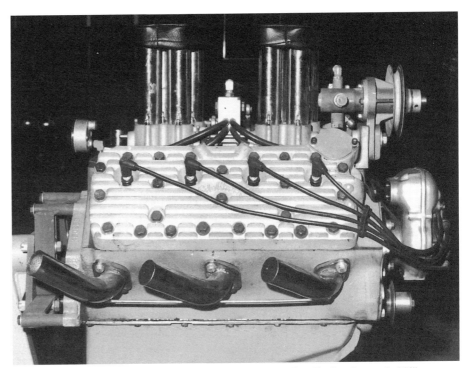

The 1970s also saw a resurgence of nostalgia flathead racing. During that period Mike McCloskey and Greg Jordan of the United Flathead Racers Association fielded an injected flathead in a digger. Below: Not to be outdone, this supercharged flathead was campaigned by Wayne Atkinson of the Utah Salt Flats Racing Association at Bonneville. Yes, "late-model" sheet metal surrounds Atkinson's decidedly un-late flatmotor. (But I'll never tell.)

much at home in a street roadster as it was in a dry lakes racer. The Ford flathead V-8 had surpassed all other engines in both arenas as the powerplant of choice, and it would remain so until the mid-1950s.

The death knell was sounded by the postwar overhead valve V-8 engines. First it was the Cadillac and Oldsmobile OHVs that debuted in the 1949 models. Then to a lesser extent it was the 1951 Chrysler, and finally the 1955 Chevy. They dug the grave, nailed the coffin shut and shoveled the dirt on top, at least as far as all-out competition was concerned. By 1956, fewer and fewer flatheads were showing up in any winner's circle.

Resurgence of the time-honored flathead in modern street rodding really took hold in the early 1980s. A prime example of the state of the art at that time (and today) is this resto-rodded 1940 DeLuxe Ford coupe owned by Bill Schmidt of New Orleans, Louisiana. Edelbrock-equipped with a "3/4-race" cam, the otherwise stock-bodied coupe is exquisitely detailed. Photo courtesy Don Winn.

Today, amateur engine builders like Jim Bremner (above) and professionals like Mark Kirby (right) are turning out flatheads that reflect the best of both the traditional and modern street rodding worlds. Efficient induction and electrical systems are but a few of the improvements foisted upon the 1930s brain child of a notoriously stubborn Henry Ford.

Flathead power was losing favor with street rodders at about the same rate. By the early 1960s the small-block Chevrolet V-8 was king. Some 50 pounds lighter, it had the same general dimensions and produced more than enough horsepower for the street in its mildest form. The average rodder began to feel out-of-step if his car was powered by a flathead Ford. In the 25 years following the introduction of the Chevy, you couldn't give a stock flathead away. Even street rods with full-dress flathead power were noticeably rare at rod runs. Young spectators at such events had to be informed that the strange-looking engine with the thin, finned aluminum heads covered with shiny "acorn" nut covers were what hot rod motors looked like in the good old days.

The flathead was a bewhiskered ghost of the past.

The Flathead and Modern Street Rodding

Then rampant nostalgia reared its grey-haired head, and the perception of proper street rod power began to change. Beginning in 1980 or so, street rodders running flatheads were no longer merely humored; they were regarded as bearers of the torch of tradition.

Today, flatheads are almost the "in thing." Almost. Many street rodders who pride themselves on having a daily

driver are aware of the indisputable reputation of the average old-timey flathead—a hot-running little devil that couldn't hold its own against a stone-stock OHV, even if it were given every advantage the speed-equipment industry has to offer. When it comes to horsepower, cubic inch for cubic inch, the flathead just isn't engineered as well as the typical OHV.

But that's not the real reason some nostalgia buffs are gun-shy about building one. It's street reliability. That is, smooth, tractable power from 0 to 60 MPH . . . and a temperature gauge that stays within the "Normal" range (180 to 200F) hour after hour on the road.

Admittedly, the average homebuilt, mildly modified flathead has its work cut out for it if it has to go head-to-head with a stock 300 or 350 cubic inch OHV V-8 engine in terms of street reliability. This is not to say that a reliable street flathead can't be built. For our purposes, and in that context, reliability is a relative concept. One man's flathead should only be compared to another man's flathead.

Well, here we are, 65 years since the flathead was introduced to the motoring public. It has become evident that a significant percentage of practicing street rodders are interested in building a flathead for the street. They just don't want problems. They don't want an engine that runs hot, starters that drag, generators that will or will not charge a battery, mechanical fuel pumps that quit delivering whenever they feel like it, or neat-looking carburetors that pee gasoline all over the place!

You guessed it, today's street rodder is a practical fellow who loves hot rod tradition, but not to the point of cutting off his nose to spite his face. He wants to eat his cake and keep it too. Can't be done? Who sez?

A flathead Ford V-8 can be built that will be reliable, cool-running and good-looking in the old-time, traditional way. Yet it can still have enough horsepower so as not to denigrate the whole concept of hot rodding. And in the truest hot rod tradition, much of it can be done at home. All it takes is patience. First, you must have the patience to locate the best block possible. Then the patience to prepare that block properly and to see its assembly through to completion in a precise, orderly fashion. The bottom line is this: if you want yours to fully satisfy you, it can't be just an "average" flathead.

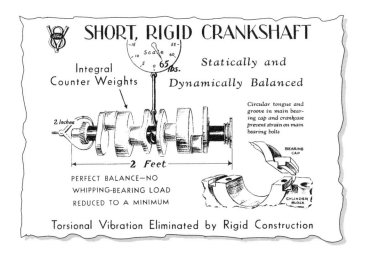

Top: This full-dress flathead of the late 1990s is not a "full-race" killer motor inasmuch as the owner/builder chooses street rod runs rather than a race course to show off his nostalgic creation. The most popular settings seem to be within the grille and firewall of a roadster. And why not? A classic fenderless roadster will always provide the most prominent display of the preeminent classic hot rod engine. Lower photos: Typically, two carbs or three top off an Edelbrock or Offenhauser manifold with Edelbrock or Offenhauser finned aluminum cylinder heads as a side dish. Alternators have replaced generators for the most part, but the vast variety of header designs often define the personal tastes of the owners. Photos courtesy Casey Charles.

The raw material is available; there are plenty of flatheads out there. Brand-new parts and reconditioning services abound. And all the performance equipment you could realistically want is just a phone call away. No need to spend years along the swap-meet trail looking for an intake manifold or a pair of cylinder heads, unless of course you must have an original Morrison side-by-side manifold and original Eddie Meyer heads.

You just have to know where to begin . . .

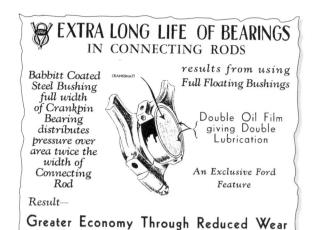
GENERAL SPECIFICATIONS

Ford

Ford sales literature and service manuals were sometimes at odds on "advertised" maximum horsepower and torque figures.

Year	Disp. (cu.in.)	Bore/Stroke	BHP @RPM	Torque (Ft. Lbs.)	@RPM
1932	221.0	3.062x3.750	65@3400	139	@1500
1933	221.0	3.062x3.750	75@3800	145	@1500
1934	221.0	3.062x3.750	85@3800	147	
1935	221.0	3.062x3.750	85@3800	147	@2000
1936	221.0	3.062x3.750	85@3800	147	@2000
1937	136.0	2.600x3.200	60@4200	94	@2500
1937	221.0	3.062x3.750	85@3800	150	@2000
1938	136.0	2.600x3.200	60@3500	94	@2500
1938	221.0	3.062x3.750	85@3500	155	@2200
1939	136.0	2.600x3.200	60@3500	94	@2500
1939	221.0	3.062x3.750	85@3500	155	@2200
1940	136.0	2.600x3.200	60@3500	94	@2500
1940	221.0	3.062x3.750	85@3500	155	@2200
1941	221.0	3.062x3.750	90@3800	155	@2200
1942	221.0	3.062x3.750	90@3800	156	@2200
1946-48	239.4	3.187x3.750	100@3800	180	@2000
1949	239.4	3.187x3.750	100@3600	180	@2000
1950	239.4	3.187x3.750	100@3600	181	@2000
1951	239.4	3.187x3.750	100@3600	187	@1800
1952	239.4	3.187x3.750	110@3800	194	@1800
1953	239.4	3.187x3.750	110@3800	196	@1800

Mercury

Year	Disp. (cu.in.)	Bore/Stroke	BHP @RPM	Torque (Ft. Lbs.)	@RPM
1940	239.4	3.187x3.750	95 @3800	170	@2100
1941	239.4	3.187x3.750	95 @3800	176	@2100
1942	239.4	3.187x3.750	100 @3800	176	@2100
1946-48	239.4	3.187x3.750	100 @3800	180	@2000
1949-50	255.4	3.187x4.000	110 @3600	200	@2000
1951	255.4	3.187x4.000	112 @3600	206	@2000
1952	255.4	3.187x4.000	125 @3700	218	@1700
1953	255.4	3.187x4.000	125 @3800	218	@1700

Ford Engine Configurations

1932-mid 1936
21-stud heads, water pumps in heads, full-floating rod bearings, poured babbit main bearings, timing gear pressed onto camshaft

mid-1936
21-stud heads, water pumps in heads, full floating rod bearings, insert main bearings, timing gear pressed onto camshaft

1937-early 1938
21-stud heads, water pumps in block, water outlets center of cylinder heads, full-floating rod bearings, insert main bearings, timing gear pressed onto camshaft

Late 1938-48
24-stud heads, water pumps in block, water outlets center of cylinder heads, full-floating rod bearings, insert main bearings, timing gear bolted to camshaft

1949-53
24-stud heads, water pumps in block, water outlets center of cylinder heads, individual rod bearings, insert main bearings, two oil holes in each crank rod journal, timing gear bolted to camshaft. Distributor moved to top right front of engine. Bolt-on bellhousing

Mercury Engine Configurations

1939-48
24-stud heads, water pumps in block, water outlets center of cylinder heads, full-floating rod bearings, insert main bearings, timing gear bolted to camshaft

1949-53
24-stud heads, water pumps in block, water outlets center of cylinder heads, individual rod bearings, insert main bearings, two oil holes in each crank rod journal, timing gear bolted to camshaft. Distributor moved to top right front of engine. Bolt-on bellhousing.

REFERENCES:

Batchelor, Dean. *The American Hot Rod.* Osceola, WI: Motorbooks International, 1995.

Oddo, Frank. "Back When Drag Racing Was Fun!" *Street Rodder Magazine,* February 1975. pp. 48-53.

Oddo, Frank. "Karl and Veda Orr: Hot Rod Pioneers." *Street Rodder Magazine,* January 1976. pp. 34-37.

Oddo, Frank. "The Elvis Presley Roadster." *Street Rodder Magazine,* March 1978. pp. 29-30.

Oddo, Frank. "Tanks For The Memories." *Street Rodder Magazine,* July 1993. pp. 70-80.

Oddo, Frank. "Stuart Hilborn: From The Lake Bed To The Brickyard." *Street Rodder Magazine,* December 1993 pp. 134-139.

Thacker, Tony. *'32 Ford-The Deuce.* London, England: Osprey Publishing Limited, 1984.

Serious nostalgia: Mike Russell's classic '50s fenderless cream-and-red roadster. Engine has rare Frenzel supercharger and Elco Twin heads. Spark plugs are fired by a Nash Twin 8 distributor on a right-angle adapter at the front of the engine. Previous owner James Moomjean used the car as a rolling billboard for his used-car business in Merced, California. Allen Osborne photographed the car at the Pleasanton Good Guys meet in 1996.

DOUBLE-PUMP COOLING SYSTEM

Safe—Under the Most Trying Conditions

2 WATER PUMPS

EXHAUST OUTLET WATER COOLED

A Wall of Water encloses each cylinder

Valve Seats are also protected, preventing valve distortion

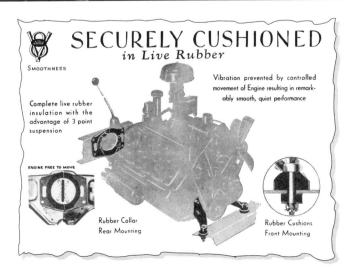

SECURELY CUSHIONED
in Live Rubber

SMOOTHNESS

Complete live rubber insulation with the advantage of 3 point suspension

Vibration prevented by controlled movement of Engine resulting in remarkably smooth, quiet performance

ENGINE FREE TO MOVE

Rubber Collar Rear Mounting

Rubber Cushions Front Mounting

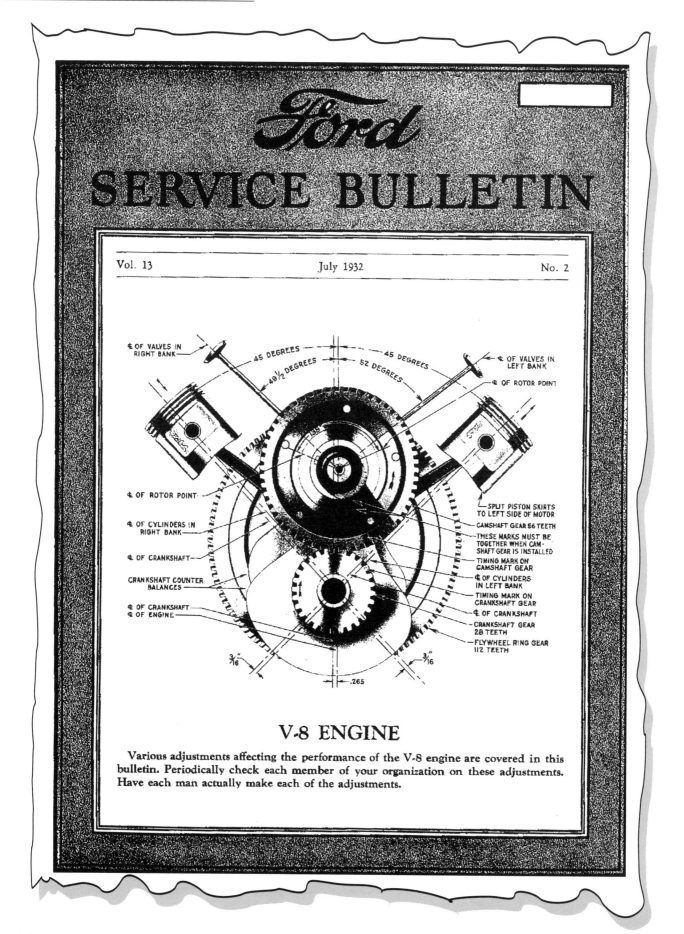

V-8 ENGINE

Various adjustments affecting the performance of the V-8 engine are covered in this bulletin. Periodically check each member of your organization on these adjustments. Have each man actually make each of the adjustments.

Early in the game, Ford alerted field personnel of the asymmetry of the new V-8. Note variances in the centerline of the crank and engine block.

2 Buying & Disassembling a Flathead

Will building a modern, high-performance flathead V-8 for a traditionally styled street rod be difficult or expensive? No, at least no more difficult or expensive than building a high-performance small-block Chevy or Ford. With one significant difference—and that's finding suitable building material. After all, the Ford Motor Company hasn't manufactured a new flathead engine block since 1953.

Today, the street rodder who wants a great flathead under his hood must be willing to go the extra mile to get all of the reliability he's come to expect from the average late-model small-block. The first step of that extra mile is selecting the best flathead block he can lay his hands on: the ever elusive "cherry."

Is the "cherry" flathead block more than elusive? Is it really an illusion, at best a deceptively glorified memory of the past? It is well known that the most notorious fault in the design of the flathead V-8 is the exhaust ports snaking through the bowels of the block. Couple this intensely heat-producing arrangement with thin water jackets and you can see why the late Clarke Cagle summed up the design and execution of the flathead block as: "Bad castings!"

A number of years ago, Cagle, a builder of high-performance and racing flatheads pointed out that many rodders subjected their flathead-powered cars and trucks to hard usage in the 1940s and 50s. This combination of design and abuse is why the vast majority of flathead blocks have a half-

dozen or so cracks in the valve and cylinder-bore areas. Fortunately, most can be repaired.

The real problem is the crack that defies repair. These are the ones running down the side of a cylinder, or well into the port. Some can't be fixed, at least not for a reasonable price.

Once you accept the fact that you will be fighting an uphill battle in the

They're out there, squirreled away in collectors' barns and in antique auto parts emporiums. Some are worth rebuilding, some are not. When you buy from a private party, you take your chances, often without return privileges. It behooves you to make a frugal cash offer.

Hopefully you will look at as many flatheads as possible before making a decision. The best often come from a knowledgeable collector who acquired it for himself. That way you have his earlier judgement as well as your own to rely on.

13

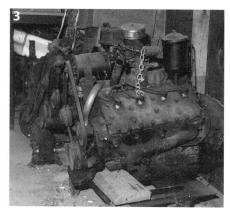

This complete 1950 truck engine (8RT) was the one I settled on after discussing my needs with the owner, fellow Forties Limited club member, Dewey Smith. The engine even had 4 original spark-plug wires still attached! No matter, I would not know what its innards looked like until it was completely disassembled.

Once we got it to our work shop, "The Cave," my son Angelo promptly mounted it on my Oddo Motor Roller for ease of disassembly.

The first step in the disassembly of a complete stock engine is to loosen the generator-support-bracket nut from the stud. Then you can drop the belt and remove the generator from the manifold.

search for a good, rebuildable block, you have to know where to look, and what to look for. A tough assignment, but one that shouldn't deter you if you really want flathead power. First off, forget scrounging through wrecking yards. Ordinary wrecking yards haven't stocked flathead V-8s since the early 1960s. Consequently, you are going to be looking to vintage automobile parts dealers and private collectors. Both must be approached in different ways, so let's take the dealer first.

I think it is safe to say that the professional dealer is more knowledgeable than most private sellers, and often the easiest with which to do business. However, because of the economic realities of the used-anything business, don't expect giveaway prices. It is not reasonable to think a dealer in antique automobile parts is any less interested in making an honest profit than a dealer in other collectibles such as postage

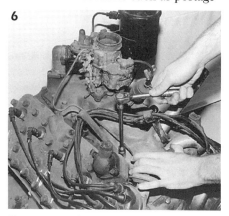

Next, remove the spark-plug wires and looms from the intake manifold and the distributor cap (or *caps,* as the case may be) from the distributor.

stamps or coins.

The dealer is likely to have the engine or block on the floor, and it is also likely to be clean. (Grease guards against rust, but it's not the most attractive way to market inventory.) Beyond that, the street rodder needn't be concerned with the stock intake manifold, cylinder heads, fuel pump and exhaust manifolds. In fact, it is better if these parts have been removed. Then he can inspect the short block more thoroughly. If he is handy with a set of micrometers, he can even measure the cylinder bores.

Although some stock parts are to be deep-sixed, no matter what their condition, it is still preferable to get all the bolts, studs and other bits of fastening hardware. Not because you are going to use them again, but for reference. You just don't want to pay a premium for them. You are really buying only a complete, rebuildable short-block and oil pan.

A block that will be an asset and not a liability is where the street rodder with a good working relationship with a vintage parts dealer comes out ahead. It's tricky, but ideally you want to be able to take the block to a machine shop for hot tanking and Magnafluxing. You also want return privileges if the block doesn't pass muster. Some farsighted vintage parts dealers even do that for you, and tag parts with the Magnaflux certification. Of course the cost is passed on to the final consumer (like everything else in a free-market society). However, just think of the peace of mind that gives the buyer when he shells out the big bucks for a block, crank and a set of rods.

Because we did not plan to reuse the original intake manifold, carb and fuel pump, it was removed as an assembly. A speed handle with an extension gets the job done quickly and efficiently.

9

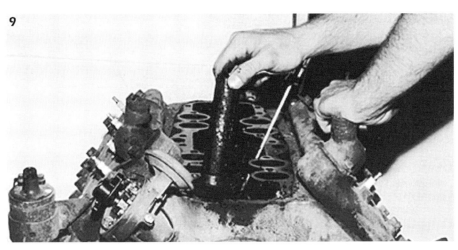

Remove the breather tube and (on the earlier engines) the oil relief-valve assembly.

11

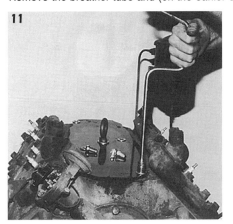

12

14

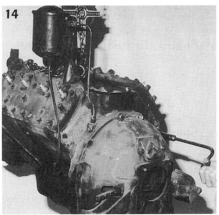

In the case of a '49 or later engine, remove the bolts that secure the bellhousing and pull it free from the alignment pins.

16

15

The factory-recommended procedure for removing the pressure plate and clutch disc is to press the end of each clutch-release lever down. Insert a 3/8-inch piece of wood between it and the pressure plate to relieve the tension. Or, just remove the bolts from the pressure-plate cover and lift the clutch assembly away from the flywheel!

Remove the safety wire, bolts, and flywheel-dowel retainer from the flywheel. Then lift the flywheel from the crankshaft. If necessary, use a soft hammer to lightly tap the flywheel first on one side, then on the other until it comes loose.

10

A Motor Arts Flat-Lift was then assembled and installed on the intake-manifold-gasket surface, the engine hoisted, oil drained, and my Motor Roller removed.

13

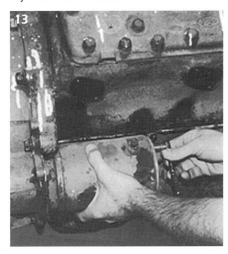

Remove the bolt that secures the starter bracket to the oil pan. Loosen two bolts that hold the starter to the flywheel housing until they are free from the housing. Remove the starter.

17

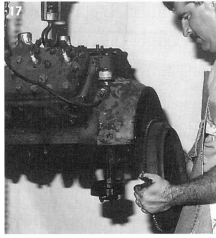

The heavy, dished flywheel on older flatheads is a bit more awkward than the more modern flywheel that came on later engines.

Bolt holes for a bolt-on bellhousing allow the '49 and later engine to mount directly onto a conventional engine stand. This is just one of the many reasons I prefer the later engine to earlier models. (For those builders interested in pre-1949 engines with the integral bellhousing, both Antique Auto Parts and Motor Arts offer fixtures which use the exhaust flanges to attach the block to an engine stand.) The thicker cast idler-gear cover on 1949-53 engines may interfere with aftermarket flywheels. A thinner steel plate was used on earlier engines.

Three basic types of distributors have been used over the years, the one and two-cap design driven directly by the cam, and the modern "post-hole" design used 1949-53. I prefer the latter because of the ease of maintenance, although I do like the earlier cylinder head design. Fortunately, a like-minded builder can both keep his cake and eat it too if he uses a 1949-53 block! More on that later. For now, disconnect all remaining wires from the coil, and remove it and the bracket. Disconnect the vacuum line from the distributor and remove the distributor.

The stock so-called "oil filter" won't be used as such on our flathead, but some folks like its looks enough (especially when it is chrome plated) to use it for an on-engine mini tool box. Maybe you will want to do that, so remove it and the handsome factory tubing carefully. Disconnect the oil-return and oil-intake lines from the filter with tubing wrenches so as to not distort the fitting nuts. Remove three nuts that hold the filter to the cylinder head, and remove the filter. Careful, we're talking messy here.

I probably wouldn't stress the condition of a tired engine so forcefully had I not participated in the purchase of more than one useless flathead in the course of my hot rodding years. I learned my lesson the hard way. I wouldn't buy a flathead block from my best friend unless I was promised return privileges if it didn't satisfy me. That's hard-nosed Yankee tradin' from a Southern boy, I'll admit. But no matter where you live, there are many flatheads around. You have street rodder friends, so put the word out you want one. You'll be surprised at the availability. Because you already know some of them are junk, you simply must be choosy. Keep looking until you find a good one.

Buying a flathead from a private party *is* a little different from buying one from a dealer, however. Joe Seller is not likely to give you a money-back guarantee unless he *is* a good friend. And, if you are looking at a complete engine, chances are he doesn't want you to tear it down right there on his garage floor. (Which *doesn't* imply he is trying to hide something from you.) What it does mean, however, is that you are buying a "pig-in-a-poke," so it behooves you to follow the ancient axiom that says loudly, "buyer beware!"

There are many things to check before and after you shake hands on a tentative purchase. Unfortunately, you won't be able to do each and every inspection while you squat there in Joe's garage. Some will simply have to be done after a full disassembly. That's why you want to make your cash offer as close to the bone as possible if you don't get return privileges in the bargain. That way, if you do haul home a junk block you know your losses going in. Now let's get on with things to watch for.

Long before you put a mike in the bores or get the block Magnafluxed, you want to apply some common sense to the purchase of an engine that is more than 40 years old. If it's still in the car or truck, whether it's been *in* the barn or out *behind,* it should be regarded as one with a strong possibility of ongoing internal corrosion. Just as with the vintage tin that once surrounded it, the engine can very easily be a victim of the "rust never sleeps" syndrome. For instance, water left sitting in the jackets for decades will contribute to thinning out the crankcase between the exhaust ports and the oil pan.

The same is true for an engine out of the car and lying on its side. One flathead Redi-Strip Derusting returned to Jim Bremner and me in the mid-1980s had huge gaping holes in several ports. Apparently it was left on its side for several years. Trapped water rusted away most of the metal forming the ports. The ports were a thin shell of rust and scale with only a web of cast iron. The Redi-Strip process had done its job well and electrolytically dissolved the rust, but then the ugly holes appeared!

Now it's time for the great unveiling, the removal of the cylinder heads. If you found your engine in complete form as I did, you are unquestionably concerned about possible cracks in the block. As mentioned in the text, cracks of some kind are simply unavoidable, but hopefully they are repairable! At any rate, cylinder heads on pre-1949 blocks are usually secured with studs. Later models use bolts. Remove the nuts or bolts and lift each cylinder head and gasket from the block. Rent or borrow a stud puller if necessary on those that have become corroded. If they are really "tough," liberally dose with Liquid Wrench® for at least two days. Save all hardware for reference.

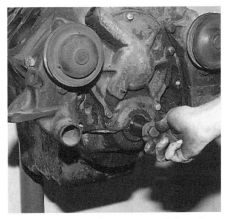

Remove the lower pulley with an impact wrench if one is available. (The "centered" force is more effective than that afforded by hand tools.) You may have to tap the pulley off with a soft hammer. Run the special bolt back into the crank snout.

Remove four bolts that hold each water pump to the cylinder block, and remove the pumps. Don't forget that one of these bolts is only accessible for removal through the pump inlet opening. Again, an impact wrench is handy for such work.

 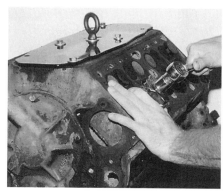 

The next operation is to ream the upper part of the cylinder to ease the removal of the piston/rod assemblies. The ridge reamer is another tool that can be rented or borrowed if you don't anticipate regularly working on high mileage motors. Operation of the tool is straightforward. Once it is adjusted to the bore size and fitted snugly in the cylinder, a ratchet is used to rotate it. Ream the ridge down a few thousandths of an inch past the worn part of the cylinder bore.

Remove the bolts securing the oil pan to the block (save 'em) and lift the pan. Betcha five dollars you will see dirtiest mess in the world. Few engines can equal the accumulated sludge that a poorly filtered (from the factory) flathead can charge up in less than 100,000 miles. All that will be rectified in your rebuild, of course.

 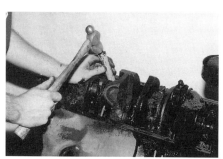

In original engines you will find either cotter-pinned rod nuts or locking caps. Remove them and the cap (taking care not to mix caps with different rods). Tap on the connecting-rod bolt with a brass hammer until the cap is free. Push the piston and connecting rod out of the cylinder, using a foot-long piece of wood. (An old broom handle cut in sections works great.) Be careful that the connecting-rod bolts do not scratch the crank although it will be reground later. Developing careful habits now will pay off later. Drop the assembly through the block into a waiting hand.

One giveaway clue that would "de-select" a contender even before a careful inspection is if the spark plugs were removed, or if the carb or intake manifold had been missing for a long time. Moisture and condensation will certainly have added to the corrosion caused by the water remaining in the jackets for several years.

Along about now you may have come to the conclusion that this chapter has a decidedly negative sound, and you're not at all sure you want to build a flathead anymore! That is not my intention. Unfortunately, I can't tell you with any assurance that any given circumstance predicts a good usable block. I can only point out the traps an

unwary buyer might fall into, and the things you should look for as predictors of an unusable block.

Finding a usable block *is* possible. Sharp shoppers do that all the time. Most either buy a known entity from a friend or make an "up-front" deal with a reputable dealer to take back a turkey. Nevertheless, the ultimate

Remove the remaining piston assemblies, then remove the timing cover from the block. Remove all the crankshaft bearing-cap bolts. (Tap them with a soft hammer if they resist.) Lift the crankshaft from the cylinder block. Next, remove the lock wire and bolt from the oil-pump-mounting flange. Remove the pump assembly from the cylinder block. The pump may not come out easily from an engine that has seen many years of service. Tap it lightly with a soft hammer to remove it from its recess in the block. Be gentle, the pump is fragile, and the housing will break if mishandled. Remove the lock wire and bolts that hold the oil-pump-drive cover to the block. Remove the oil-pump-drive cover, gasket and idler gear from the back of the block. Again, an engine that has seen severe service may not give up its innards without a fight. In stubborn cases, the idler-gear shaft located within the crankcase (arrow) may have to be driven out with a drift punch.

Removing the crankshaft assembly and oil pump is a piece of cake compared to breaking down the valve assembly in an engine that has never been taken apart. Not only do you have the problem of years of caked-on sludge and baked-in varnish, a cantankerous design and limited working room adds insult to injury. Because cam-bearing removal is a job for the machine shop, as is the hot-tanking of this very dirty engine, we stepped aside and let the old master Allen Hail of Hail's Automotive Machine Shop (648 W. Williamson, Fullerton, California 92632) do the entire job. Allen started by taking pressure off the valve assembly with a valve-spring compressor. Once done, the spring retainer lock keys or "keepers," used with one-piece valve guides are removed and the valve withdrawn. Next, the guide must be forced down its bore to release the valve-guide retainer (commonly called a "horse shoe" clip). Tap it gently from the top side with a suitable tool to drive the guide straight down. (In this case an old ratchet extension and socket were used to jar it loose from the varnish and corrosion.) Drive the guides down until the retainer can be removed from the guide. When it is free, you can slip the guide out. Do this on all valves that are in a closed position. Turn the cam until all the valves that were open are closed, and repeat the procedure.

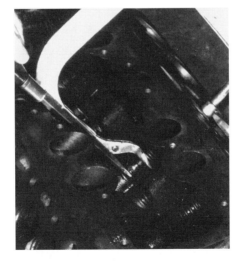

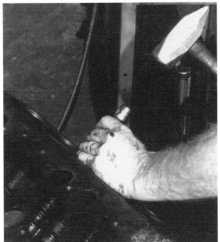

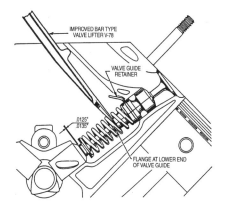

Remove the oil baffles by placing a screwdriver under each and prying its mounting clamp off the oil manifold. Remove them from the block.

Turn the block bottom side up and tap out the lifters so that the cam won't snag on them.

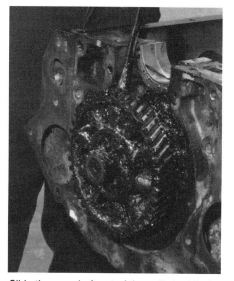

Slide the camshaft out of the cylinder block. If it resists (sometimes the wear on the cam bearing itself will leave ridges) you may need to encourage it a little with a stout screwdriver or pry bar.

Bend the tabs on the camshaft-gear lock ring out of the way to get to the four bolts securing the timing gear to the cam. Clamp the cam in a vise and remove the bolts. Often the timing gear is reusable. If not, however, replacements are available.

responsibility as to whether you should purchase this or that flathead block is yours. Take any shortcuts, or the seller's word that it was a great little engine that didn't burn a drop of oil when he pulled it out a few years ago, and *you* risk getting burned.

In 1994, I had the pleasure of doing a series of magazine articles on the flathead with Mark Kirby, one of the country's premier early V-8 builders. We were talking about the best flathead material for a street rod power plant. "I don't know how it got started, but there is the old rumor that the wartime flathead block was better, at least in terms of dimensions. I doubt it. Henry would not have gone to the expense of tooling up for production of the military block, then scrapped it and do another set of tooling for 1946."

Mark hunched over in a mock stance of the Duke of Dearborn, "'Here, we're gonna do cars again, but let's not use this thick block we built for military equipment. Let's put it aside and do some new tooling.' Ford would not have done that, it just wouldn't make sense. But military specifications *are* much higher, always the best when it comes to metallurgy. The military always demands the highest quality material in the product because it is going to be subjected to such abuse. In any case, the military block is usually identified with an X, Y or Z cast on the back of the bellhousing where the 59AB would be. They were also very common in the pickups built right after the war, the 46s and 47s."

Until some enterprising soul sends cast-iron samples to a test lab to see if the alloy in military blocks *is* any different from the passenger-car blocks, we may never know if Ford really used more chrome and nickel in the military casting. "No matter. The walls are not thicker like the old timers believed. The military specs were higher than Ford used in pre-war blocks, and I think they doubled the tensile strength of the grey iron for military purposes, but the wall thickness is about the same."

As a contributor to the automotive press, I'm always looking for the *best* street rod material, be it a World War II

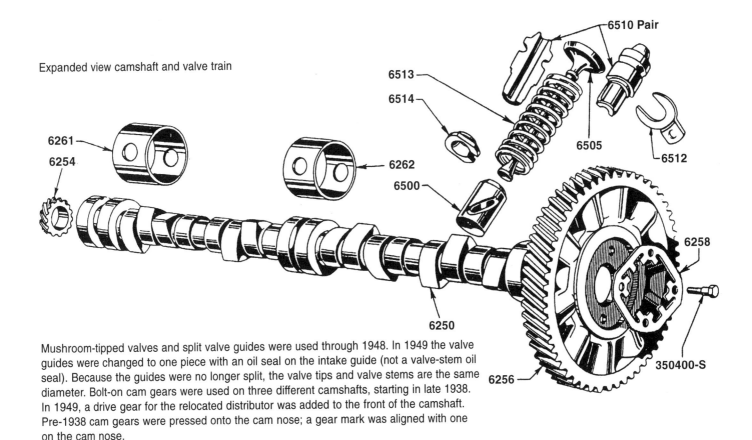

Expanded view camshaft and valve train

Mushroom-tipped valves and split valve guides were used through 1948. In 1949 the valve guides were changed to one piece with an oil seal on the intake guide (not a valve-stem oil seal). Because the guides were no longer split, the valve tips and valve stems are the same diameter. Bolt-on cam gears were used on three different camshafts, starting in late 1938. In 1949, a drive gear for the relocated distributor was added to the front of the camshaft. Pre-1938 cam gears were pressed onto the cam nose; a gear mark was aligned with one on the cam nose.

cylinder block or a newly manufactured transmission. Nevertheless, I don't want to be too exclusive in what I pass on. So I asked Mark if he thought a street rodder itching for a reliable flathead block to build in the 90s should hold out until he found a gen-u-wine military casting.

"The most desirable street engine *is* something made during or right after the war: 1942 to 1946 or 1947. But I think the 59A, 59AB, 59L 59C, X, Y, Z or 8BA are almost identical with regard to casting thickness and material." He paused for a minute, then went on . . . "The 1939, 1940 and 1941 Mercury blocks are also good street rod blocks. The pre-war Merc had a 3-3/16-inch bore. The Ford, however, had a 3-1/16-inch bore, and they are not suitable for a street rod. The 3-1/16-inch block will not take a big bore. I like to stay at 90 to 100 thousandths wall thickness on a street motor. When you start getting thinner than that, it's going to oblong. You have 48 head bolts in a flathead, and most are located in a bad spot—close to a cylinder. When we go for the

big bores, we better have some strength, there will be a significant amount of stress, possibly leading to distortion in service. Anyway, if it says 59, buy it. It's a good street rod motor. That broadens our block hunting to a pre-war Merc block or a postwar Ford or Merc block."

Mark knew of the trouble Jim Bremner and I had run into when we were looking for a good, rebuildable flathead block a decade earlier, but he didn't seem too concerned. He had, after all, purchased hundreds of blocks over the years. He bent over one and pointed into the exposed crankcase. "I always look in the webs, between the valves, and down in the seats. I make a totally visual check. If it's cracked, I'll see it. Later, if I uncover a hairline crack when I am relieving the block, maybe I'll stop and not use it. But that's only happened to me once or twice. Cracks from valve to cylinder are edgy, but many of these blocks have minor cracks. That's common."

I asked him about more extensive repair to a block that might have one

or two troubling defects. "Flathead blocks are prone to cracking in the combustion area because they have been severely overheated so often back when there were no pressurized cooling systems. If you got to 220F, you were in danger. Boiling water creates steam that goes to the highest and hottest spot in the block. Steam pockets gathering in the combustion area lead to severe and extreme temperatures—that's what damages and cracks the blocks. Of course, with modern pressurized systems you can raise the temperature without creating steam and doing damage."

Engines Used in Book

The acquisition of the primary engine used as a "demo" for this book, a 1950 truck motor, came gratis by way of my long-time friend, Dewey Smith. Dewey simply has more engines than he could ever possibly bend, spindle or mutilate in his many street rods. This engine, from now on called the *8RT*, was removed from its factory home years ago and had never been

Finally, the old cam bearings must be removed. This is always a job for the local machine shop. Have them do it before the first step down the long road of our several cleaning procedures and options, the hot tank.

rebuilt. It still had vestiges of the original Ford green engine paint, and four original spark-plug wires! (Folks were very frugal in those days.)

The second engine was not exactly free. It came attached to a 1941 Ford pickup with 37,994 original miles on the odometer. I acquired the engine (and the truck) after some hardnosed haggling with the third owner. Both the second and the third owner, however, had never driven the truck on the street. Only the original owner, a Minnesota farmer had done so as demonstrated by the 1972 license plates still in place. But that's another story.

The 1941 engine was complete and running. I actually *drove* the pickup into my shop for the teardown. Once on the floor, the disassembly of two engines began. Did you think that a book on rebuilding a flathead would require a chapter on disassembly? Nevertheless, I photographed the procedure just in case there were flathead enthusiasts among the readers who had never knocked down the old-timer.

After all, it's a dirty job as you will see in the photos. Somebody's got to do it, however, and who better than you? Besides, the best way to put something back together is to learn about it as you take it apart. Do it at your leisure, make notes and take pictures for future reference.

Unquestionably, the *supercharged* flathead really makes the mouth of a sometimes modern, sometimes traditional street rodder water. Once exceedingly rare on a boulevard cruiser, the advent of the affordable B & M blower kit has put it within the reach of anyone with a craving for the ultimate hot rod induction.

Inspecting & Derusting The Cylinder Block

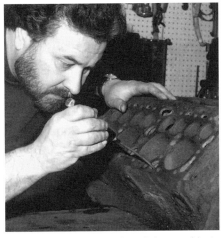
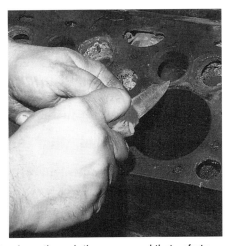

'Tis a rare flathead that hasn't been subjected to abuse through the years, and that unfortunate legacy can't be detected without a careful inspection of the block. Even before the obligatory preliminary cleaning in the local machine shop hot tank, you should measure the cylinder bores with a vernier caliper to be sure it has not been overbored to excess. Many rebuilders feel 0.125 inch over standard should be considered maximum. Remember, whatever you buy will need yet another "clean-up" bore. Look for cracks around stud holes, down the cylinders, valve pockets and water jacket inlets. Always check cylinder-bolt holes to see if the threads have been damaged or stripped out. Major defects can sometimes be detected without a technical analysis. Mark Kirby is unequivocal, however. "If there is a crack between the valve and the cylinder, pass!"

There are four distinct methods of cleaning an engine block. Only three of them, the alkaline electrolytic immersion, the mild acid dip and the thermal method, clean internal rust out of the block. I'll get to those in a bit. The old stand-by, the caustic-soda hot tank method, is where the prudent rodder begins after he has removed everything fastened to the block including cam bearings and oil-galley plugs.

A hot tank is in the corner of nearly every automotive machine shop in the country. Not only is it readily available, the service is cheap. Although not the final cleaning, it is good enough so the machine shop can thoroughly check the block for cracks and damage that could prevent the rodder from going any further. That's where the magic of Magnafluxing comes in.

Magnaflux® is the trade name of the original non-destructive magnetic-particle inspection. In this process a magnetic field is established, then a finely grained iron powder (often suspended in light oil) is applied in and around known trouble spots. If there are no surface or subsurface defects in the area of inspection, the magnetic force lines travel in an uninterrupted parallel path. If there is a crack, the lines of force will deviate around it. When a surface defect exists, the flux lines create a small north-south swirl and the iron powder accumulates.

Perpendicular defects are identified by using different types of magnetic coils that encircle the critical inspection areas.

Magnaflux also detects subsurface defects if they are not too deep. A shallow subsurface defect will disrupt the magnetic flux lines and detour them around the defect, causing the iron powder to collect on the block. Naturally, a well-experienced operator is required to "read" something as complex in shape as an engine cylinder block. Not only that, it is helpful if he has some idea of where the critical areas are on a particular engine.

The personnel in most engine-rebuild shops wouldn't have any problems with a small-block Chevy. But, most of them weren't even born when flatheads ruled. That's why it is worth your while to observe the testing if possible. Establish an amiable working relationship with the technician before the tests. Then, armed with the information you get from the accompanying photos, you can make sure the block is thoroughly inspected. (Be tactful, don't imply that you know the Magnaflux operation better than the technician, just that perhaps you are more familiar with the idiosyncrasies and problem areas of a flathead block.)

Once your local machine shop has given you a "thumbs-up" on the Magnafluxing, the block is ready for some serious de-rusting via your choice of alkaline immersion, acid dip, or oven baking.

The Redi-Strip® Company, with

After visual and measuring checks indicate that you can continue forward in your pursuit of a rebuildable block, the next step is a preliminary cleaning in the venerable caustic-soda "hot tank" in preparation for the real indicator of success, magnetic-particle inspection. Properly known as Magnafluxing, this proprietary service requires considerable experience. I assigned my 8RT block to Allen Hail's Automotive Machine Shop in Fullerton, California for the relatively inexpensive, but always indispensable evaluation. Under Allen's watchful eye, apprentice machinist Scott Emley first checked out the lifter valley, then the exhaust valve ports, and finally the crankcase. These areas *must* be free from defects.

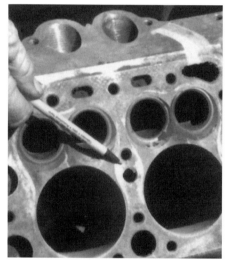
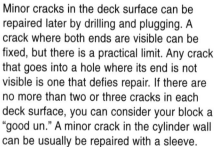
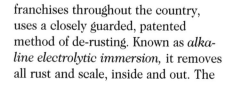

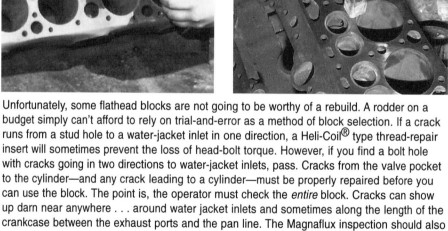

Minor cracks in the deck surface can be repaired later by drilling and plugging. A crack where both ends are visible can be fixed, but there is a practical limit. Any crack that goes into a hole where its end is not visible is one that defies repair. If there are no more than two or three cracks in each deck surface, you can consider your block a "good un." A minor crack in the cylinder wall can be usually be repaired with a sleeve.

Unfortunately, some flathead blocks are not going to be worthy of a rebuild. A rodder on a budget simply can't afford to rely on trial-and-error as a method of block selection. If a crack runs from a stud hole to a water-jacket inlet in one direction, a Heli-Coil® type thread-repair insert will sometimes prevent the loss of head-bolt torque. However, if you find a bolt hole with cracks going in two directions to water-jacket inlets, pass. Cracks from the valve pocket to the cylinder—and any crack leading to a cylinder—must be properly repaired before you can use the block. The point is, the operator must check the *entire* block. Cracks can show up darn near anywhere . . . around water jacket inlets and sometimes along the length of the crankcase between the exhaust ports and the pan line. The Magnaflux inspection should also cover the front of the block. In my original *Street Rodder Magazine* flathead series more than a decade ago, we went through *nine* blocks before finding one worthy of rebuilding. I'll never forget the late Clarke Cagle who helped us saying, "Even in the 1950s if your block wasn't cracked, you weren't considered smart . . . just lucky!"

franchises throughout the country, uses a closely guarded, patented method of de-rusting. Known as *alkaline electrolytic immersion,* it removes all rust and scale, inside and out. The process takes place after a caustic soda bath similar to automotive machine shop hot-tanking.

The chemical opposite of an alkali is an acid, right? Well, the opposite of an alkaline immersion is a mild hydrochloric acid immersion. That's where the opposition ends, however. If you didn't know what was in the tank in which your block is immersed, and

We're talkin' yesterday's motors here, and manufacturing techniques that may have been on the cutting edge 50 years ago often won't cut it today. The flathead is notorious for core-sand residue, and it can clog water jackets adding to overheating problems. To get a better idea of what frequently occurs, Kirby pasted modeling clay in one of his cylinder block cut-away sections where sand collects (arrows)and is ultimated impacted by scale and the long-term use of block sealer. Most of the sand is accessible through the water-jacket openings in the deck surface. A careful and thorough poking and scraping with a sharpened iron rod is the only way to really be sure that you are giving the flathead back its maximum cooling capacity. It is preferable that this is done after hot tanking, but *before* sending the block to a specialty shop for chemical or thermal cleaning.

Now your block is ready for a serious bath. The machine-shop hot tank was great for a quick and easy degreasing, but it won't get rid of rust and years-old scale. And there's plenty of both in every flathead block. There are two chemical methods of eliminating rust and scale. Both require a complete immersion in a big, smelly old vat. However, the bubble baths respectively used by the two are as different as night from day . . . or alkali from acid. The Redi-Strip® Company has been a long-time favorite for cleaning out accumulated debris. Their method is the electrolytic alkaline immersion, where huge generators mounted near each tank drive an electric current through the solution in a manner not unlike electroplating, only the result is just the opposite. The immersed flathead block acts as the cathode (the negatively charged electrode) and rust molecules are released or "dissociated" from the block and bubble up to the surface of the electrolyte. Before you bring your block in, however, you must remove all non-ferrous items from the block such as cam bearings. They will soften in the process. Remove all screw-in plugs to open the internal passages for the electrolytic solution to circulate freely. There are Redi-Strip facilities located in two dozen cities around the country. (For the location nearest you, contact the national headquarters in Illinois at 708/529-2442.)

The mild acid dip is on the opposite end of the spectrum. Here, an *internally* rusty block is immersed in diluted hydrochloric acid. When the "pot watcher" is confident that all rust and scale have been removed, the work piece is dipped in a neutralizing solution, then vigorously hosed down. Southern California rodders have been patronizing Ron Usrey's PSC Painting Stripping Corporation of America (10051 Greenleaf, Santa Fe Springs, California) for years, and that's where my latest block got sanitized.

Whichever your choice, alkali or acid immersion, you won't be disappointed with the results. The engine block, both inside and out, will be as rust-free as possible. Not only that, other flathead accouterments such as the oil pan and steel bolt-ons will be cleaner than you could ever hope to get 'em at home.

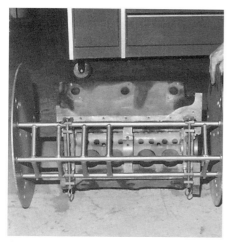

One of the most modern engine block and component laundering methods is that developed by the AmPro Company of Plain City, Ohio. Called *thermal cleaning,* this highly efficient, three-part patented system consists of a thermal degreaser, an airless blaster and a shaker. I brought my own 8RT block to Jim Grubbs Motorsports (28130 Avenue Crocker, #331, Valencia, California 91355) where the first step was to stuff it into a huge rotisserie-like basket. It was then put into the degreaser where it was "thermally dried," that is, all the oil, grease, rust and calcium deposits were turned to dust. In other words, the block is oven-baked while it slowly rotates.

The block looked doggone clean to me at that point, but it was then taken from the oven by hoist and loaded into the airless blaster and fed stainless steel media. This part of the process only takes about ten minutes.

In the final phase, the block is again moved by hoist from the blaster to the shaker. Here, the loose media is shaken out and the block allowed to cool down. Total time for drying, media blasting, and shaking is approximately 55 minutes. The result is an absolutely clean piece finally ready for machine work. (And why not, after poking, submerging, baking and shaking my poor 8RT must have felt like it had literally gone through the wringer! Simple machining must have looked like a picnic!)

if you didn't know the name of the company you were in, you probably couldn't tell the difference. You pay your money and you make your choice; a choice largely dependent on what facility is nearest you.

The traditional caustic soda "hot-tank" is usually located in the dirtiest, grubbiest part of an automotive machine shop. For good reason too, it's the dirtiest, grubbiest part of the engine-rebuilding process. That's why the environmental-pollution powers have been on the owners of auto machine shops like gravy on rice. One screw-up in using or disposing of the caustic soda and other hazardous chemicals, and the shop owner can be looking at a stiff fine. It now costs the same (or even more!) to dispose of the chemical as it does to buy it in the first place.

The necessity of cleaning engine blocks within the parameters of environmental protection laws has "mothered" a relatively new service, the thermal-cleaning system. The value and efficiency of this method will not be lost on the rodder who wishes to return a classic flathead to the street.

The AmPro® brand of thermal cleaning uses a three-stage system: (1) a thermal degreaser, (2) an airless blaster and (3) a shaker. An overhead crane moves the work pieces (block, crank, heads, manifolds, etc.) in a holding fixture from unit to unit. Typically, the bare cylinder block is clamped into the fixture, then placed in the degreaser and slowly rotated while it is heated to 350F. The average engine is baked for 15 minutes. If it is really dirty, it may go for 20 minutes at a boosted temperature of 550F. As the end of the first phase of the process nears, the operator opens the oven and looks for telltale smoke. If there is no sign of smoke, all of the oil residue has cooked off.

The block, still at more than 200F, is taken from the oven and placed in the airless blaster. There, it is rotated and stainless-steel media (shot) is tumbled throughout. This gentle abrading process removes surface rust and some internal scale.

The block, still in its holding fixture, is next placed in the shaker where any loose shot is shaken out and the block is slowly cooled to room temperature. When done, the block is as clean as new with no damage.

At this point I am compelled to clear up a misconception I've run into from time to time. Namely, that modern block-cleaning methods may do more harm than good to an old-timer like a flathead. These misconceptions arise because the owner is usually unaware of just how much rusting had occurred in his block *before* cleaning. When he sees daylight shining through what he thought was solid cast iron, he yelps in pain. What he didn't know was that rust and scale impaction had created an illusion of solidity. I realized this in the 1980s when I retrieved what I thought was a good flathead block

from a Redi-Strip tank. I peered into the ports of the block only to find them peppered with perforations.

After your block has passed visual inspection—then a Magnaflux inspection, and has come out of the cleaning process smelling like a rose, there's still another test: the high-pressure water block check. This procedure is not ordinarily necessary on a block that was not previously over-bored. If yours is on the outer limits of displacement lust, it is a good idea to pressure test it just to be absolutely certain you have a builder.

Here, the block is sealed and cold water is pumped through the jackets under pressure. Although the block and water are not heated, any perforations or cracks not previously detected

will spring a leak . . . or at least drip a drop.

That's about it for determining the condition of a Ford V-8 flathead block. It has to be recognized that not even modern technology is perfect. There will always be the hidden joker. Sometimes an engine just has to be assembled, filled with oil and water, then brought to operating temperature before some gremlin makes itself known. When that happens, you have to console yourself with the street rodder's equivalent of "racing luck."

That's why I stressed a rigorous evaluation and cleaning of the block before you start the machine work. Do so and you are way ahead of the game.

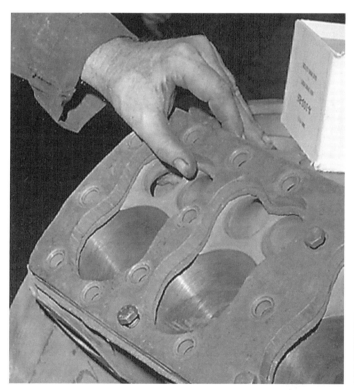 

A concern of long standing with the flathead re-builder is a stable block after boring. The racers of yore were always trying to get a few more cubic inches out of the block, and sometimes they went too far. The wall thickness of a standard-bore block is about 0.300 inch in the center of the cylinder, and the minimum safe wall thickness is 0.090 to 0.100 inch. Even a block bored out to 3-3/8 inches is still going to have a wall approximately 0.180 inch thick. This is adequate, but just to be sure, consider the high-pressure water check. If your existing bore is 3-5/16 to 3-3/8 inches, it would be wise to make this test before you go any further with the machine work. Most metropolitan areas have an industrial engine rebuilder. If you're lucky, one will be able to test old Ford engines. Cyclone Excelsweld Company had the deck and water-pump plates necessary to test pal Terry Smith's 59AB a few years back. Currently Excelsweld USA is at 1231 - 16th Avenue, Oakland, CA 1/800-743-HEADS.

Each water-jacket segment must be sealed, then the operator pumps water in under high pressure. If there are leaks in the cylinder walls, tell-tale squirts will appear. The operator's close scrutiny assured Smith that his flathead block had passed muster with flying colors even though there were several small, scary pits in the bore. Following benediction, pits or no, Smith could begin the reassembly of his flathead when he was ready.

Finally, there is one more thing to do before your block and components go to the machine shop. A plug is staked into the oil passage at the end of the crankshaft. It is a good idea to remove it and clean out the passage by hand before sending the crank out for its regrind. Bend and sharpen a piece of rod to do the job. It may take an hour or so, but this is up to you. (The crankshaft grinder is not going to mess with it!) When the passage is clean, run a drill down in the hole, which is also likely to be clogged. Do this to each journal. When you drop the crank off, ask the shop to chamfer the oil holes. Crank prep is critical. Oil passages have to be clean, otherwise the engine won't oil properly and bearing wear will be accelerated.

Reconditioning the Cylinder Block & Selecting Critical Components

After Magnafluxing and a thorough cleaning, it is time to select the bottom-end components and commission the necessary machine work for their assembly. It is a task that can be daunting.

The restorer has it made; he doesn't have to spend time and energy pondering over such formidable considerations as cylinder bore and crankshaft stroke. Ford did that for him. He is only concerned with reliability.

The street rodder, on the other hand, not only needs and wants reliability, he has to build in a certain amount of performance. And if he is prudent, cost-effectiveness.

To keep up with OHV-powered rods on a weekend club run, the flathead is going to have to develop more low-end torque than it does in its "natural state." And the only practical way to get more torque out of any engine is to increase its displacement by boring and possibly stroking. Let's look first at the question of a moderate overbore.

Flathead blocks considered most appropriate material for street-rod motors are those with a standard 3-3/16-inch bore. These include the 1939-53 Mercury and the 1946-53 Ford offerings. Now, it has long been held that any of these could be safely bored 0.1875-inch oversize. There is always the possibility of encountering an occasional "core-shift" block in which one or more cylinders were originally cast "out of kilter." And wall thickness may be a bit too thin for a *safe* 0.1875-inch overbore. Let's not borrow trouble; we've got enough to think about with-

The crank (top) has the conventional parting line on it (chalk mark outlines it). Other casting methods leave several parting lines that seem at odds with one another. Nevertheless, the engine builder need not fear component reliability as long as no metallurgical flaws are detected during Magnafluxing and the journals measure in the safe range for regrinding.

out conjuring up the improbable.

Hold on—I just said you can safely overbore 0.1875-inch. But I don't recommend it unless it is needed to get rid of scrapes and gouges in the cylinder. I suggest a more conservative overbore because you're going to need the remaining meat to keep distortion-free cylinders to hold good ring seal (reduce blowby) for a longer time—and survive high-HP output. No sense building an engine that is on the "ragged edge" to start with.

Naturally, you must settle on a conventional bore size for which pistons and rings are available. As of this writing you can still buy replacement stock-type 4-ring pistons in 0.020, 0.030, 0.040, 0.060, 0.083 and 0.100 inch oversizes from TRW and Silv-O-Lite. Aftermarket piston makers offer pistons up to 3-3/8 inch bore size in modern three-ring configuration for whatever stroke you choose to use. Every size is not necessarily available upon demand, so an early investigation is prudent.

For my engine, I chose a conservative 3-5/16-inch bore. But what about stroke? Better stated, what about the crankshaft itself?

Since its introduction in 1949, the 4-inch stroke Mercury crank has been the hot rodder's favorite. If you are purchasing your crank separately, don't be dissuaded by what looks deceptively like a giant chip. Many cranks have them, and it is just a casting artifact. Although a cracked flathead crank is not common, don't shell out any rubles until it is Magnafluxed and measured as to "re-grindability."

The Crank

When the dramatically redesigned Ford and Mercury models were introduced to the American public in late 1948, everyone was excited. The hot rod fraternity rejoiced. Sure, they liked the updated styling; but more to the point, the engine was also redesigned. Not so much as the surrounding sheet metal, but redesigned nonetheless. The coolant outlets were in a different location as was the distributor. These, and a few other variations were minor—the long-stroke crankshaft in the Mercury was what set the performance crowd on its ear.

The Merc four-inch crank was a surefire way to pump up the volume of not-so-well-endowed engines. Unless the rodder was flush enough to walk into a dealer and plunk down $80.95 for a brand-new crank, he had to wait until Merc engines started to show up in wrecking yards.

"Stroking" was popular with the hot rod crowd long before the 1949 crank appeared, however. The stock Ford 3-3/4-inch crank to 1942 had a journal diameter of 1.999-inches, and used a 7-inch (center-to-center) rod designated by the factory as a "21A." The stock Mercury crank from 1939 to 1948 also had a 3-3/4-inch stroke, but its journal size was 2.139 inches. It still used a 7-inch rod. The factory designated the Merc rod as the "29A." The extra 0.140-inch-larger connecting-rod journal on the Merc crank meant it could be safely ground down to Ford diameter and simultaneously ground off-center. That's why the "eighth-inch" stroker became popular. The Merc block with its larger-from-the-factory

cylinder bore, stroked Merc crank, Ford 21A rods and appropriate pistons became the hot set-up after WW II—at least until the Merc 4-inch crank hit the scene. The 1949-53 Merc crank, and the shorter stroke 1949-53 Ford crank used rods designated 8BA, 0BA or 29A. (Journal diameters on all were 2.139 inches, but 8BA and 0BA rods could only be used with insert bearings and on journals with two oil-feed holes.)

In the years since 1949, the 4-inch stroke Merc crank has taken on almost mythical proportions. Some folks just don't consider a flathead a hot rod engine unless it has the "long arm." Obviously, with only a four-year production and a very high demand, a 4-inch crank commands a premium price today.

There's an interesting sidebar to the 4-inch crank story. Let's call it part of the "flathead folklore." This is, of course, the rampant but erroneous belief that some or all of the Merc 4-inch cranks were forged steel. The *original* 1932 V-8 cranks were forged, but from 1933 the company used only "Special Ford Cast Iron Alloy".

Sometimes the term "Cast Steel Alloy" was used. Recent discussions with Jim Homrich, a Michigan toolmaker, whose father was a Ford pattern maker for many years, throw some light on how the forging misconception possibly came to be. Ford used two casting techniques. One was the "cope-and-drag" casting which uses a two-piece mold. Therefore the "parting line" is straight down the length of the crank. The other is called the *stackable core casting*. Eight or nine molds are bolted

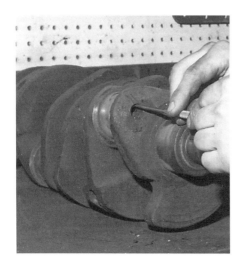

As mentioned earlier, clean out the oil passages *before* and after your crank is reground. The *amount* of regrinding is first determined by your local machine shop, then usually done by a shop specializing in this type of work. There, the crankshaft is carefully inspected and tested for alignment and for journal and crankpin wear and roughness. Alignment is checked while supported in V-blocks and slowly rotated with a dial indicator reading the journals. Any misalignment of the crankshaft (not common in a flathead crank) can usually be straightened in a heavy press. The shop relieves (or grinds back) the journal and grinds in new crankpin radii (where the crankpin curves up to the crank cheeks). This will prevent bearing failure from "radii ride." The original radii are duplicated in a street engine, but high-performance cranks may get a little more. (The rounder, the stronger.)

together in a modular fashion, resulting in several parting lines at irregular intervals. Because a crank cast in this fashion looks "different," early hot rodders jumped to the erroneous conclusion that it was a forging.

As an added incentive to misconception, Ford did come out with a forged crank in early 1948. The engine was called the Rouge 337 "EQ" Series. Listen to these quotes from the February 28, 1948 *Dealers' Service Bulletin:* "The cylinder bore is *3 1/2 inches* and the *stroke 4 3/8 inches.* The piston displacement is 337 inches. The pistons are of aluminum alloy . . . and the 90-pound crank is of alloy steel, *drop forged* and is fully counterbalanced with six integral counterweights." Obviously, this was not your run-of-the-mill flathead. It was slated for the new F-7 2-1/2 ton and F-8 3-ton trucks introduced that year. Flathead historians will immediately recognize this limited description as similar to the 1949-51 Lincoln flathead.

So much for the fictional forged Merc crank. Besides, it really doesn't make all that much difference to the street rodder. My sources agree that all flathead cranks are solid, substantial units, and the street rod engine builder should never look down on the 3-3/4-inch crank.

Modern engines are "over-square," that is, the bore diameter is greater than the length of the stroke. Yet, just because the rodder doesn't want to pay the premium for a 4-inch Merc crank assembly, doesn't mean he won't have a high-performance motor if he does everything else properly. Mark Kirby said it well when he pointed out shorter-stroke motors have their place. "We pick up more efficiency by slowing the piston speed down in the flathead because it is such a slow burner anyway. It's easy to outrun the flame travel, so there are advantages to a short-stoke engine. The closer to square you can get (where stroke equals bore) the better off you are."

There is another performance index to consider when evaluating the cost-efficiency of the 1949-53 Mercury 4-inch stroke crank—the factory's vital statistics!

Variations between models, and from year to year, can be attributed to factory tweaking for *advertising* gains. Even so, there is only an average gain of about 21 foot pounds of torque for the additional quarter inch of stroke and 16 cubic inches of displacement. The above is not to rain on the parade of the street rod-engine builder who in his heart of hearts really wants a 4-inch Merc crank. It is presented to further inform him, so he can judge for himself if each engine dollar is well spent.

Identifying Cranks

And there he is, looking over a bunch of cranks laid out on a dirty blanket at the Sunday Go To Meeting Hot Rod Swap Meet. The shifty-eyed character half-asleep in the lawn chair says some cranks are four-inchers. Can you believe him? Again, Mark Kirby to the rescue. "Ninety-nine percent of the time, if you have a 3/8-inch plug (in the journal), it's a 3-3/4-inch-stroke crankshaft. If you have a 5/8-inch hole, it is a Merc 4-inch. But I have seen one Canadian crank with a 4-inch stroke with a small hole. Nevertheless, if you can get your finger in it, it's probably a Merc stroker. By the way, don't worry about surface rust, you can safely go 0.040-inch undersize, even 0.050 inch. (But it is difficult to find bearings for a 0.050-inch undersize crank.)

After much consideration, I decided to bore my engine to 3-5/16 inches, and stick with the stock Ford 3-3/4-inch crank and the rods that came with it. The displacement is 258.510 inches. Like ol' Henry himself, I still like an engine as close to "square" as practical.

I might have changed my mind however, had Motor City Flathead come out with their long-awaited 4.250-inch newly cast nodular-iron crank before building the 8RT. This brand-new production crank uses either 8BA or 29A rods. With the 3-5/16-inch bore and the new MCF crank, the displacement would be a hair under 293 cubic inches. For those with a 3-3/8-inch bore and the MCF 4-1/4-inch stroker crank, the displacement is a whopping 304 cubic inches! "Now that," as Mae West said, "is something to see!"

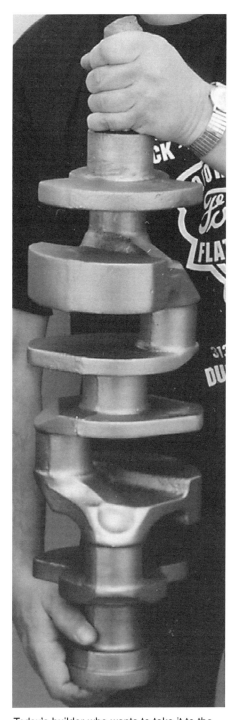

Today's builder who wants to take it to the max, and wants a *really* long stroke has to look no farther than Motor City Flathead. Again, Mark Kirby surprised even the skeptical with his proprietary stroker crankshaft. The handsome unit, shown here in the raw, is cast of super-tough nodular-steel alloy with a *four and a quarter inch* stroke. The MCF crank is designed to use 29A or 8BA 2.139-inch-journal connecting rods and special stroker pistons. The latter have a shorter compression length (the distance between the center of the wrist pin and the top of the crown). Test engines indicate that the piston is stable in the bore.

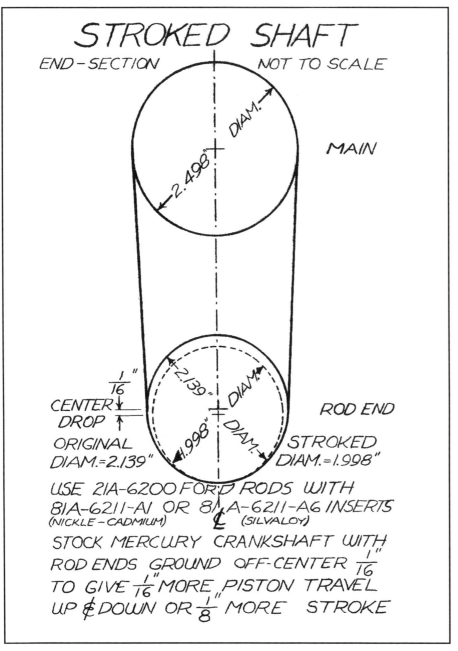

Out of the past: Drawing from California Bill's Hotrod Manual (1947) illustrates the then-popular 1/8-stroker modification to the 1939-48 Mercury crankshaft. All 1932-48 Ford and Mercury crankshafts have only one hole in each connecting-journal and require the use of full-floating rod bearings as illustrated on page 85.

Displacement Chart

Bore inches	Stroke inches	Displacement cubic inches	Bore inches	Stroke inches	Displacement cubic inches
3-1/16	3-3/4	220.92	3-5/16	3-3/4	258.48
3-1/16	3-7/8	228.28	3-5/16	3-7/8	267.10
3-1/16	4	235.65	3-5/16	4	275.71
			3-5/16	4-1/8	284.33
3-3/16	3-3/4	239.31			
3-3/16	3-7/8	247.29	3-3/8	3-3/4	268.38
3-3/16	4	255.27	3-3/8	3-7/8	277.33
3-3/16	4-1/8	263.24	3-3/8	4	286.27
			3-3/8	4-1/8	295.20

Courtesy of Offenhauser Sales Corp.

Pistons

OK, we then know we are going to re-use a stock crank and rods. Not so with the pistons. Pistons, rings and bearings are the consumables in engine rebuilding. That is, they are always replaced with modern upgrades. Several piston manufacturers are still cranking out slugs for the stock and high-performance market. (See Buyers' Guide) Let's pause for a moment, and point out a few more interesting flathead idiosyncrasies.

One is the off-center position of the crankshaft in relation to the block centerline when you are looking at it straight on. The other is the fact that although Ford originally used a long-skirt, 3-ring (two compression rings, one oil ring) piston, during a mid-life crisis in the 1930s, a fourth ring was added, presumably for oil control and stability. Kirby has a few thoughts on this . . .

"Today, we know how to control expansion rates and bore taper. Back in the 1930s and 40s they were still learning. Today, with our modern technology, we know what all the expansion rates are, plus we have machinery that holds taper. If you pull an old motor apart, you can take a telescope gauge and find as high as 8, 9 or 10 thousandths taper in the bore. Much of that is wear, and that fourth ring keeps oil from splashing up. But was the ring perhaps added to stabilize the piston in the bore because of the rod angle created by the offset of the crankshaft?"

Aftermarket pistons for the flathead have followed the modern short-skirt design with two compression rings and one oil ring since the 1950s. Nothing new there, but, "Nobody else offsets the wrist pin. In the Motor City Flathead piston design, we offset the pin location 50 thousanths. Now, by bringing the driver's-side piston pin closer to the block centerline—toward the passenger side—at top center our rod is straight up, and it has a better start on its way down. Moving the pin over like we're doing, a straight push down, and the piston cocks less, giving quieter running.

"Look at a stock block and you'll see the ports on one bank are shifted over from a true centerline. On one bank,

On left is the traditional replacement piston for the restorer. It is slotted and has two oil-control rings, one down near the bottom of the long skirt. While it is commonly accepted that the "extra" ring was for better oil control, it probably was for better stability in the bore. Today, the lightweight 3-ring piston at right is far more common.

I chose Motor City Flathead's modern, hypereutectic cast pistons for my 8RT. These unique slugs have the wrist pin offset 0.050-inch left of center. This provides more piston stability and smoother operation than the stocker or the conventional 3-ring competition piston. MCF also undercuts, grooves and slots the piston for heat separation. (Piston dome temperatures can run as high as 500F while skirt temperatures are only about 200F.) MCF uses a permanent mold rather than a sand casting for a stronger, denser piston. They also polish the domes to reflect heat and reduce carbon build-up.

the deck surface almost touches the seat. This is because one set of valves is at 52 degrees, and the other set is at about 49 degrees. Sometimes people think their block was machined wrong, and try to match it to the valves. You can expect to get in trouble doing that because the valves are on two different angles. The driver's side is canted more than the passenger side. Although the relief on the driver's side is deeper that the relief on the passenger side, it is the same volume-wise. If you ran a compression check on one of our motors you wouldn't find more than three or four pounds variance."

Piston Pin Weight

Aftermarket pistons for your rebuild may have heavier-wall piston pins than the originals. The answer is to toss the heavy-wall pins and substitute stock pins. If you are planning a rebuild, this is a good item to look for at swap meets. One thing you don't want is to be adding more reciprocating weight. Keep your pistons and pins as close to the original stock weight as possible.

The Connecting Rods

If you heft a flathead's long, skinny rod with its integral bolts, you notice how different it is from its short, stubby late-model counterpart.

Nevertheless, original flathead rods are what the typical street rod engine builder is going to use. If you are concerned about 40- or 50-year-old connecting rods in your "brand-new" engine, just remember that the Ford

Motor Company was in the forefront of automotive metallurgy from the Model T forward. The flathead's rods are heat-treated, carbon-manganese steel forgings that will bend before they fracture. They are very forgiving. Doubling stock horsepower output in a high-output performance engine will *not* overstress them. They can also be used (after reconditioning) without the need for polishing and shot-peening.

The Machine Work

Shortly after my 1950 8RT truck block was sanitized, I delivered it to Allen Hail's Automotive Machine Shop (648 W. Williamson, Fullerton, CA 92632). Allen and his crew have done all the machine work on my engines since the early 1970s. Allen, however, has much more experience than that paltry 25 years or so. He cut his teeth on precision automotive machining in the late 1950s, and many of his

Stock pin at left weighs 2.5 ounces (71 grams). Aftermarket pin with heavy wall weighs 4.3 ounces (122 grams). Using the heavier pins would add almost a pound of reciprocating weight. Always use pins no heavier than the original stockers.

apprenticeship motors were flatheads.

It might come as a surprise to some readers, but many younger automotive-machine-shop employees have never even *seen* a bare flathead block. All V-8 cylinder blocks are similar when they're turned upside down. Right side

Stroker cranks need stroker pistons

When a stroker crankshaft is installed, the crankshaft's longer throw raises the piston higher in the cylinder bore at top center and brings it lower in the bore at bottom center. A stock piston used with a stroker crankshaft will come out of the block at top center. The top piston ring may pop out into a relief or pop out above the top of the block.

Because the connecting rod length and the stroke of the crankshaft are fixed, the piston manufacturer positions the pin so the piston dome or crown and the top ring will end up where they are supposed to be at top center. The piston should rise to the top of the block at top center.

When ordering pistons, the manufacturer must know the bore size and the stroke that is to be used. If there is a 1/2" stroke, the piston pin will be located 1/4" higher in the piston. The top of the piston may be marked 1/4 L.C., meaning 1/4" low crown.

NOTE: In some competition engines, the piston dome rises into a corresponding recessed area in the cylinder head. Again, the piston pin must be located so the piston dome or crown and the top ring will end up where they are supposed to be at top center.

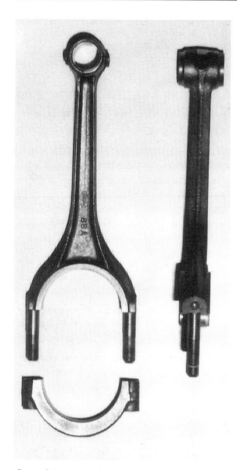

One of the most durable components in a flathead is the connecting rod, and reconditioned stockers are fine for the street. However, flathead piston speed is high because of the long stroke and that makes reconditioning mandatory. The pin diameter is only 0.750-inch, not significant enough for long service loads. So the small end always wears out. The big end typically goes "out of round" about 3 to 4 thousandths of an inch.

In the 1950s, strokes of up to 4.50 inch were available, although those beyond 4.250 were considered "edgy." The traditional engine builder who wants the additional cubic inches only a long-arm can provide can't miss with the 1949-53 Merc 4-inch-stroke crank. However, the 4-incher is more difficult to come by these days, and commands a premium price.

Perfection in the area where the cylinder head meets the cylinder block is crucial to a performance engine. Therefore, re-surfacing the block, sometimes called *decking,* is a standard rebuild operation. The block sits on a precision ground bar running through the main bearing saddles to keep the head gasket surface (which is to be milled) absolutely parallel with the crankshaft axis. Here a machinist's level is used to make sure the gasket surface is parallel with the cutter.

up, however, flathead V-8s don't look like anything manufactured in the last 45 years! The guys working in the machine shop behind the auto parts store who bang out OHV valve jobs every few hours may even stiff-arm a

The reader who is unfamiliar with the aluminum-silicon alloys used in cast street pistons might be interested to know more about them. The point of silicon saturation in aluminum is known as eutectic, and it occurs when silicon level reaches 12 percent. Aluminum alloys with silicon levels below 12 percent are known as hypoeutectic. The industry standard for common hypoeutectic pistons has only been about 9-percent silicon, although there is a slow movement toward eutectic pistons.

Alloys with silicon levels above 12 percent, and ranging as high as 18 percent, are known as hypereutectic. This alloy is considered the premier grade in cast pistons. In addition to greater strength, scuff and seizure resistance, the hypereutectic alloy improves groove wear and resists cracking in the crown area where operating temperatures are severe. Hypereutectic aluminum will exhibit about 15 percent less thermal expansion as compared with conventional piston alloys.

A knowledgeable machinist will take as little as possible off the gasket surface because of the flathead's thin deck. Depending on warpage and scratches, he wants to keep as much material on the deck as he can for rigidity and gasket sealing. Standard procedure is to take from 0.003 to 0.007" off the worst side. If that cleans it up, he takes that much off the other side. The same amount must be removed from both surfaces to keep the deck heights the same.

time-consuming, low-profit job such as you will be lugging in.

It therefore behooves the flathead enthusiast to check around before he settles on one particular automotive machine shop. As I said, not everyone will want the work. More importantly, you won't want to give the job to just anybody. You want a ready, willing and interested machinist with lots of experience.

Don't get me wrong. I'm not saying that the flathead V-8 is a particularly complicated motor. It is a bit temperamental and needs to be treated with just a little more sensitivity than a small-block Chevy. The problems I described earlier—cracks and rustaways—clearly tell you that. Just remember that this old duffer was designed more than 65 years ago and produced with industrial technology that is now at least 45 years old.

Crankshaft Grinding

The crankshaft takes a beating in normal service because of the greatly varying loads and thrusts imposed on it. This causes the main journals and crankpins to taper or wear out of round. This is to be expected and only means the crank needs to be reground for undersize bearings. A special lathe called a *crankshaft grinder* is used to recondition the journals and crankpins to extreme smoothness. Journals and crankpins are then polished by hand with a very fine crocus cloth. Crank regrinding may be done at your local machine shop, but it is usually sent to a larger, specialty machine shop. If you get the chance to visit such a shop, do so. It can be very interesting.

Rebuilding Connecting Rods

Connecting rods are something else. Their reconditioning is usually done at the local level. The rod undergoes several evaluations including Magnafluxing, a check of the alignment and the condition and fit of the piston bushing. In addition, drilled oil holes in the connecting rod are inspected to make sure they are open.

Following a satisfactory Magnaflux, the rod is mounted on an arbor in the alignment fixture and the rod cap is replaced. A V-block is placed over the piston pin and moved in against the faceplate. The V-block will not fit squarely if the rod bearing and piston pin are not in perfect alignment. A rod can be bent by the uneven loading of a tapered or worn crankpin, and depending upon the degree of misalignment, must be either straightened or replaced.

If the machinist thinks the rod can be saved, a straightening bar is inserted in the piston-pin bushing and force is exerted in the proper direction to align the rod. It is bent a little past the straight position and then back to straight again to relieve the stresses that were set up while it was in service and during the repair process.

Some automotive machinists simply demand the replacement of bent connecting rods assuming the rod is only temporarily straightened with the bar and may drift back to its bent condition. If you have as much confidence in your machinist as I have in mine, you will follow his advice.

Worn pin bushings are standard in a flathead. They are pressed out with an arbor press. Burrs on the bushing-bore edges are removed with a hand scraper or a tapered burring reamer. A new bushing is pressed in, then swaged with a tapered mandrel. Finally, the bushing is honed to size.

On the "big" end of the rod, the machinist can only cut the mating surface of the cap, but that's enough to make the full journal "hole" smaller. With the cap replaced, Scott then precision-honed the big end of the assembled rod back to size. Our rotating and reciprocating, stock stroke, bottom-end assembly was now ready for the balancing shop.

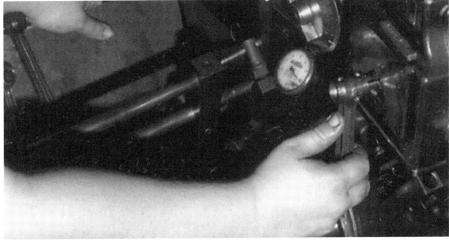

After rebushing the small ends, the honing operations begins. Scott Emley first expanded the hone until the stone began to take off metal. Then he expanded it farther to within 0.003 to 0.005 inch of the finished size, giving a precise clearance between the piston pin and the pin bushing.

The "eyebrow" in this cylinder (arrow) was cut by the top ring during the first service life of this block. Gouging is caused by the piston wobbling slightly as it changes direction during operation.

"There's no substitute for cubic inches." Increase the displacement and you increase performance, the hot rodder's mantra since the mid-1930s. Sixty years later, it is still the significant first step after bolt-ons. The cylinder boring machine (called a *boring bar*) is clamped on the block, usually over the worst-worn cylinder to ensure that it will clean up and accept an oversize piston. Increasing the bore size can also be done with a power hone. Then the block may be clamped absolutely squarely to the power-hone head via a bar placed through the main-bearing caps to ensure a square bore. Some professional builders use a boring plate to apply head-like torque (and stress) to the block during boring and honing.

The power hone takes out the last few thousandths of material. If you looked at a cylinder wall microscopically after it has been bored (we are told), it would look like a plowed field. The boring tool literally rips out the metal. The hone precisely grinds away that roughness. Back in the 30s, and even the 40s and 50s, honing was a hand job. Flatheads were newer then, but modern machine-shop technology has vastly improved. An experienced machinist can "guesstimate" accurately just when the last few thousandths of an inch have been removed. My block was finish-honed with a piston-to-wall-clearance of 0.0025-inch. A racing engine with solid-skirt pistons would require more clearance.

Align-Honing the Block

During my visit with Mark Kirby at the Motor City Flathead facility in Michigan, a number of machining topics came up. One was the need for align-honing a well-used flathead block. Mark does not believe it is necessary to align-hone as long as you use the main caps that originally came with the engine. "You never need to align-hone a street rod block, unless aftermarket steel caps are used, or if there is a cap mismatch. If you are not using the caps that came with the block, you must align-hone. Of course, a full-race, high-RPM engine is another matter."

Three Main Bearings

Then there is that major design element that many feel is a significant design flaw, the three-main-bearing bottom end. Kirby emphasized his feelings on the subject. "We have done our homework relative to what works and what doesn't work in the basic flathead design, and we don't want to reinvent the wheel. The Novi (Indy racing motor) had three main bearings and lived! We make a support for the main cap—an I-beam that will not flex." It is *not* necessary to put an aftermarket cap support on a street engine. Yet the center bearing does get stressed in performance driving, so I decided to install one on my own engine. Let's get back

to the nitty-gritty of machining the block and related components.

Incidentally, Tony Baron makes a cross-bolted center main girdle with cap, plus heavy-duty front and rear caps for the serious flathead racer.

Cylinder Boring

'Tis a rare flathead cylinder block that would not need to be re-bored during a rebuild. And it would be a rare street rodder indeed who would settle for the stock 3-3/16-inch bore even if he had that exceptional block!

We've already discussed the practical overbores, but you might be interested in the actual operation. Before the machine shop rebores the block, the main caps are replaced and the bolts drawn up to the specified tension. If this is not done, the bores may distort when the crank is reinstalled. With the caps on during the boring operation, any distortion of the block tends to be held constant.

The cutting tool is carried in a rotating bar that feeds down the cylinder as it rotates. The first cut is a roughing cut, followed by a finishing cut. The machinist then finishes the job by power-honing the last three or four thousandths with very fine stones. When the bore is 0.030 inch or less power honing is an alternative to using a boring bar. Power honing is

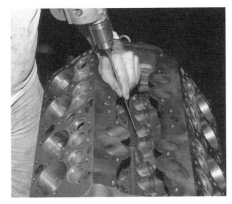

Alan Anderson marked the lifter bores in the 8RT where he would drill holes to simplify adjustment of the new lifters. A very long bit is used to reach down into the valley. Size of the bit is arbitrary, but 1/8 inch is large enough to slip a pin punch through the bore boss into the lifter depression. Center the hole on the bore boss, about 5/8-inch down. When the lifter is on the heel of the cam lobe and the valve is closed, the adjusting nut will be accessible just above the boss. White arrows point to holes in lifter bosses.

accomplished under a constant flow of oil to carry away the debris and keep the bores reasonably cool so they don't tend to distort.

Balancing The Rotating and Reciprocating Mass

When the typical street rodder decides to build a power plant for his pride and joy, he immediately becomes dollar-conscious. If you were to press me for a guess, I'd have to say that although motor reliability is unequivocally demanded, it isn't nearly as visible as paint, upholstery and other accouterments for the car proper. Consequently, parting with the extra money for something as intangible as engine balancing sometimes gets outweighed by other more visually pleasing considerations.

Now, it is true that precision balancing is not so critical that the motor won't run properly at street cruising speeds. Nonetheless, vibration, reflected only in a mild lack of smoothness at low RPM, is a bearing killer when you're honking it on.

For instance, original flathead-crank assemblies were balanced at the factory to about 20 grams static unbalance. (Static unbalance exists when the center of gravity of a rotating mass does not lie on the axis of rotation, but at a distance from it.) Centrifugal force (the exertion that impels a rotating mass, or part of it, outward from the center of rotation) increases as the square of the RPM increases. Simply stated, tripling the RPM increases the centrifugal force nine times. That adds up to a bunch of

The final machine shop operation on the block is installing the camshaft bearings. New babbit-lined bearings are placed on the driving tool and carefully driven into the block, the rear one first. The machinist must make certain that the bearing oil holes line up with those in the cylinder block bearing bores. The block can now come home.

pounds at 3000 RPM on the Interstate!

The elimination of such "tolerable" unbalance can significantly lengthen the service life of bearings and seals, more than compensating you for the cost of a precision electronic balancing job. A conscientious technician such as Andy Miron of the Anaheim Balance Shop (1842 S. Lewis, Anaheim, CA 92805) can keep tolerances below a half gram and 14 gram-inches respectively. Consequently, it's easy to see why a blueprinted and balanced flathead is going to run a lot more smoothly than a stock original.

The first step in a precision engine balance is to weigh each component. A record is made of the type of pistons, rings, and rod bearings and their weights. When the lightest piston in

the set is identified, it becomes the standard for the remainder. Each heavier piston is chucked in a lathe and material removed from its inner skirt pad to make its weight equal to the lightest. Ordinarily, the rings, pins and bearings do not vary much within their sets, so usually no alteration to them is necessary.

Weighing and balancing the connecting rods is more complicated. Both the big and little ends must be weighed separately by suspending one end of the rod and reading the weight of the other end on the scale. The weight of each end of each rod is brought into line by removing material on a deburring machine. Three separate unit weights must be equalized—the big end, the little end, and the total rod

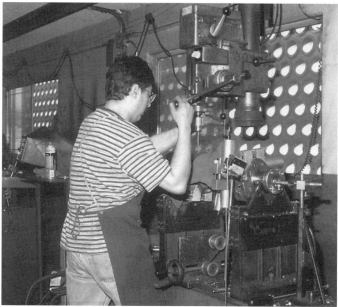

By design, the flathead is internally balanced, which means that only the crankshaft, rods, pistons, one set of crank and rod bearings, and one set of piston rings is all that needs to be sent to the shop. This is a real boon to the street rod builder who has not yet selected a drive train. The flywheel and clutch assembly, or the automatic-transmission flex plate, can be brought in later. Mechanical balancing of an engine's rotating and reciprocating parts is necessary because the centrifugal force acting on them must be equal in all directions around the radial axis of the crank. Only then can the assembly rotate freely and with minimal vibration. After making sure all pistons weighed the same, and all rods weighed the same, Andy Miron mocked up a crank assembly with bob weights and put it into motion. The electronic magic of the balancing machine changes the rotating deflection of the spinning crank into up-and-down motion.

The amplifier of the balancer is sensitive to 0.004 ounce-inch. The unbalance meter indicates the amount of unbalance in the crank assembly directly in ounce-inches. A strobe lamp illuminates reference marks for locating the heavy points during balancing. Unlike the pistons and rods, which can only be lightened, some weight may have to be added to the crank counterweights. When this is needed in the flathead crank (which is internally balanced and therefore quite heavy) the technician merely fills existing balance holes with a bit of welding rod or heavy metal. Excess weight is drilled out. After each weight change is made, the crank assembly is returned to the balancing machine, rechecked, and perhaps altered again. It can be a tedious job.

If you run a high-lift camshaft with Chevrolet valves (they are 1/16" longer than stock), you may find it difficult to reach the adjusting nut on the adjustable lifter. Make a trial assembly after the cam bearings are installed and the valve seats are ground. Install the camshaft and the lifters and valves for one cylinder. Using light springs will make the installation and checking easier.

1. Measure the clearance on the intake valve with the lifter on the heel of the cam lobe to see whether it needs to be increased or decreased. If you can get the wrench onto the adjusting nut to turn it as you hold the lifter against turning with a drift punch inserted through the hole in the lifter boss, everything is OK. If the adjusting nut is too low in the bore to reach with the wrench, then the top of the lifter boss can be ground off as required to provide wrench clearance. Repeat the check for the exhaust valve.

2. Or, instead of grinding the lifter boss top, turn the camshaft to raise the lifter so you can reach the adjusting nut. Make an adjustment, then turn the camshaft back to place the lifter on the heel of the lobe and check the adjustment again.

NOTE: The wrench used for tappet adjustment is typically ground to reduce the depth of its opening to provide clearance for turning.

weight. When removing material, good judgment—based on experience—is critical, otherwise one could spend many hours at the deburring machine.

Once the pistons and rods have been weighed and balanced, it's time to do the crank. For it to rotate smoothly in its bearings, the crank must be in balance both statically (at rest) and dynamically (in motion). The unbalanced forces generated in a rotating crank assembly are measured in ounce-inches. One ounce-inch is an ounce of weight an inch away from the crank's axis (or a third of an ounce 3 inches away from the axis). Naturally the crank can't be rotated in the balancer with the pistons and rods bolted to it, so bob weights that duplicate the weight of the piston/rod assemblies are used. For V-8 engines the bob weight is built to 50% of the reciprocating weight

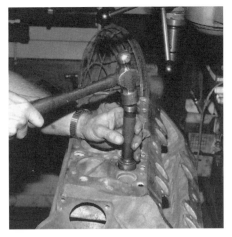

The new valve seat ring is driven in, and held tight with a compound that is both a sealer and ceramic-type glue. Because of the type of valve guide used in flathead blocks, a special pilot must be used. The pilot base resembles the valve guide.

"Everything about a flathead valve job is unique and special. Not every shop will even have the proper pilots." So said the late Clark Cagle. The standard flathead seat angle is 45 degrees for both intake and exhaust valves. And, perhaps more than any other machining operation, experience is critical. When a seat is worn or damaged, it must be cut out, or, if there was no seat to begin with, a recess has to be cut in the block for one. Alan Anderson, a machinist at Hail's is shown replacing a seat on the 8RT.

Alan is now ready to start grinding the seats. The grinding-tool pilot fits in the guide hole. The pilot holds the alignment necessary to grind a 45-degree seat, 0.060-inch wide. This geometry is still considered the most practical for street use.

and 100% of the rotating weight of the piston assemblies.

By the way, flatheads are "internally" balanced engines. The flywheel and clutch assembly can be balanced as an independent unit, and when worn or damaged, it can be replaced with another separately balanced unit.

Finally, when the balance shop returns your crank, pistons and rods, you are ready to begin the assembly of the short block!

Replacing Worn Valve Seats

What makes a flathead a flathead is the location of the valves in the cylinder block. Because the exhaust seat is blasted by extremely hot gases exiting the combustion chamber, it is made of a special heat-resistant steel alloy. The insert ring is set into a counterbore in the block, and when it has become

worn, it can be serviced by a valve seat grinding machine. When it is damaged, it can be removed and a new one installed. Special seat pullers are made for OHV cylinder heads, but for flatheads, Hail's Machine uses a punch on the accessible backside to remove a bad seat. This acceptable method has been in use for years, but like so much in the flathead, requires some experience.

Obviously it is extremely important for the valve to seal all the way around the seat. If there is a leak, there will be blow-by and rapid valve failure will result. Therefore, the valve, the valve seat and the valve-guide must be all be perfectly concentric. Furthermore, the face angle of the valve must either match the seat angle or there must be a slight interference angle.

The valve seat grinder uses a rotating stone of the proper shape and

angularity. (Cutters could be used, but it's quite a hassle to properly position the block on the work table.) The stone is kept concentric with the valve seat by a pilot installed in the valve guide. After preliminary grinding, upper and lower cutting stones or cutters are used to narrow the valve seats to the desired width. The remainder of the valve story is covered in a later chapter.

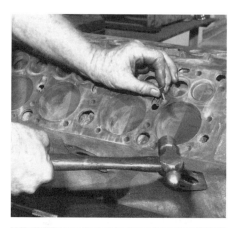

Minor cracks in the block can be repaired by your local automotive machine shop. The "fix" is a tapered cast-iron plug that seals the crack and prevents it from migrating farther. The first step after locating the crack via the Magnaflux is to centerpunch, drill and tap a hole (or holes) in the crack. Normally, a 13/64-inch or 5/16-inch drill bit is used.

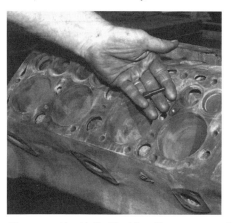

Plugs used by Hail's Machine Shop are manufactured by Irontite Products of El Monte, California. There is a fine "pipe" thread (a wedge shape) on the plug. So the more pressure exerted during installation, the tighter the seal. The plug is simply screwed in like a bolt.

One of the more pesky cracks in my 8RT was just below a valve seat. We had to replace two seats in the block. Allen, however, was able to do a plug repair. As few as three solid threads will hold the plug. The most important thing about any crack repair is that the machinist repairs *all* of the crack. If even a trace remains, it is going to continue to migrate. Often the machinist must drill more than one hole in a crack, then he has to peer into the holes to make sure that he is corralling all of the crack. Admittedly, cold-plugging a crack is not as good as welding, just cheaper and more convenient. If Allen has a cracked classic cylinder head, he sends it out for welding rather than plugging it. Welding involves preheating the entire work piece before welding. It is more expensive as well. A one-inch crack costs about $50 to plug, and from $150 to $200 to weld.

There are two different ways of removing the excess, and it's a judgment call. If the machinist is not too worried about part of the broken-off edge ending up below the surrounding surface, the plug is simply broken off. If the plug is on a gasket surface, and he doesn't want a shallow spot, he will cut it off with a hacksaw, and then peen it over. If the crack is in an area such as the valve pocket, it won't make any difference. Sawing it off, however, does make the finished job prettier.

FORD GENERAL SPECIFICATIONS

Year	Model	Bore & Stroke	CID	Comp. Ratio	HP @RPM	Torque Lb.Ft. @RPM	Oil Press. Lb. @MPH
1932	V-8 18	3-1/16 x 3-3/4	221.0	5.50	65 @3400	147 @1250	30 @30
1933	V-8 40	3-1/16 x 3-3/4	221.0	6.30	75 @3800	147 @1250	30 @30
1934	V-8 40	3-1/16 x 3-3/4	221.0	6.30	90* @3800	147 @1250	30 @30
1935	V-8 48	3-1/16 x 3-3/4	221.0	6.30	85 @3800	144 @2200	30 @30
1936	V-8 68	3-1/16 x 3-3/4	221.0	6.30	90* @3800	149 @2000	30 @30
1937	V-8 78	3-1/16 x 3-3/4	221.0	6.20	85 @3800	153 @2200	30 @30
1938	V-8 81A	3-1/16 x 3-3/4	221.0	6.12	85 @3800	146 @2000	30 @30
1939	V-8 91A	3-1/16 x 3-3/4	221.0	6.15	85 @3800	155 @2200	30 @30
1940	V-8 01A	3-1/16 x 3-3/4	221.0	6.15	85 @3800	155 @2200	30 @30
1941	V-8 11A	3-1/16 x 3-3/4	221.0	6.15	85 @3800	153 @2200	30 @30
1942	V-8 21A	3-1/16 x 3-3/4	221.0	6.20	90 @3800	156 @2200	30 @30
1946	V-8 69A	3-3/16 x 3-3/4	239.4	6.75	100 @3800	180 @2000	30 @30
1947	V-8 79A	3-3/16 x 3-3/4	239.4	6.75	100 @3800	180 @2000	30 @30
1948	V-8 89A	3-3/16 x 3-3/4	239.4	6.75	100 @3800	180 @2000	57 @40
1949	V-8 8BA	3-3/16 x 3-3/4	239.4	6.80	100 @3600	180 @2000	57 @40
1950	V-8 0BA	3-3/16 x 3-3/4	239.4	6.80	100 @3600	181 @2000	57 @40
1951	V-8 1BA	3-3/16 x 3-3/4	239.4	6.80	100 @3600	187 @1800	57 @40
1952	V-8 B2	3-3/16 x 3-3/4	239.4	7.20	110 @3800	194 @1900	57 @40
1953	V-8 B3	3-3/16 x 3-3/4	239.4	7.20	110 @3800	180 @2000	57 @40

* Discrepancies between Ford advertising and Ford technical literature are not uncommon during this era. The specifications noted are from the Ford Service Bulletin for January-February 1934, and October 1935.

MERCURY GENERAL SPECIFICATIONS

Year	Model	Bore & Stroke	CID	Comp. Ratio	HP @RPM	Torque Lb.Ft. @RPM	Oil Press. Lb. @MPH
1939	V-8 99A	3-3/16 x 3-3/4	239.4	6.15	95 @3800	170 @2100	30 @30
1940	V-8 09A	3-3/16 x 3-3/4	239.4	6.15	95 @3800	170 @2200	30 @30
1941	V-8 19A	3-3/16 x 3-3/4	239.4	6.15	95 @3800	176 @2200	30 @30
1942	V-8 29A	3-3/16 x 3-3/4	239.4	6.40	100 @3800	176 @2200	30 @30
1946	V-8 69M	3-3/16 x 3-3/4	239.4	6.75	100 @3800	180 @2000	30 @30
1947	V-8 79M	3-3/16 x 3-3/4	239.4	6.75	100 @3800	180 @2000	30 @30
1948	V-8 89M	3-3/16 x 3-3/4	239.4	6.75	100 @3800	180 @2000	30 @30
1949	V-8 9CM	3-3/16 x 4.00	255.4	6.80	110 @3600	200 @2000	57 @40
1950	V-8 0CM	3-3/16 x 4.00	255.4	6.80	110 @3600	200 @2000	57 @40
1951	V-8 1CM	3-3/16 x 4.00	255.4	6.80	112 @3600	206 @2000	57 @40
1952	V-8 2M	3-3/16 x 4.00	255.4	7.20	125 @3700	218 @1900	57 @40
1953	V-8 3M	3-3/16 x 4.00	255.4	7.20	125 @3800	218 @2000	57 @40

FORD VALVE SPECIFICATIONS

Year	Operating Clearance H-Hot Intake	C-Cold Exhaust	Clearance For Timing Intake	Valve Seat Angle Degrees	Intake Opens Degrees BTDC	Exhaust Closes Degrees ATDC	Valve Spring Pressure @ Length	Valve Stem Clearance (I & E)	Valve Stem Diameter
1935-38	.012	.014	.012	45	9 1/2	6-1/2	37 @ 2-1/8	.0025-.0045	.341
1939-48	.012	.014	.012	45	TDC	6	37 @ 2-1/8	.0025-.0045	.341
1949	B	B	B	45	C	D	40 @ 2-1/8	.0010-.0030 (Intake) .0015-.0035 (Exhaust)	.341
1950-51	.014	.018	.014	45	5	3	40 @ 2-1/8	Same as 1949	.341
1952-53	.014	.018	.020	45	24	14	39 @ 1.89	Same as 1949	.341

A - BTC means before top center, ATC means after top center

B - Early 1949 .012" intake, .014" exhaust. Late 1949 .014", .018" exhaust.

C - To Serial No. 8BA-622468, top center; after 8BA-622468, 5 deg. before TDC.

D - To Serial No. 8BA-622468, 6 deg.; after 8BA-622468, 3 deg.

MERCURY VALVE SPECIFICATIONS

Year	Operating Clearance H-Hot Intake	C-Cold Exhaust	Clearance For Timing Intake	Valve Seat Angle Degrees	Intake Opens Degrees BTDC	Exhaust Closes Degrees ATDC	Valve Spring Pressure @ Length	Valve Stem Clearance (I & E)	Valve Stem Diameter
1939-48	.012	.014	.012	45	TDC	6	37 @ 2-1/8	.0025-.0045	.341
1949-50	.012	.014	.015	45	10	10	37 @ 2-1/8	.0010-.0030 (Int.) .0015-.0035 (Exh.)	.341 (Int.) .341 (Exh.)
1951-53	.014	.018	.015	45	5	9	40 @ 1.89	.0015-.0030 (Int.) .0020-.0040 (Exh.)	.341 (Int.) .341 (Exh.)

FORD ENGINE BEARING DATA

	Camshaft Bearings		Connecting		Rod Bearings	
Year	Camshaft End Play, Inch	Bearing Clearance, Inch	Journal Diameter, Inches	Bearing Clearance, Inch	Rod End Play, Inch	Rod Bolt Tension, Lb.Ft.
1939-41	.003	.002	1.9990	.0017-.0036	.006-.014	40
1942	.003	.002	1.9990	.0017-.0036	.004-.008	40
1946-48	.003	.002	2.1390	.0017-.0036	.004-.008	40
1949-50	.003	.002	2.1390	.0005-.0030	.006-.014	40
1951	.003	.002	2.1390	.0005-.0030	.006-.020	40
1952-53	.007	.002	2.1385	.0005-.0030	.006-.020	45-50

Main Bearings

Year	Journal Diameter, Inch	Bearing Clearance, Inch	Crankshaft End Play Inch*	Main Bolt Tension, Lb.Ft.
1939-41	2.4990	.000-.003	.002-.006	80
1942	2.4990	.000-.003	.002-.006	80
1946-48	2.4990	.000-.003	.002-.006	80
1949-50	2.4990	.000-.003	.002-.006	100
1951	2.4990	.001-.002	.002-.006	100
1952-53	2.4985	.001-.002	.002-.006	100

*Measured at rear bearing.

MERCURY ENGINE BEARING DATA

	Camshaft Bearings		Connecting		Rod Bearings	
Year	Camshaft End Play, Inch	Bearing Clearance, Inch	Journal Diameter, Inches	Bearing Clearance, Inch	Rod End Play, Inch	Rod Bolt Tension, Lb.Ft.
1939-48	.003	.002	2.1390	.0017-.0038	.006-.014	40
1949-50	.003	.002	2.1390	.0005-.0030	.006-.014	45-50
1951-53	.003	.002	2.1390	.0005-.0030	.006-.020	45-50

Main Bearings

Year	Journal Diameter, Inch	Bearing Clearance, Inch	Crankshaft End Play Inch*	Main Bolt Tension, Lb.Ft.
1939-48	2.4990	.000-.0030	.002-.006	80
1949-50	2.4990	.000-.0030	.002-.006	90-105
1951-53	2.4985	.001-.0026	.002-.006	90-105

*Measured at rear bearing.

Earle Bruce - original owner

In all the world, can another practicing street rodder claim to have bought his pre-World War II car off the showroom floor? By Gosh, Earle Bruce can. Talk about a rod with history; Earle acquired his 1940 Ford Deluxe Business Coupe from a Los Angeles dealer in late *1939!* Not satisfied with the stock lines, he had the top chopped 2-1/2 inches and the quarter windows filled. As you can imagine, the names of the immortal Southern California custom car and high-performance luminaries who had a hand in the progression of the coupe since 1939 are legion. One is the famed Von Dutch. Perhaps best known for his *avant garde* pin striping, Von Dutch punched the four rows of symmetrically arranged louvers in the hood. That was long ago, but the flathead that nestles between the fat fenders is a lot newer, equipped as it is with Kong Jackson heads and a B & M supercharger.

Flathead Breathing and Selecting Valve-Train Components

Before we get into the flathead's camshaft and valve train proper, I want to discuss flathead airflow, and two of the most cherished performance "massages" since the mid-1940s. For 50 years, cylinder-block "porting and relieving" has been assumed to add usable power to the street motor. After all, don't the fast guys do it? Besides, unlike most "machine operations" the home builder can do it himself as long as he can borrow a Dumore grinder.

I fell into the category of the uncritical faithful; I've even written magazine how-to articles on porting and relieving in the past. I suppose it can be explained by something Ak Miller once said to me at Bonneville, "If a guy goes fast with a banana on his aerial, the next day everybody will have a banana on his aerial!"

The problem with most "monkey-see, monkey-do" behavior is that too few of us monkeys ever go to the trouble of testing a theory. Thankfully, some inquiring minds do. I know that other engine builders have done airflow experiments on flatheads, but few of them have the professional credentials of Paul Schalk, an airflow development engineer. By day, Paul wears a starched white lab coat emblazoned with the logo of a research and development firm that caters to Detroit's auto manufacturers. By night, he is one of the cohorts of Mark Kirby, the founder of Motor City Flathead. To put it mildly, these guys are engaged in the endless pursuit of flathead perfection, and Paul's expertise particularly impressed

me. I believe you will find his application of modern airflow technology to the Ford flathead V-8 very interesting.

I'm sure you've heard of airflow, but there are two kinds that interest the automotive enthusiast, one is associated with body design (aerodynamics), and the other is concerned with engine design (volumetric efficiency). It is the latter that commands our attention in this chapter. So much so, that I want to present it to you before I continue with the nuts and bolts of the book.

Volumetric efficiency is the ratio between the quantity of air-fuel mixture that enters the cylinder during its operating cycle . . . and the quantity that could enter under *ideal* conditions. Let's look at a typical street rod flathead engine of 286 cubic inches displacement. Quick division tells us that each cylinder measures 35.75 cubic inches. If it were allowed to completely fill on its intake stroke, it would take in about a quarter ounce of air. (Air at atmospheric pressure weighs about 1.25 ounces per cubic foot.) Unfortunately, the volumetric efficiency of many production car engine designs drops to as low as 50 percent at freeway speeds. In other words, the cylinders are only half-filled—hardly "high performance."

Enter the hot rodders with their make-over of those production-car engines. You know the standard tricks: bigger and better induction, larger, straighter and shorter intake manifold runners, bigger valves that lift higher off their seats . . . and stay open longer. It's all called *better breathing*, and it's

Recognizing that the flathead was not blessed with good airflow, and in stock form, its volumetric efficiency is appallingly low, hot rodders have taken up high-speed grinders in an attempt to improve it. This graceful, albeit non-conventional, relief design is the culmination of several years of professional airflow research at MCF.

been hot rodding's mainstay since the 1930s.

The 1930s? Hey, that's when the flathead was born, right? Well, here are a few words of wisdom from Paul on that subject. "I've been around airflow

Paul is intrigued by the work of British engineer Harry Ricardo who designed a cylinder head for the side-valve engine in the late 1920s (above). Note the large, hemispherical combustion chamber and the plug directly above the valve. Although the Ricardo chamber resulted in a low compression ratio, a high-lift cam could be used. With an *overhead valve* hemispherical combustion chamber efficiency as a base (1.0), the Ricardo high-turbulence side-valve chamber has an efficiency of 0.88. The efficiency of the production Ford flathead design is dismally lower. The Ford design also limits valve lift to about 0.360 inch for street use.

Paul Schalk, known to the Michigan crowd as "Doctor Flow," set up his flathead Ford V-8 airflow research bench at MCF. Using a more-or-less complete engine, he has scientifically evaluated a variety of factors critical to volumetric efficiency in the street rodder's favorite nostalgia engine. His studies have culminated in several unconventional approaches to traditional hop-up methods.

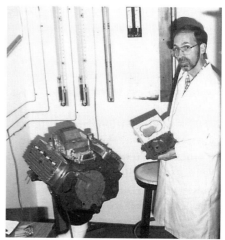

Paul developed several special pieces to analyze airflow characteristics in carbureted as well as supercharged flatheads. He is working on the design of a new three-carb manifold.

a number of years, but the flathead—well it is such a challenge. It has several problems as compared to modern engines. Breathing is a problem; combustion is another problem. The engine needs a lot of help, but it's been out of production a long time and there's no modern version. However, we're trying to take everything we've ever learned to assist the flathead in becoming a state-of-the-art motor.

Not that it's going to be high-tech. We're not really sure it *should* be high-tech with computer-controlled ignition and all of that. The motor carries a lot of nostalgia, so it should look and sound like a flathead. Yet it should run just as well as it can. Breathing is a problem that's going to take a long time to solve."

Paul showed me a rubber casting of a flathead intake port. "With this you

can get a better idea of what kind of path the airflow has. Everybody realizes it's bad. When you look at something like this you can see it has some constricted areas to breathe through."

He then showed me a piece of machineable plastic that was a casting

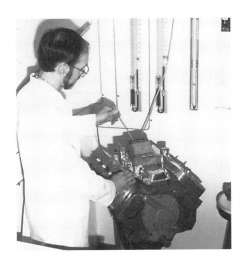

Plenum chamber and runner modification are of major importance in designing an intake manifold for optimum performance under both normal aspiration and forced induction (supercharged) conditions. An efficient modular manifold with interchangeable sub-sections would be a significant breakthrough with regard to production costs.

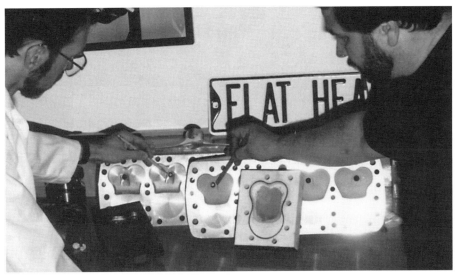

Schalk and Kirby also came up with significant improvements to aftermarket cylinder heads, particularly in the spark plug area. We'll discuss that further in a later chapter.

of the flathead's combustion chamber. "A lot of airflow is controlled by the combustion chamber, and the configuration around the valves is a very important factor. Because the valves are shrouded, air to the cylinder has to do a 180. In an overhead, it just has to get past the valves and it's right there in the cylinder.

"Everybody seems to agree that an engine needs a certain charge motion. Some people talk in terms of *swirl*, a horizontal rotation. *Tumble* is what you would commonly expect to see on a 4-valve OHV engine where the air comes in and does a barrel roll inside the cylinder. Those kinds of motion are needed and are being looked at intensely because of interest in reduced emissions.

"But what you really want inside an engine is perfectly distributed and atomized air and fuel. You want a good-quality mixture so when that thing lights off you get the best possible burn.

"If you've got a charge motion that is a little on the lazy side you can have problems. You can go to the other extreme and have too much motion, and it can burn too fast. That isn't good either. You don't want to take a severe flow loss just to generate swirl. You

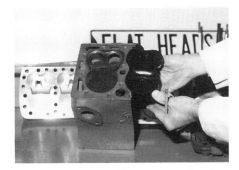

Paul uses rubber molding compound, a flexible non-hardening material, to get a better idea of the airflow characteristics of the stock flathead combustion chamber, and high performance heads on a relieved block.

have to look at the whole thing and try to strike a balance as far as how much charge motion you want, what kind you want, and what you are going to end up with for volumetric efficiency.

"In the flathead's case, we are not concerned with emissions, but we are concerned with good combustion, good power output, and good airflow.

"In my experiments we discovered certain things that we expected. Talking strictly in terms of airflow, the high-compression head flows less air than the stock head. That's to be expected. The high compression head has less combustion chamber volume, so it's more restrictive to airflow. On the other hand you are getting higher compression. That's the trade off: airflow for compression.

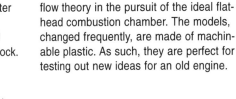

Paul's working models evaluate textbook airflow theory in the pursuit of the ideal flathead combustion chamber. The models, changed frequently, are made of machinable plastic. As such, they are perfect for testing out new ideas for an old engine.

"That would be a good thing for fuel economy, but most street rodders don't buy high compression heads for fuel economy, they are after power and performance.

"This engine suffers in many respects: split cylinders, three main bearings, and restricted breathing. The valve train is good because it is lightweight and direct-acting. Yet the camshaft lobes aren't very big, so you are limited with what you can do with lift. This engine does not have a lot of lift compared to most other engines its size. Most modern-day motors roll out as 270 cubic inchers with at least 0.400-inch valve lift. Try to open Henry's V-8 that much and the valves

Airflow Tests
Ford Flathead V-8 Relief Comparison
(on a stock engine)

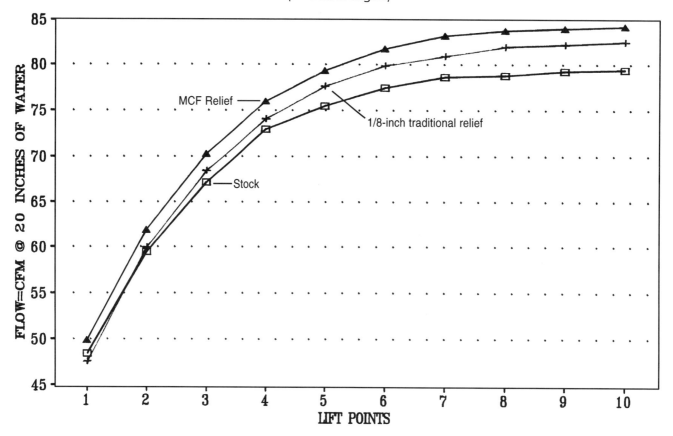

The "fixture" for airflow engineer Paul Schalk's experiments consisted of a stock block, cam, ports, valves, and cylinder head. Valve-lift points were determined by putting 10 marks on the crankshaft pulley spaced approximately 11 degrees apart. Lift points on the flow curve are not even increments because they reflect a cam-lift curve.

The cam was turned by the crank gear to activate the valves. The stock arrangement was tested first, then the block was then relieved 1/8 inch in the traditional manner and retested. Clay was added to the block to simulate the improved MCF relief for the third test.

Although differences in airflow are minimal with the stock setup as tested, they would be increased with larger valves, ports and a high-performance cam. The graph of these particular tests shows that the shortened and contoured MCF relief flows better than over extending the relief straight into the cylinder bore.

will hit the cylinder head. Typically you'll get by with 0.300- to 0.350-inch valve lift. Of course, that makes correspondingly less horsepower output."

"Unfortunately, the flathead was not blessed with good airflow. Back when it was conceived and built, airflow was not really much of a consideration as long as the engine made a certain amount of horsepower and torque. When compression ratios were in the range of 6 or 7:1, fairly low, the flathead did not suffer much of a disadvantage. It wasn't until 1949 when GM came out with their high compression,

big bore, short stroke overhead-valve engines, and high octane fuel became available, that the flathead started to suffer a disadvantage . . . more and more each year to the point where it just couldn't keep up." (Just to keep the historical record straight, flathead racers didn't have to wait until the early 1950s for competition. There were several serious competitors such as John Hartman, Marvin Lee, Wayne Horning, Harry Warner, Bill Fisher, Kenny Bigelow and Howard Johannsen, to name a few, with their Chevy and GMC OHV 6-cylinder engines that gave

the Ford boys fits long before the advent of the GM OHV V-8s!)

"We're trying to apply modern technology to this motor in hopes that it's going to run better and more reliably than ever before. It's not meant to be a replacement for all street rod engines, but for the flathead enthusiast, the goal is to give him the best possible flathead based on current information."

Paul then steered me to the well-lighted back corner of MCF's immaculate engine-assembly area. There sat a bunch of chopped-up blocks and heads, with a flathead block on a stand with

Repetitive and exact charting of airflow during all phases of the flathead's operating cycle are necessary to achieve maximum efficiency relative to combustion chamber configuration, valve lift, duration, and overlap. Information gleaned from these experiments has been incorporated into Motor City's camshaft profiles, and their unique porting and relieving procedures.

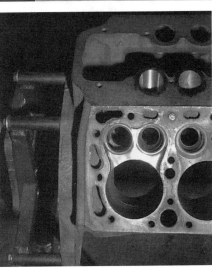

Sometime in the mid-40s (nobody seems to know for sure) Ford Motor Company started to machine a channel relief in V-8 blocks between the valves and the cylinder. The intent was obvious, to get a better fuel flow in, and conversely, to get a better exhaust flow out. The channel, known as a *relief,* ranged from 0.070-inch to 0.100-inch deep. MCF has measured several stock blocks in their accumulation and found 0.070, 0.080, 0.085 and 0.100-inch-deep reliefs! There's no consistency, not from side-to-side in the same block or in models of blocks! Factory reliefs can be found in some "L" blocks, some "59" blocks and some "Z" blocks. No matter, it appeared to be a good thing to early hot rodders. Every block modified for high performance since then has sported some variation of the stock relief job. And, knowing hot rodders, you can well imagine that if some relieving was a good thing, more relieving was better. The "standard" hot rod relief ranged from 0.125 to 0.150 inch deep. But was it such a good thing?

plastic tubes running back and forth between several gauges on the wall. "This has been lots of work, but lots of fun. This is our version of a flow bench. We use this engine block because we can check from cylinder to cylinder very quickly. We use the engine for a flow fixture and just turn the crankshaft to open a different intake valve. That way, we can check our manifold distribution without bolting and unbolting a head eight different times. We need the ability to move the spark plug around because we want to find out where it should be."

Paul then launched into a discussion of the work of the famous British engineer Harry Ricardo, patron saint of flathead airflow. He developed a high compression cylinder head for valve-in-block engines that took the automotive world by storm in the late 1920s.

As long as the quality of gasoline, lubricating oils and exhaust-valve steels remained poor, the valve-in-block (L-head) engine was the production motor of choice because of the ease with which tappets could be adjusted and the head removed for decarbonizing. The L-head's poor breathing and indifferent burning of its charge were accepted as inevitable. During that time, however, Ricardo demonstrated the possibilities of enormously improving L-head-engine combustion.

In fact, his studies encouraged many auto manufacturers to adopt the L-head configuration. Follow the money trail: its simplicity brought with it the virtue of manufacturing economy, although casting the cylinder block was more difficult. Over all, it was a "torquey" little engine renown for its flexibility and well suited for the nonsynchromesh gearbox of the day. That's a major reason why it lasted so long. Another is that there were few problems of differential expansion, that is, valve adjustment was not needed at frequent intervals.

Of course, World War II encouraged widespread development of materials and design in the aircraft industry. That resulted in a significant carryover eventually leading to the OHV engines brought into common use in the 1950s. Let me return to Paul's

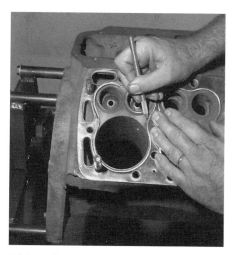

Modern research indicates the traditional relief is a poor choice. The Motor City relief retains much of the deck surface around the bore. A gentle radius leads to a lip of the unmodified deck immediately surrounding the bore. In this design, the air/fuel mixture exits the intake valve, swirls in the abbreviated channel, then tumbles up into the combustion chamber in the head. There, it can more appropriately apply its expanding force directly to the crown of the piston. This affords a direct improvement in airflow. Cutting off part of the upper edge of the cylinder in a traditional relief causes a loss of bore rigidity. The top of the cylinder needs to be the strongest area, because if detonation and cylinder distortion takes place, it is going to occur there, not down at the bottom of the cylinder. Kirby reports that the idea germinated when he took an engine apart in which the bores were so badly out of shape that the rings were pinched and broken.

Do not grind into the water gallery that runs across the top of the block. Grind only *below* the port.

All that will be cut out of the deck is the area from the valves to an eighth-inch ring encircling the cylinder. Use a gasket to scribe the heart-shaped curvature.

Be very careful not to take too deep a bite when relieving. A pair of old valves is insurance against a slip. A small cutter works best between the two. A deft touch with your finger is the best measuring instrument when determining the levelness of the grind.

insights, however.

"What Harry Ricardo did was put turbulence into that cylinder head and consequently it ran better and produced more power. I haven't found an example of that cylinder head in this country on any engine. The Ford head does not follow his general guidelines for a turbulent head, but I'm sure that they were aware of his work. The general idea was to get some turbulence in the chamber, because these chambers are notorious for being slow-burning, kind of on the lazy side. That meant running a lot more spark advance—trademark of an inefficient engine.

"Some overheads, particularly the hemis, don't have much charge motion,

although they make up for it in other areas. But the flathead was born with problems, so we have to try to work around them as best we can. We're trying to pick up where people like Ricardo left off, with the benefit of their facility." Paul then shifted into high gear. "The supercharger is probably the best thing you can do for a flathead, because it makes up for all the deficiencies.

"The supercharger is a mechanical lung. If you can't breathe well, you put on a mechanical lung and let it do the breathing for you. Some people are not going to be comfortable with a blower, however; some are going to want to stick with carburetors.

Paul then sauntered over to a work bench and picked up a time-honored artifact of the street rod flatmotor, the finned aluminum cylinder head. "Aftermarket heads are primarily designed for compression. To gain compression they took away combustion chamber volume, and in doing so, made the breathing tougher. An aftermarket head has less airflow than a stock head."

Then he switched gears . . . "What we found is that for a given valve size, a given port size works best. If you were to optimize everything in the system it would probably be a whole lot different from what we see now. It's all got to fit together . . . valve seats, valve

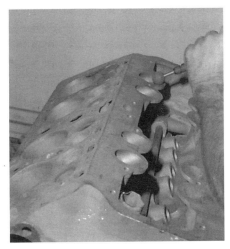

A very conservative approach is recommended for port rework. Stick your finger in the intake port and feel for a sharp edge just past the seat in the casting. If you like, smooth out the port mouth with a grinder. Stones used to relieve the block are also used to clean out the ports. Abrasive cloth wound around a slotted shank is best for polishing them. Exercise extreme caution when polishing as well as porting. Those port walls and water jackets are thin!

One last thing to do. Put a high-performance intake-manifold gasket in place and check the port match. Use the gasket as a "master." If there is a significant discrepancy, you might want to do a little fine tuning with the grinder. Don't go overboard. Save the gasket for future reference. When you get ready to install the intake manifold, you will want to match its ports to those in the master.

stems, chamber shrouding . . . a system, one package that works better than randomly throwing everything together. We may even end up with a smaller exhaust valve! It's tough to seal a chamber like the flathead's because of its irregular shape, with lots of bolts covering a big area. We don't have a nice round hole like an overhead."

Well, what does all this theory mean to a modern street rodder? Does he have to wait until the 21st Century to benefit from the sum and substance of what Paul and Mark learned at their airflow bench? Hardly, a good part of their findings is as close as right now. Let's get back to the train of thought that opened this chapter: relieving and porting.

The practical sum and substance of what I learned from all my resources is that *relieving a block for a pure street rod motor is not necessary.* Polishing out all of the sharp edges surrounding the valves is. Relieving is only justified when the end purpose is an all-out competition motor, or a street motor that will be supercharged. Even then, you may want to imitate the way Kirby does it. Study the photos and see for yourself.

In closing our discussion of relieving, here's a bit of history: The first reliefs in a factory block appeared in 1942. While they may have been added to improve mixture flow into the cylin-

ders, they were also used to solve another problem. Pre-1942 truck blocks often cracked from the valve seats into the top of the cylinders. This was because many trucks had vacuum brakes. Using the vacuum brakes caused the mixture to lean out, increasing combustion temperatures and causing thermal stress in this area of the block. The factory relief effectively cured this problem.

Porting

Finally, the second part of the traditional attempt at improving airflow is porting. As with the relief, port enlargement and polishing is a traditional do-it-yourself operation. As such, countless hours have been expended by hands-on street rodders. Was it just busy work with no appreciable gain? Quite possibly!

If you are so inclined, and want to be able to say that your block is at least polished, if not ported, here is an efficient compromise. Stick your finger in the intake port. You'll feel a sharp edge just past the seat. If you like, smooth out the mouth of the port with a grinder. This is a standard feature on a MCF-prepared block. "The combination of cleaning up the stock port so the air can follow the turn smoothly, with our Superflow Valve, meets the needs of most street rodders. That alone is going to give them a good-run-

ning street engine."

The Cam

Armed with the realities of scientific airflow analysis, one should be able to zip right on out and buy the exact cam he needs for his street flathead. Yeah, sure. Cams are one of the most durable bull-session topics whenever flathead rodders congregate. Just listening to a couple of flatsters looking over a cam layout at a swap meet is often downright entertaining. No matter what grind they are perusing, the conversation turns more to what used to be in the "old days" rather than what may be useful in the here and now.

Not only that, buying a used *aftermarket* flathead camshaft along the swap meet trail is, more often than not, an exercise in false economy. Even if it looks good, there are potential problems. Sometimes the cam has a weathered data sheet attached. Sometimes not. Even then, who knows if the data sheet is for the cam to which it is attached. There are some exceptions, however. One of them is the original, verifiable, Iskenderian 404 radius-tappet cam. According to Kirby, "It's wild-sounding and drivable with a big motor. It's a good mid-range cam if you build a full-race motor for the street."

There must have been a dozen flathead cam grinders in the old days, but today that number has dwindled down to a precious few. Of that few, none have so deservedly earned the "pioneer" title as Ed Iskenderian. The "Isky" name and cigar have been synonymous with flathead valve actuation since the end of World War II.

Today's flathead enthusiast is a bit different from the flathead hot rodder of the 40s and early 50s. (Well, maybe *more* than just a bit.) In those days, when the flathead-powered hot rod was either the means of daily transportation, or at the other end of the spectrum, a racer, the engine builder installed a cam that was very mild or absolutely hairy. No middle ground. Even the guy who occasionally went to the lakes or the drags didn't want more cam than he could live with on the way to work or school Monday through Friday. And the serious racer sure didn't want some street grind in his "gow machine."

Motor City Flathead, fully aware that most of today's potential customers are neither daily drivers nor serious racers, has non-traditional grinds that incorporate the best of both worlds without the short-comings of either. "If the customer were to put a mild street cam in a full dress, multi-carbed engine he's not going to be happy, because he doesn't have that sound (the lopey idle) that everybody loves in a flathead."

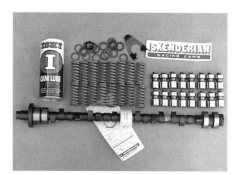

The Isky catalog doesn't list quite as many different grinds as it once did, but according to Motor City Flathead, "If a fellow is building a mild engine, he's a good candidate for an Isky 88 or 77, something like that, it's a great combination. Isky's 400 Jr. is also a good performing cam."

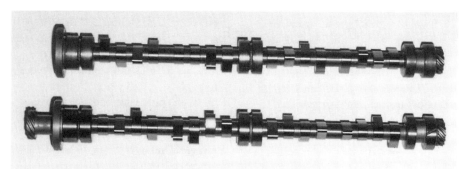

Motor City Flathead carries all the traditional brands that are still available, but they have also developed their own grinds for today's street rod market. Their proprietary cams are manufactured nearby in Michigan. The lower cam with the integral distributor gear is for the 1949-53 engine with the "post-hole" igniter.

1949-53 Ford valve at left is exactly the same size as the 1.5-inch-diameter Chevrolet V-8 small-block valve on the right. Chevy 1.5-inch intake and exhaust valves are drop-in replacements for the flathead Ford V-8. So you can choose high-buck aftermarket valves, or pick up cheaper ones at your Chevy dealer or local auto parts house. The Chevy valve-stem keepers work with the flathead valve-spring retainers.

That's why up front advice on a specific motor is often a very necessary part of what makes a satisfied cutomer.

Motor City Flathead is a resource for any flathead cam still available as well as their proprietary grinds.

Motor City Flathead has three proprietary grinds—the MCF 3/4, 7/8 and Full Race. The 3/4 grind is a good choice for a 3-5/16 x 3-3/4-inch engine of about 258 cubic inches. It's also a good street choice even if the engine displacement is a bit larger. "It's also a good cam with a 3-3/8 x 3-3/4 engine. If the customer wants to put 2 deuces, or 3 deuces or a 4-barrel carb on his engine, he's got the cam, he's got the sound, and he's still got driveability. Even if he is running an automatic; it's just a nice combination."

Heavy-duty valve springs are cataloged by Isky, Speedway Motors and Motor City Flathead. It is always best to buy your springs recommended by the manufacturer of your cam.

The Rest of the Valve Train

The camshaft is only part of the valve-train picture. The remainder is the valve assembly. Original Ford valves were made of chrome-nickel alloy steel. If that rings a bell, it is because it is the metallurgical composition of austenitic stainless steel[1]. Kirby, however, suspects that in later production engines, Ford used a higher nickel content in the exhaust valve because of the more severe demands placed upon it. "Most later-production intake valves are magnetic while the exhausts are *non-magnetic.*"

Kirby also believes Motor City Flathead has improved upon that formula. "We use high-nickel content stainless steel for both our intake and exhaust valves. They are better than stock. It would be foolish not to use the best available modern valves." That's Motor City Flathead for you, always trying to go the competition one better. Even if the competition is ol' Henry himself. I used their valves in my own 8RT.

The major detriment of the typical American overhead valve engine is the complexity and weight of its valve train: lifters, pushrods and rocker arms, and the heavy valve springs required to keep everything in place during high speed operation. The Ford flathead doesn't have to deal with all that.

There are valve lifters to be sure. (Although FoMoCo originally called them *push rods* for some unknown reason.) However, they are very thin-wall castings and much lighter than the typical OHV lifter. And, because the valve and spring assembly is perched right above the lifter, there is no need for real pushrods, rocker arms or killer valve springs.

Those of you who cut your teeth on OHVs, and the substantial valve springs required for even a mild street cam, will be surprised to learn flathead factory specs only called for 36 to 40 pounds per square inch seat pressure. In fact, this specification stayed the same from 1932 through 1953!

"We all know that these are lawn-mower engines, and they don't breathe very well." Kirby smiled, and shook his

Original Ford "pushrod" at left cannot be used with a high-performance cam unless you weld material onto the valve stem to create correct clearance. That's how they did it in the "good old days." Traditional Johnson adjustable tappet at right is no longer made. Photo on page 72 shows the currently available adjustable tappet with original Johnson adjustment wrenches. Current lifters have depressions instead of slots on the outside surface.

---

(1) Although there are more than 40 types of stainless steel, they are classified in three broad divisions based on their predominant crystalline structures: ferritic, martensitic and austenitic. Austenitic is the only one of the three that contains a significant percentage of nickel, typically from 6 to 36 percent. It is extremely tough and ductile in the welded state. *Stainless steel with a low percentages of nickel is magnetic, and is often considered inferior for high performance use.* Stainless steel also contains a minimum of 11-percent chromium. It is the surface layer of chromium oxide that makes it corrosion-resistant.

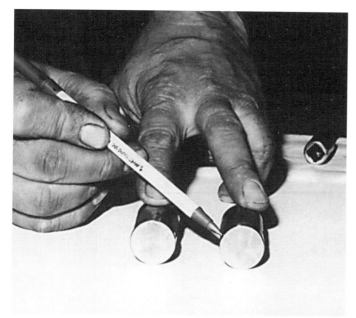

The adjustable lightweight lifter on the left has a sharp-edged machined chamfer as it comes from the box. Motor City Flathead hand polishes a smooth radius around the leading edge of the lifter. This radiused edge is not to be confused with the full radius on the lifter face of the Iskenderian non-adjustable, non-rotating, keyed tappets for competition cam grinds. Is hand polishing a radius busy work or what? What's the significant difference between a machined chamfer and a hand massage? "When you start chamfering, you are coming in 20 or 30 thou each way. That's a lot on a one-inch diameter tappet, and it's stealing part of your cam; it's opening a few thousandths later." Kirby reports that in the past, some traditional cam grinders excessively chamfered the lifters they supplied with their cams. Just one of the reasons a smart swap meet shopper will look over valve gear offerings very carefully.

"The cam grinds that we currently use are as big as we can get out of a 1-inch-diameter tappet. That means that when you run anything other than a stock cam, you really need all of the lifter surface area. We're maxed out with most flathead cams. We know this edge (the leading edge) is critical; it can gall the lobe. To prevent that, we make a nice radius all the way around the edge of the tappet. We remove the stock chamfer and turn it into a polished radius.

The cam gear held in Kirby's left hand is fiber with an aluminum center. Kirby advises against its use. The bonding often loosens and changes the timing. The aluminum one-piece gear (right hand) is far preferable. You might be as lucky as I was, the original cam gear in the 8RT was in excellent shape and I reused it. Not to worry, though . . . replacements are available for the needy.

Most readers already know that the internal combustion engine is merely an air pump. One traditional way of improving its efficiency is to install bigger valves. Kirby points out that his on-going testing has suggested a significant warning. "In valve sizing, we find that we lose airflow between bigger valves and the head gasket. Most people are going to be very happy with the (stock) 1.5-inch intake and exhaust valves. Only the guy who is getting a little carried away will go to a 1.60-inch intake valve." Well, I guess that ends that, no beating around the bush here.

* * *

Trick valves or stock, performance-minded street rodders still have to face up to the realities of today's unleaded gasoline. Fortunately, this is not a significant concern for the flatheader. According to Kirby, the restorer need not worry about unleaded gas. Many stock flathead blocks have seat inserts that are satisfactory from the factory. "Most (but not all) 59s have seats. Some truck motors and the early 8BA stuff have seats. But some later 8BAs don't." Over and over, there is that refrain of unaccountability when trying to pin down a production standard for any of the 22 years the flathead was manufactured. Factory-installed high-tungsten chrome alloy steel valve seat

head in mock amazement at the never-ending paradox of the quintessential hot rod engine. "Yet, in essence, the flathead is an overhead cammer. It doesn't have a heavy valve train or complicated geometry to contend with." True, Kirby's upside-down overhead-cammer analogy ends at the valve *per se*, but it is still something for street rodders to ponder in their next bull session.

* * *

inserts (rather than in-block machining) are just another example. "There's no explanation for any of this," sighs Kirby.

"Anyway, if you are going to be thorough and you are going to build a hot rod engine, you want to make certain you have seats on the exhausts. The intakes are not critical because the valve is not getting hot or cherry red and pounding the seat during operation. The intake has a cool charge rolling over the seat all the time. Remember, (tetraethyl) lead was once used as a fuel additive (to reduce detonation), but it also acted as a cushion. When the valve slammed shut, the blow was cushioned. No lead, no cushion, and you start pounding out the seat. Today, most commercial engine rebuilders install valve seats that are harder than the cast iron in all engines.

Those of you who remember when flatheads powered most street rods will no doubt remember the "cam wars." Everybody was quick to drop the name of their favorite grinder to impress the guys hanging around the burger joint. There was only one significant name in lifters, however: Johnson Lightweights. You can't use stock, non-adjustable Ford lifters (push rods if you like) with a re-ground cam. During re-grinding, material is taken off the cam-lobe heel. In a flathead, some method of "replacing" the material becomes necessary. Although there were overlength or "tipped" valves (or you could weld material onto the end of the valve and grind it flat), the preferred method was, and remains, an overlength, *adjustable* tappet.

Johnson Lightweight Tappets simply dominated the market in the 40s and 50s, but they are no longer made. No need to fret. There's an adequate substitute for street rods. Nevertheless, tappets manufactured today have a machined chamfer on the leading edge. You probably thought that was okay. Kirby doesn't. He radiuses the edge by hand. A lifter with a radiused edge rides the cam lobe easier, smoother and more safely.

* * *

So there you have it, the final (?) word on flathead airflow and what you can reasonably do to improve it. Unfortunately, not all traditional "speed secrets" and cam grinds will return a performance profit to the modern street rodder. Chose your grind prudently, and if you must err, err on the side of conservatism.

Why The Relief?

The first reliefs in a factory block appeared in 1942. While they may have been added to improve mixture flow into the cylinders, they were also used to solve another problem. Pre-1942 truck blocks often cracked from the valve seats into the top of the cylinders. This was because many trucks had vacuum brakes. Using the vacuum brakes caused the mixture to lean out, increasing combustion temperatures and causing thermal stress in this area of the block. The factory relief effectively cured this problem.

Hotrodders typically used the top of the top ring as a guide for the bottom of the relief. They coated the cylinder wall by the relief with Dykem Machinist's Blue, then scribed a line across the top of the top ring with the piston at top center.

Tony DiCosta's Hot Rod & Custom Supply offers every imaginable chromed, polished and functional acessory for any flathead. This beauty sports a finned oil-fill tube, stainless-steel wire looms, alternator and coil mounts and polished three-carburetor air cleaner. Photo courtesy Tony DiCosta.

TABLE ONE

Iskenderian Flathead Cam Timing Specifications

Grind	Type	Intake	Exhaust	Lift (In.)	Duration
77-B	3/4	20-60	60-20	0.320	260 Degrees
Max #1	3/4	17-52	57-12	0.360	249 Degrees
88	Full Race	24-60	64-20	0.320	264 Degrees
1007-B	Track	20-55	15-60	0.355	255 Degrees
1007-LD	Impactor	22-67	65-24	0.370	269 Degree
1017	Track	26-67	67-26	0.355	273 Degrees
400 Jr.	Track	18-60	60-18	0.400	258 Degrees
404-A	Constant Acceleration	20-62	62-20	0.400	262 Degrees
431	Accelerator Track	25-69	69-25	0.422	274 Degrees
433	All-Out Competition	29-71	71-29	0.410	280 Degrees

These traditional Iskenderian Cam specs are presented for general information only. The only Isky grinds currently available are 77-B, Max #1, 88, 400 Jr., and 433.

Isky recommendations are as follows:

77-B;   Good low-speed and mid-range power cam. Good idle.

Max-1:   Good low-speed cam when using stock carburetion and manifold. Good idle.

88:       Good mid-range cam for high-performance street use. Fair idle.

400 Jr.: Competition use, oval track and drags. Lopey idle.

433:      All-out competition use, drags. Lopey idle.

TABLE TWO

Motor City Flathead Cam Timing Specifications

Grind/Type	Intake	Exhaust	Lift (In.)	Duration
3/4	29-72	72-29	0.370	282 Degrees
7/8	29-72	72-29	0.390	282 Degrees
Full Race	28-73	73-28	0.420	282 Degrees

Motor City Flathead recommendations are as follows:

3/4 Grind: Good street characteristics in engines up to 260 cubic inches displacement. Lopey idle.

7/8 Grind: Good street characteristics in engines up to 276 cubic inches displacement. Lopey idle.

Full Race: Good street characteristics in engines up to 286 cubic inches displacement and larger. Lopey idle.

Ron Williams

Lest you think all flatheads are tenderly street-driven marsh-mallows, here's Ron Williams' truly non-wimp '27 T dragster with a rompin' stompin' flathead. Engine is 296-CID, 3-carb Weiand manifold, Weiand heads, Ross pistons and an Iskenderian 400 camshaft. Competing in the flathead/inliner class, it ran 12.868 seconds ET at 106.373 mph in its best outing during 1996. Wheel-standing photo at Indianapolis 1996 flathead/inline class finals. ©1996 by Mark Bruederle. Other photos courtesy Ron Williams. That's Ron with the roadster and a closeup of the engine. Car is pictured on the back cover.

To Bill
From
Ron Williams
'96

Tony Baron - fast flatheadder

Following in his father Frank's footsteps, Tony Baron has created an entirely new line designed for new levels of flathead performance. Also like his father, Tony is a dry lakes and Bonneville racer and his supercharged flathead set a record of 199.041 mph in 1995.

The Baron-equipped engine in Tony's belly tank lakester as it ran at the 1996 Muroc Reunion meet.

Beauty with function: Cylinder heads 3-1/2 inches tall hold a gallon of water. When used with pop-up pistons, they can provide high compression with adequate transfer area for mixture flow. Although this intake manifold is equipped with 4 Weber downdraft carburetors, Baron also offers a plenum top for two 390-cfm Holleys, a throttle-body top for fuel and electronic fuel injection.

6 Building The Bottom End: Installing The Crank & Cam

The right way to build a bottom end for a street rod flathead starts with a clean, well-lighted corner of your garage that is not dusty or drafty. I assume you already have the standard accouterments of a street rodder's garage, i.e., a work bench, drill press, bench grinder and hopefully an air compressor. It is understood that you have, or will acquire, all the hand tools you will need. There's one thing you may not have—a small table on which to lay out the engine parts, so you can keep them clean, well organized and quickly found. A card table is too weak. You can buy a substantial fold-up "banquet table" from the local warehouse home or office improvement store for about $35. Tape a few sheets of poster board on top of it and you can use it later for a backyard barbe-cue! Or, make a substantial bench out of lumber with a plywood or galvanized-metal top.

Before you can get underway, you will need a few assembly items such as white grease, Plastigage®, protective rod sleeves, etc. (See Table 1.) You probably have laundry detergent and access to hot water. With no more ado, let's have at it.

Nothing gets out metal chips and the recently acquired grinding dust, dirt and grime like solvent, followed by a hot soapy scrubbing. First rinse the block thoroughly with clean solvent (away from your assembly area, of course). Make sure to get all the dirt out of the webbing and cylinder recesses. Then use heavy towels and laundry detergent. Lay your hands on a special stiff bristle long-handled cleaning brush. You will need it to clean the oil galleries. The brush is available through auto parts houses and tool suppliers. When you are satisfied that the block is as clean as you can get it, hose it off. Dry it with compressed air or paper towels. When using air, wear safety goggles. Lightly oil the cylinder bores and other machined surfaces. Finally, protect the cleaned and oiled block from airborne dust with large garden plastic bags. They're cheap and easily torn, so use two or three. Don't forget to tape the open end closed.

Next clean the crankshaft thoroughly. The oil passages and sludge traps you cleaned out before hot-tanking are dirty again, this time with grit and grime from regrinding. Clean them again, first with solvent, then with hot soapy water. Dry with compressed air or paper towels. Put a little Loctite® on the new freeze plugs and carefully drive them in with a blunted tool so you won't punch holes in them. I often use a deep socket of the appropriate size. Stake them over to prevent them from falling out when you hit those high notes in second gear. Oh yes, even though your hands may look clean, they really aren't. Wash them frequently.

In a perfect world, you would now begin the assembly of your engine. In reality, many street rodders doing a rebuild as a hobby will not be able to get back to the project right away. Build a simple crank cradle to support the crank longitudinally. Pad the supports with foam rubber. Shoot a light coat of cosmoline or heavy oil on the bearing surfaces. The cradle helps to reduce crank sag, and the cosmoline protects the fresh machining. Wrap the crank in plastic for final protection. Now, if you are away from the project for several weeks, you won't have to worry about your parts.

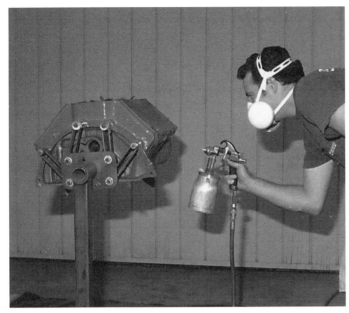 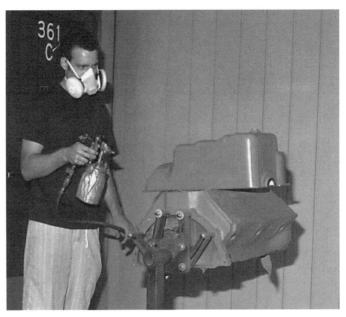

Doesn't the flathead that will power your rod deserve something better than a "quickie" paint job with a $4 hardware-store spray can? Engines get dirty and greasy; even the best of 'em. After the first trip to the quarter car wash, spray-can paint starts to go away. Why not treat your engine with a modern, ultra-durable automotive finish? Angelo is a fan of PPG two-part acrylic-urethane paints and reducers. (Reducer is just a fancy name for expensive thinner, but make no mistake, you gotta use the good stuff.) Mixing paint is like following a cake-baking recipe. If you don't mix the proper ingredients in the proper proportions you will get something other than what you expect. The recipe you need is on the can. While there are several kinds of reducers, what you use depends on ambient temperature at the time of painting. It should be noted, if it is colder than 60F, forget driveway painting. Angelo mixed one part PPG K 200 Primer Surfacer and 1 part DT 1865 Reducer. Then he added one part K 201. The latter is the catalyst or hardener. If you didn't put this in, your paint would stay gummy—it would never dry. The batches were mixed in clean, one-gallon cans, then strained before shooting. Please note, guys. Whatever you do, don't risk your health by painting without a really good face mask. It is an absolute necessity. Borrow or rent the proper safety equipment if you don't feel the cost of purchase is justified. (But it is!) The engine block was taped off before painting. The spraying was done in the Cave's driveway, but make sure this is legal in your community. With the new acrylics, weather is not a problem so long as the ambient temperature is above 60F. Allow 24 hours for drying. In case you're wondering, the block, pan and water pumps were painted a custom-mixed Snap-On® red. No funky green for me!

Now we start down the road of short-block assembly. The first step is to lubricate the cam journals with motor oil. A mixture of STP® and oil is okay for this task. Then, reinstall the oil-gallery pipe plug (removed for block cleaning) behind the cam gear. Put a little bit of gasket sealer such as Permatex® on the plug.

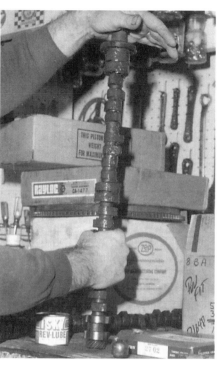

The cam installation is not tricky, but perhaps you noticed that your own 1949-53 cam does not have a distributor drive gear! Don't fret, some aftermarket 8BA types came that way from the manufacturer. Jim Bremner's Isky didn't have a distributor drive gear. Using a standard puller, Jim removed the gear from the original cam, then lightly tapped it on the new bumpstick with a piece of pipe and a hammer. The fit should be snug, but not tight. The cam journals and lobes were then slicked up with moly assembly lube.

Slide the bumpstick in carefully so the lobes do not scratch the soft metal of the bearings. Installing the cam before the crankshaft allows you to reach right down in there to grab and guide the back end. It is relatively easy to nick the lobes or the journals on the many sharp edges in the crankcase.

The cam should rotate freely without any drag. As long as it does, you can turn your attention to the crank.

The first thing is to replace the crankshaft drive gear, oil slinger and key. A piece of steel tubing makes a fine driver. (And an old Captain's chair holds the crank firmly as the gear is driven into place.)

Beginning in 1950, flathead cranks used a sleeve on the snout. It's a press fit with a little spiral groove. Note the direction of the groove—pointing *toward* the crank. It is very important that you start it this way otherwise oil will leak past.

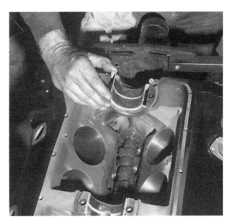

With all parts cleaned, reworked and cleaned again, start assembling the short block. First, verify the correct sizes for each main bearing. The size is usually marked on the back of the bearing shell. Check all new bearings against the old for locking lips, oil grooves and oil holes.

Sometimes you'll get a bearing where the oil hole in the bearing doesn't quite match the oil hole in the block. The bearing in the photo partially covers the hole. The bearings can be off because of machining tolerances in both the block and the bearing. Remember, everybody's variables tend to stack up.

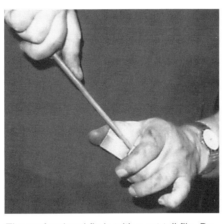

The professional fix is with a rat-tail file. Do it on an angle so the bearing surface isn't marred.

1932 through mid-1936 engines had poured babbit main bearings.

When you are fully satisfied with bearing fit, but before installing them permanently, wipe off each case bore, then the back of the corresponding bearing with a high quality paper towel. It is best not to use a cloth rag or cheap towel because they leave fiber. Install the upper main-bearing halves in the crankcase saddles and snap them into their seats. Be sure each locking lip nests in the recess. Spread a few drops of oil over the bearing surfaces with a *clean* finger.

It is not necessary to align-bore the block so long as you use the block's original main caps. Do not install the lower oil-seal retainer and rope seal. Wipe the crankshaft journals with a high quality paper towel, then carefully position the crank on the bearings. The crank is heavy, so be sure you hold it parallel to the case bores as you gently lower it into position. Take care because the thrust-bearing surfaces can be damaged. Once the crank has been laid, give it a gentle spin to be sure there isn't any major problem. The crankshaft should turn very easily.

Early flathead blocks used main-cap studs, but the 8BA blocks use capscrews (bolts). Trouble is, not all capscrews were created equal; there are *front bolts* and there are *back bolts.* Front bolts on a flathead are full-shouldered, i.e., not designed for a washer. Washers are used on the remaining bolts.

The front and center caps are sometimes confused by flatheaders. The bolt hole is in the center on the center cap, and the hole is slightly offset on the front cap. Although the caps are not marked, many engine builders stamp them. It is obvious that the rear cap can only go on one way, but it could be twisted around, remember that it has to be tang-to-tang.

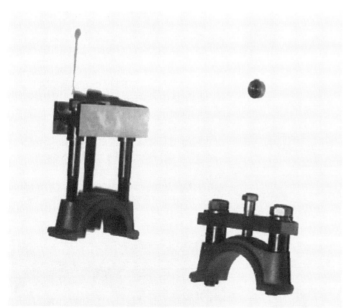

Some folks feel the three-main-bearing bottom end is a significant design flaw. Although most mild, carbureted street rod flatheads shouldn't experience any problems with stock main caps, those who opt for greater displacement may be at risk because the center bearing does get stressed a bit. Mark Kirby re-emphasized this a few years ago when he told me, "The flathead is rugged, it'll take a lot of abuse before it lets go, but the center main is the weak link when you start to build horsepower. It just can't take the load of 4 cylinders on that one bearing. For years speed merchants offered a 1/2-inch-thick main-cap strap with a 3/8-inch bolt in the center that pressed against one point on the cap (shown at left in left photo). Unfortunately, the bolt/strap would act as a splitter when a strong enough downforce was applied." Motor City Flathead to the rescue. "Our version of the old strap is an I-beam carved out of a piece of billet steel. It is designed not to flex, and we make a foot to spread the bolt-applied load. Rodders should note that there is more than one main-cap style. Measure and tell us how wide it is. Sometimes the cap has to be milled."

Original main-bearing-cap bolts are fine for street engines. Install the main caps, and run the bolts (with oiled threads) in finger-tight. Tap each cap with a plastic or leather mallet to help it find its natural position. Then, using a heavy screwdriver or pry bar, force the crankshaft forward until the rear faces of the thrust flanges are properly aligned. Don't put oil on the thrust face because it could give a false end-play reading by as much as 0.002-inch. When the thrust flanges are aligned, tighten all of the nuts/bolts alternately to fairly snug. Then, final tighten each nut/bolt to the proper torque limit specifications in three steps: 60 foot pounds, 80 foot pounds, then 100 foot pounds.

After the nuts/bolts have all been torqued, rotate the crankshaft by hand. If there are no alignment problems and everything has been done properly up to now, the crank should turn reasonably freely. Now check the crankshaft end play. The correct end play is built into the thrust bearing. But to be sure it is within specified limits, check it with a feeler gauge. From 0.002-inch to 0.006-inch is acceptable. That's the good news. The bad news is that you have to remove the crank to install the upper half of the oil-seal retainer in the cylinder block.

The stock rope seal for the front of the pan is shown on page 90 (with oil filter).

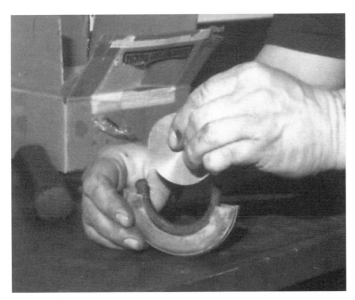

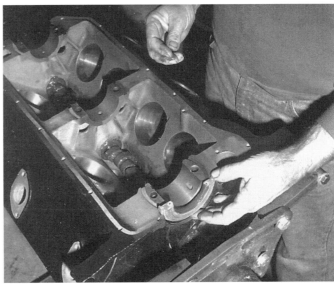

Flatheads aren't blessed with a nice modern rubber lip seal. You have to shape the rope seal a little bit. To make the installation easier, soak the rope seal in motor oil for a half hour. Use a piece of aluminum stock about 2-1/2-inches in diameter for an insertion tool "and smack it with a hammer!" Trim the ends of the seal flush with the face of the retainer before the retainer is installed. Mark suggests laying a bead of auto silicone on top of the seal ends. "When we set this baby in there, we know we will have a good seal!" Even so, if you find a drop or two of oil under your car down the road, don't be discouraged. As Mark says, "People just have to understand this is part of the beast, but there should never be any puddles." Note: A modern seal for the timing cover and pan is illustrated on page 75.

Wipe off the crankshaft journals with paper towels one last time, then carefully re-position the crank on the bearings. Again, take care lest you damage the thrust bearings. Yeah, that crank definitely starts to get a little heavy about now, so a helping hand is appreciated.

A generous serving of white lithium grease on the mains is good insurance, especially if you think it might be some time before you run the engine.

Re-torque the cap bolts or nuts just as methodically as you did the first time. There is a natural apprehension with a 45-year-old engine that some in-block threads may have been stressed one time too many. If you get a mushy one, you'll feel it. In other words, you can't back off now. Correctly torqued main cap bolts or nuts are essential. If some in-block threads are weak, the problem was there before you started.

One more spin test on the crank to ensure all is well, and you're ready to proceed to the next step, installation of the remainder of the valve train.

Bob Whitehead - Flathead "Investor"

You've noticed Bob Whitehead's name appearing throughout this book--and for good reason. He is a serious collector of flathead antiquitaria and some of his more interesting acquisitions illustrate the historical commentary. Bob's multi-car garage in Bella Vista, Arkansas is not simply a repository of ancient aluminum artifacts. It also houses his street rod collection. And, because no rod shows off an imposing motor better than a Deuce, I've included his full-fendered roadster to prove that man does not live by engine alone.

Stationed on the West Coast during a stint in the Air Force in the early 1960s, Bob spent his off-hours working at Gene Winfield's custom body shop. He wisely plowed his meager earnings back into this roadster. A true 1950s type rod (1939 Ford trans, 1940 Ford rear end), the Edelbrock-equipped 276-CID 59AB powers a real steel car with profitable returns that would make any ordinary financial portfolio blush with shame.

Bob's passion within a passion is his love of the Ardun conversion. This original, outfitted with modern Weber carbs, has powered first this, and then that of his street rod collection. Dunno what it will go into next, but I suspect any surviving moonshiners would give their eye-teeth for it.

Well, what do you expect a serious collector like Bob to do with all that stuff. How about building a few spare engines such as this 59AB with a modern T-Bird huffer, and a "fotogenic" flathead complete with "beehive" oil filter (lower left).

Now retired and living the life of a country gentleman in the Ozarks, Whitehead pursues his life-long passion of collecting flathead memorabilia. No, Arkansas is not a secret repository of V-8 goodies, he travels 'round the country to all of the big swap meets searching out rare and pristine examples of what was once commonplace.

Bill Herbert - Innovator

Bill Herbert, a long-time aficionado of flatheads, owns this head-turning flathead-powered 1934 roadster. 59A-style ignition and heads are used on an 8BA block. He made his own magnetically triggered ignition to provide sparks plus trigger pulses for a 500-cfm 2-barrel Holley Pro-Jection fuel injection. A Kong Jackson intake manifold and heads add to the beauty of this creation. A Winfield SU-4 camshaft handles the valve motion. Exhaust exits via Fenton headers, of course. Bill is a 27-year member of the L.A. Roadsters club which holds the annual Fathers' Day meet at the Los Angeles County Fairplex.

Not content to wait for a fuel injection specifically designed for the flathead, Herbert adapted the Holley ProJection in 1995. The performance is outstanding!

Polishing those genie Halibrand wheels is a never-ending task, but don't they look great?

John Bradley - Fastest Flathead Dragster

John Bradley started drag racing in 1946. By 1952 he had his first dragster--a 4-cylinder Cragar Model B that turned 115 mph. Once he changed to the flathead V-8 in 1953, he won so many races that he became known as *Mr. Flathead*. John campaigned a twin-engine flathead dragster from 1958-62. He was inducted into the International Drag Racing Hall of Fame in 1994.

On the line at Sacramento Raceway. Engine here had 8 exhaust ports. Car weighs only 850 pounds and has turned 151 mph with a 9.30-second ET. Photo by Ron Burch, Drag Race Photographer ©1990.

This engine has only 8 exhaust ports. John usually adds 6 extra ports for a total of 12 exhaust ports. The two center cylinders are completely separated. Hilborn injectors remade by Bradley, Mallory Mag-Spark 3 ignition on a home made drive. Billet heads are hand made by John. Potvin 425 cam actuates 1-11/16-inch valves. Ross pistons with Total-Seal rings on Cunningham rods. Girdle and main caps by Doug King. Clutch is an L & T Double-8 slider. Only high gear is used. Fuel is 98% nitromethane with 2% alcohol. Photos courtesy of John Bradley.

1957 at Cordova, Illinois where John was the Top Fuel Runner-up. Equipment included Isky 404 camshaft, 1-11/16-inch valves, Jahns pistons, Edelbrock heads and 4-carb manifold, Schiefer clutch and flywheel. Harmon & Collins magneto. 6 extra exhaust outlets. John won 50 Top Fuel Eliminator Awards in 1957-58 with this car.

Finishing The Valve-Train Installation

Installation of the valve assembly looks complicated to the street rodder unversed in the vagaries of the old Ford side-valve engine. In reality it is no more complicated than the comparable procedure in an OHV engine. Some parts and the spatial relationships are different, though. The valve spring, valve guide and valve are all one assembly that drops into the engine block as a unit.

Then you have to pull the guide down to get the horseshoe-shaped valve-guide bushing retainer in (sometimes called a *crowsfoot*). This is done with a special, long-handled tool properly called a *valve lifter*, but generations of hot rodders have called the thing a *pickle fork.* The pickle fork is inserted into notches in the lower end of the guide to compress the valve spring.

The valve guide bushing retainer (see figure 1) is inserted to lock the assembly in position. If a hole has been drilled in the lifter boss (shown in a previous chapter), all that is needed to

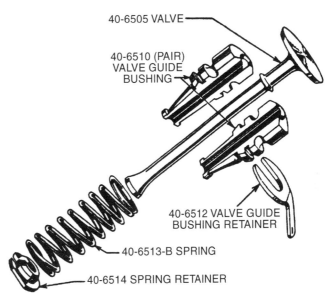

40-6505 VALVE

40-6510 (PAIR) VALVE GUIDE BUSHING

40-6512 VALVE GUIDE BUSHING RETAINER

40-6513-B SPRING

40-6514 SPRING RETAINER

Figure 1

Figures 1, 2: Exploded drawings of the camshaft and early valve assembly taken from Ford Service Bulletins. Ford used split guides through 1948, then went to solid guides and a more-or-less conventional valve stem with split keepers because the split guides tended to move apart, galling and destroying the valve-guide bore. Figure 2 shows both the bolt-on cam gear as used from 1939-48 and the 1932-38 press-on gear with a mark that was aligned with a mark on the cam nose. 1939-41 "short nose" 21A cams are used with a specific timing cover and distributor. 1942-48 "long nose" 91A cams also require a specific timing cover and distributor. It is important to keep similar parts together so the distributor fits correctly and turns freely. 1949-53 cams have an extended nose with a distributor drive gear. Cornhuskers Rod & Custom offers a bolt-on extension for 21A and 91A cams to add the gear drive for a post-type 1949-53 distributor.

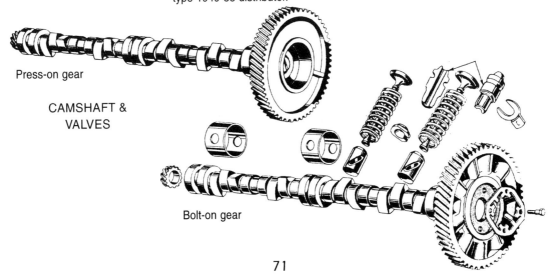

Press-on gear

CAMSHAFT & VALVES

Bolt-on gear

Figure 2

71

The layout of some cam-installation hardware and the remainder of the valve train. Pictured is the aluminum camshaft timing gear, solid one-piece valve guides, valve-guide retainers, and a gear lock-ring with special shouldered bolts.

One more check to make sure the oil-gallery plug has been installed.

Install the timing gear, and although it can only go on one way, make sure the timing marks are lined up.

Install new lock-ring with its special bolts, and tighten. The hammer is wedging the crank so it doesn't move during tightening. Bend the locking tabs over. It is sometimes worthwhile to have an extra lock-ring handy. If a tab breaks, use a new lock-ring.

adjust the lifter is a thin, open-end wrench and a drift punch. If there is no hole in the boss, a special, but inexpensive, set of wrenches is available from the lifter supplier. One is used to hold the lifter, the other to turn the adjustment screw.

Johnson adjustable lifters (tappets) were hollow with large "windows" in the side (see photo, page 53). There was no problem using the punch through a hole in the lifter boss because the punch fit into one of the windows. Currently available tappets have a little cast-in depression that the punch can jump out of, so this can make tappet adjusting more than a lit-

tle frustrating. If worse comes to worst, you can always try using the wrenches, but you won't like it.

No matter which method you use, it's an awkward procedure. Guys with

big mitts get frustrated. Sorry 'bout that, it's one of the reasons this is called a *knuckle-busting hobby*. At any rate, there's no better way to learn than by doing, so have at it . . .

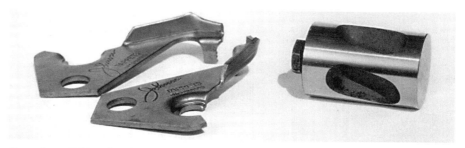

Currently available adjustable tappet with a set of original Johnson adjustment wrenches. There are depressions instead of slots on the outside surface. Bear down on the punch that you insert through the lifter boss as you adjust valve clearances. Otherwise, turning the adjusting nut may force the punch out of the depression. Photo courtesy Gene Scott, Antique Auto Parts.

Just as a matter of clarification, the new MCF Power Valve is on the left, the middle and right are 8RT originals. You can see that the OEM valves have a ledge (arrow) on the stem. This is just another old Ford artifact, modern valves don't have it or need it. Ledge is also shown on figure 1.

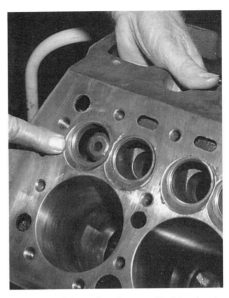

Lube a lifter tappet and drop it into the boss. Then lube a guide and make sure it slides freely in the bore.

If you are running a mild cam and the grinder does not specify an installed spring height, you can proceed. Lightly lubricate and build the valve assembly. Shims can be added to obtain a desired spring height. Typically, Chevrolet valves will require shims. If the valve spring has closely wound coils at one end, that end goes toward the guide. A rubber seal encircles the solid valve-guide bushing to eliminate oil being sucked into the incoming air/fuel mixture. Oil in the mixture promotes detomnation and carbon build-up. The exhaust guide does not have a rubber seal. Valve-stem seals can also be installed on the intake valves.

Let me add a few calming words here for the meticulous. There is no doubt that for maximum confidence in the precision of your valve timing, the cam should be degreed. Degreeing, however, requires a dial indicator and a bit of experience in its use or false readings will occur. The probability of a poorly indexed cam (direct from the grinder) is so remote as to render concern pointless. Relax.

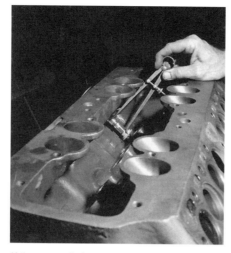
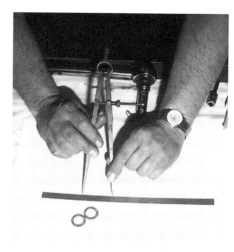

If the cam grinder recommends precise "installed valve-spring height" this is what you do. Install a light spring to hold the valve, spring, spring seat, guide and guide retainer (everything necessary to simulate a loaded valve assembly) in place. Measure the distance between the spring seat and the retainer with a pair of dividers and a scale (steel ruler) to determine the installed valve-spring height. Shim as necessary to meet cam specs.

Make sure that you understand which groove the horseshoe/crowsfoot guide retainer fits in, and that the valve guide does indeed fit.

Close-wound coils at one end of the valve spring should be placed toward the guide.

Rotate the cam until the lifter is sitting on the heel of the lobe. Compress the spring and guide with the pickle fork in the groove, using the top of the block for a leverage fulcrum. Pull the guide down far enough so the guide retainer will go in.

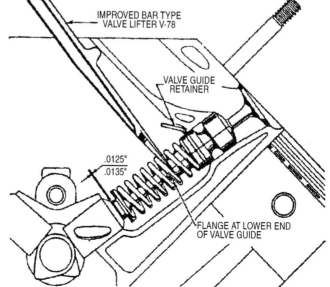

IMPROVED BAR TYPE
VALVE LIFTER V-78

VALVE GUIDE
RETAINER

.0125"
.0135"

FLANGE AT LOWER END
OF VALVE GUIDE

Figure 3

 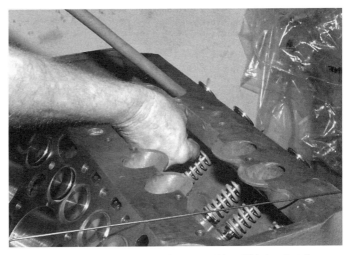

When installing the intake valve assemblies, it is sometimes easier to reach through the intake port to do the same thing. This is what the other end of the pickle fork is for. Either way, just make sure that the horseshoe retainer is securely in place before you release the spring.

After all valve assemblies are in place, but before they are adjusted, drop back to the front of the engine and install the oil slinger and sleeve on the crank. And let's take a look at a couple of new pieces that just may turn your crank.

Ever eager to keep their modern-day customers happy, Motor City Flathead developed a straight-cut cam-gear set. The more nostalgic among us love the whine of straight-cut gears.

Betcha never saw one of these before. VEO Products (1000 Piner Rd., Ste. G, Santa Rosa, CA 95403) has an aluminum-bodied, 360-degree neoprene-lip oil seal for the timing gear cover and oil pan. Their motto is, "Just say nope to rope" and that says it all. It fits all 1928-53 4-cylinder and V-8 engines, and when properly installed, prevents oil leaks. Note the oil-drain hole. When the seal is installed, make sure the oil-drain hole is on the bottom so oil can drain back into the pan. VEO's oil seal is closer to a modern seal design and easier to install than the traditional rope seal. I strongly recommend using this seal for your rebuild.

At this point, it is a good idea to reinstall the timing-gear cover to prevent cam walk that can upset the valve adjustment. Carefully slip it over the oil seal and into the recess in the block. Our die-cast aluminum cover has been modified, but we'll discuss that in detail later.

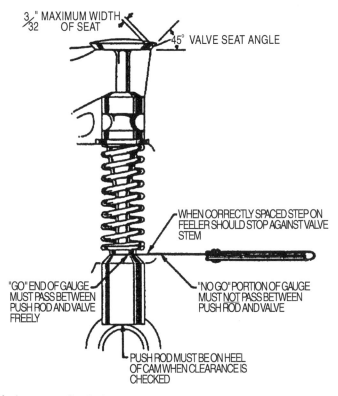

$\frac{3}{32}$" MAXIMUM WIDTH OF SEAT

45° VALVE SEAT ANGLE

WHEN CORRECTLY SPACED STEP ON FEELER SHOULD STOP AGAINST VALVE STEM

"GO" END OF GAUGE MUST PASS BETWEEN PUSH ROD AND VALVE FREELY

"NO GO" PORTION OF GAUGE MUST NOT PASS BETWEEN PUSH ROD AND VALVE

PUSH ROD MUST BE ON HEEL OF CAM WHEN CLEARANCE IS CHECKED

Check clearance between the lifter and the end of the valve stem with a feeler gauge. Stock clearances are shown on page 42. Specs will be a little different for a re-ground cam. They are supplied with the cam. The cam I installed calls for 0.012-inch intake clearance, and 0.014-inch exhaust clearance. By the way, this cold adjustment is just fine for most street work. The procedure is repeated for each valve. At this point I suppose you are wondering just which cam I selected for my 8RT. After much thought, and in line with my conservative everyday street driving, I chose the MCF 3/4 grind with 0.370-inch lift and 282-degree duration. I like 'em quiet and docile on the street.

Assuming the lifter bores have been drilled, you'll only need a thin 7/16-inch open-end wrench, a drift to hold the lifters, and your feeler gauges. Again, don't forget to rotate the crank until the lifter to be adjusted is riding on the heel of the cam. (The quick and easy way to be sure, is to rotate the crank until the valve is fully off its seat, then a half revolution more. At that point the valve drops, and the lifter is on the heel of the cam.) Next, insert the drift through the hole in the lifter bore and on into the depression in the lifter.

Also see sidebar, page 38.

8 Installing The Piston/Rod Assembly

After the cam and crankshaft have been installed, the home-builder can turn his attention to filling those empty cylinders with the rest of the plastic-wrapped goodies in the box that came back from the engine balancer.

We've already pointed out that the street rodder doesn't have a practical alternative to those 45-year-old long-legged stock connecting rods, and they simply must be reconditioned. We also discussed modern piston metallurgy, and Motor City's new age piston-design answer to ol' Henry's interpretation of the DeSaxe Principal back in 1931, i.e., the 0.265-inch offset of the crankshaft. We haven't, however, taken notice of the piston rings. Now is the time.

The traditional, and most commonly available flathead compression ring is 0.0938-inch (3/32-inch) thick. Well, the Motor City pistons we are installing in the 8RT are cut for 0.078 inch compression rings. That may startle some of you who equate thickness with strength, and have heard stories about flathead rings breaking. Don't fret about that, we'll circumvent that problem when we grind the end-gap in our rings.

Kirby believes the smallish flathead bore size makes a thinner ring the best choice for normal street use. He is even experimenting with 0.062-inch rings. He reasons thus: "We always want minimal ring drag on the cylinder walls and the flathead doesn't need massive rings. The Japanese are running rings as thin as 1 mm (0.0394-inch) on small pistons. The 0.078-inch

You will need a place to assemble the piston/rod unit, and although your regular work bench can be used, I've found that a small, mobile, easily cleaned "dedicated" engine-building bench with the specific tools needed is more efficient. My own bench has a box of high-grade Scott WypAll® wipers, a roll of high-grade Scott® Shop Towels, and shelves for acetone, motor oil, assembly lube, and white grease. The top of the bench is covered with inexpensive stick-on floor tiles and mounts a small vise on one end and the ring gapper on the other. Below the bench is a tool drawer and a storage cabinet for parts, gaskets and the like.

ring is proven, and is better than 0.093. And as soon as our field tests indicate that 0.062-inch rings work, they will be offered. The oil-control rings we use, either 0.156-inch or 0.187-inch are what everybody uses."

Finally, the builder must choose chrome or cast-iron rings. Chrome rings are the highest grade, and worth it in an extremely dirty environment, but they are expensive. I selected cast iron for the 8RT. MCF's compression rings are made by the company that manufactures their pistons, but they use Grant oil-control rings.

There really isn't much more to jaw about, so let's get our hands oily.

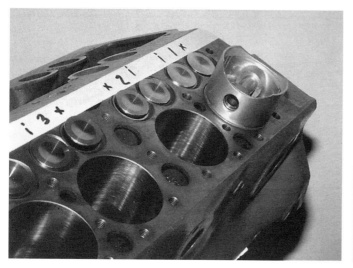
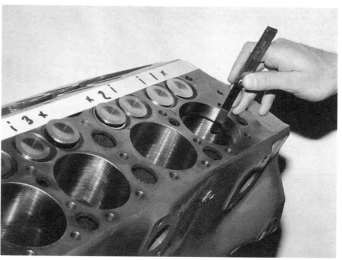

The top of each compression ring has to be matched to the particular cylinder in which it will be used. Therefore, the end gap (which allows for heat expansion) must be as precise as possible. Fit one ring at a time. Put a ring into the cylinder, then square it to the bore with a new piston. Determine what the "out-of-the-box" end gap is with a feeler gauge. By the way, the strip of masking tape across the deck identifies the cylinders. When you are whirling around the block during assembly, it is easy to forget which hole is which.

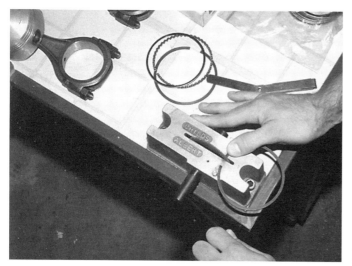
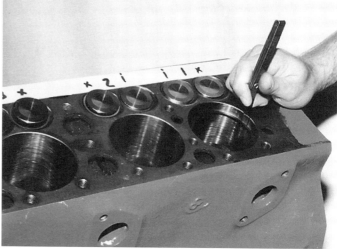

Grind *one end* of the ring ever so carefully to obtain the proper gap. I have used a Childs & Albert gapper for years, and I know from experience how rough the cutting wheel is. (One full turn grinds off about 0.002-inch.) The maximum end gap is 0.016-inch in a normally aspirated street engine, with a minimum end gap of 0.012-inch. (The rule of thumb is 0.004" per inch of bore.) The rings in my 8RT with its 3-5/16-inch bore were gapped at exactly 0.014 inch. The new gap is measured by carefully fitting in the feeler gauge and holding it parallel to the cylinder wall. If you are building a supercharged engine, remember that blower heat requires opening the gap a bit more. The ring manufacturer is the best resource for that information.

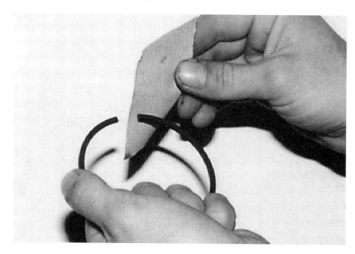

When you have gapped one cylinder's rings, *lightly* deburr the rough edges of the end you cut. Use a piece of 400-grit sandpaper. Don't overdo this step, or you chance losing compression.

All flathead rods are bushed and pin-fitted by the machine shop, but they come back to you bolted together and a bit dirty. Clamp them in a *padded* vise and remove the cap. Again, do one rod at a time to avoid mix-ups.

Use a stiff-bristle toothbrush and a sharp pick to clean the grime from the bearing-tang nest and around the integral rod bolts. Paint thinner is an acceptable solvent. Work outside to avoid noxious fumes, and wear gloves if your skin is sensitive. Angelo is tough, so he didn't wear gloves, but as soon as each rod was cleaned in solvent, he washed his hands, the rod, piston and pin in hot soapy water. He then dried the parts (and his hands) with compressed air.

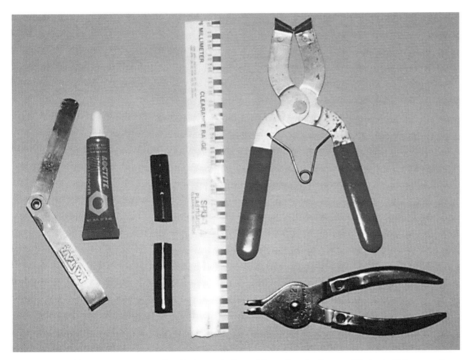

I'm sure you knew you were going to have to invest in a few tools specific to building engines to complete your project. In addition to the feeler gauge, you will need a ring expander and a pair of special pliers for the wrist-pin circlips. They are available from any auto-parts store as is a length of rubber tubing (for crankpin protectors), Plastigage® Clearance Indicator and Loctite® High-Strength Red Threadlocker.

The most important tool is the ring compressor (squeezer). There are several varieties, and the auto-parts store will be glad to demonstrate them. My personal favorite is the machined, tapered, aluminum sleeve. You simply can't break a ring with one of them, and you sure can with universal squeezers. Sleeves are commonly available in speed shops, but guess what? None will fit the flathead "pee-wee" bore! Hey, necessity is the mother of invention or something like that, right? That's why I prevailed upon Motor Arts (P.O. Box 9902, Brea, CA 92822) to add them to their catalog of unique flathead equipment.

Assembly begins with oiling and inserting the wrist pin through the piston and rod. Note well the "FRONT" inscription on the piston and the cylinder number stamped on the big end of the rod. When you eventually sink the piston, you want the word "FRONT" at 3 o'clock, and facing the front of the engine. In addition to this, you want the stamped number on the rod visible to you from the *outside* of the cylinder block. This is not merely convention; it is purposeful. It is to accommodate the offset of the piston pin, and to make sure the machined chamfer on the big end of the rod (and bearing) is in the proper relationship to the radius of the crankpin for proper oiling. Next install a circlip in the piston at each end of the piston. Take care to ensure that the clip is seated in the groove. Even young eyes can be fooled, so break out that magnifying glass to check that each clip is seated. I have seen the damage caused to engines by a clip that worked loose.

  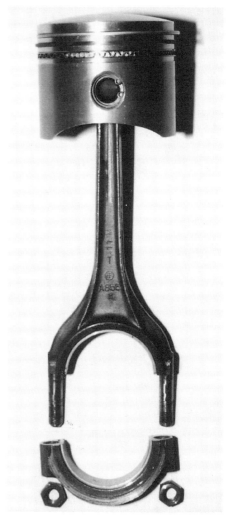

Now you're ready to install the piston rings. Clamp the rod in your padded vise and install the oil ring first. Be sure the ends of the expander ring are visible and properly butted, and the gap is above the piston boss area. Install the top and bottom rails over the expander with their gaps 180 degrees apart.

Use the ring-expanding tool to install the second and top compression rings. Look closely at the rings, there will usually be a dimple or some kind of marking indicating the top side of the ring. My rings had a tiny "C" stamped in. Be gentle, no need to open the rings any larger than the circumference of the piston. Rings have been known to break.

Use a Scott WypAll to wipe out the rod bore and the back of the bearing insert upper half. Install the bearing in the bore, making sure the tang nests properly in the recess. Spread engine oil or assembly lube on the bearing surface.

The fully assembled piston/rings/rod/bearings assembly ready to sink. Individual rod bearings can only be used on 1949-53 crankshafts with two oil holes in each crankshaft rod journal. They *cannot* be used on 1932-48 crankshafts with only one oil hole in each crankshaft rod journal.

Oil the rings and full surface of the piston and slip it through the tapered end of the ring sleeve. Gently close each ring gap with your thumbs as you are pushing the piston into and down the sleeve. The same procedure is followed if you are using an adjustable universal type ring squeezer. An inch or so of the skirt should extend past the squeezer so you can guide the piston into the cylinder.

Full-floating Bearings

Gotta stop right here for you guys building a 1948 or earlier engine with a stock crank and original "full-floating" rod bearings. One full-floating bearing services both connecting rods on the crankpin, so the top bearing half is placed directly on the crankpin before the piston/rod assembly is installed. Simply dab a tiny bit of white grease on the bearing surface that fits to the crank pin to hold the bearing steady and proceed. Full-floating rod bearings are illustrated on page 85.

Before you install the piston assembly, wipe the cylinder clean with an acetone-soaked WypAll, then oil it well. The best thing to use to oil the bore is your hand. You can feel the bore to make sure you're getting full coverage.

Slip the rubber crankpin protectors on the rod studs, then turn the block so the deck surface is level with the world. Rotate the crank so it is at the bottom of the throw. Carefully slip the rod down the bore. Make sure the piston and rod reference marks are in correct relation to the front of the engine.

Carefully slide the piston skirt into the bore so that the loaded ring squeezer sits squarely on the deck. Gently tap the assembly down the bore. With your thumb and forefinger wrapped around the journal, grab the rod studs and guide the rod into place. Make sure the rod studs do not touch and damage the crankpin while the rod is being installed.

Wipe off the connecting-rod-cap bore and the back of the lower bearing insert. Install the bearing into the cap, again making sure the tang nests properly. Spread assembly lube or white grease on the cap bearing surface, then install it. Put a little Loctite on the threads and turn the nuts down a little more than finger-tight. Be sure the rod cap and blade markings are on the same side. The same general procedure is followed for rods with full-floating bearings.

Continue tapping the piston crown gently, and keep an eye on the bearing to make sure it stays in place. Firmly seat the rod bearing on its crankpin.

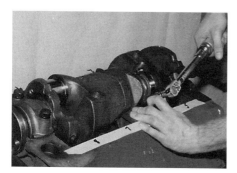

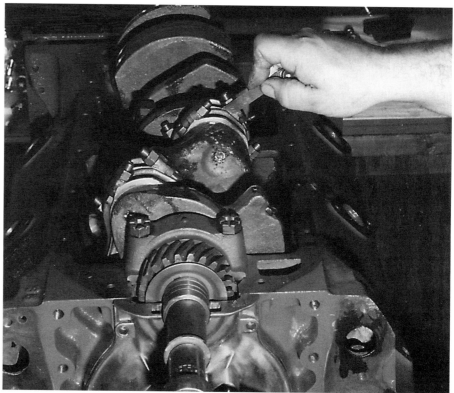

Tap the cap with a plastic mallet to firmly seat it in its proper position. Then tighten the rod nuts to 45 foot pounds. Be exact, too much torque will distort the cap. Install the remaining piston/rod assemblies in the same manner. As a final check, and to save possible trouble later, recheck the reference marks to be sure all parts are in the proper position. Recheck the cap nuts to ensure correct torque limits and finally, be sure the crankshaft still turns nice and easy.

And now for a few "safety" checks. True, at this point, there's not a lot you can do about side clearance between original, well-used rods. Yet, it never hurts to verify a good fit. The normal range is from 0.007 to 0.012 inch. Rods that have been in the engine all its service life are not likely to be too close, but there is the off chance that a rod may have been *overclearanced* sometime in the engine's dark past. If you run into either too much or too little, telephone your machinist. Decisions here are a judgement call, and his is the best judgement.

As long as the crank assembly turns over smoothly with no problems, you can be reasonably certain the machine work was done properly. However, if you want to be absolutely sure, Plastigage the tolerances. Plastigage Clearance Indicator is a thin strand of wax available in three color-coded thicknesses. The "Green," with a 0.001- to 0.003-inch clearance-evaluation range, is normally used on street motors. It can be used at any stage of the assembly process, but always when the engine builder senses an unusual drag while rotating the crank by hand. Its application is extremely simple. Remove the crank or rod cap and wipe the bearing surface clean. Lay a strip of Plastigage across the width of the journal and re-install the cap to torque specs. Then remove it again. Tear a piece of the paper sleeve the Plastigage comes in, and using the "piano keys," measure the "squished" wax strip. You can feel confident if the strip measures at or around 0.0015-inch. If not, well, discuss it with your machinist before you go any further.

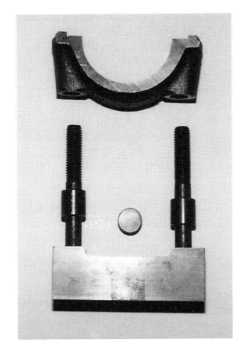

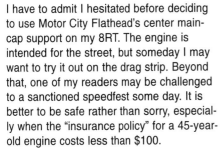

I have to admit I hesitated before deciding to use Motor City Flathead's center main-cap support on my 8RT. The engine is intended for the street, but someday I may want to try it out on the drag strip. Beyond that, one of my readers may be challenged to a sanctioned speedfest some day. It is better to be safe rather than sorry, especially when the "insurance policy" for a 45-year-old engine costs less than $100.

MCF advises home installers that there is a variety of flathead main caps. If any trouble is encountered when fitting the support, the customer's cap will be "massaged" at no cost. Part of the *routine* procedure, however, does involve filing or milling a flat on the curve of the cap where the support foot rests. Bob Schweder of BC & Sons Fabrication (361-C Oak Pl., Brea, CA 92821) spot-faced the 8RT's cap for a professional-looking installation.

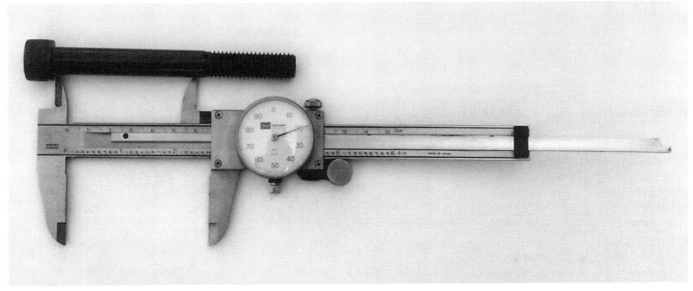

New Grade-8 socket bolts come with the cap support, and to make sure that they would not bottom out in my block, I measured the combined thickness of the support and the cap, and verified that 3/16-inch of the bolt shoulder (just before the threads end) would seat in the crankcase web as required on a stock installation.

The cap and support were then torqued to specs (60-80-100 foot pounds). The foot was centered, and a liberal dose of Loctite was applied to the threads of the 3/8-inch bolt that locates the foot. The bolt was run down finger-tight only. That is, *no* load is put on the cap. While the Loctite was still wet, the bolt was centerpunched in several places around the support to further ensure that it would not back off in service.

Installing the Oil Pump and Idler Gear

The next chapter discusses adding a full-flow oil filter and installing the oil pan. If you are not going to install a full-flow filter with its special oil pump, now is the time to install the oil pump. I recommend a new short-body pump with helical gears. This type was introduced in 1950. You will need the matching short-body pickup, as illustrated on page 88. Use the original bolt with new lock wire to hold the pump to the block.

It is not necessary to use a high-volume pump.

Now look at the back of the block. Install the oil plug (not used on all blocks) and the idler gear shaft (if it was removed). Install the idler gear and add the cover with its gasket, bolts and lock wire. A bit of white grease on the idler-gear shaft and gear teeth would be a good plan.

Oil-Pressure Relief Valve

On 1932-48 blocks install the oil-pressure relief valve at the front of the block. (See photo).

Fuel-Pump Pushrod Hole

If you will not be using the stock fuel pump, the hole for the fuel pump pushrod must be plugged. (See photo).

Install Oil Baffles

Install the two oil baffles in the lifter area.

Installing the Oil Pan

Use the photos in the next chapter as a guide to install the oil pan. The captions provide tips on gasket sealers to help avoid oil leaks.

1932-48 blocks have a second oil-pressure-relief vavle in addition to one in the oil pump. This second spring-loaded relief valve at the front of the block consists of a ball-shaped end, a spring, and a retaining cap. Photo at left shows threaded hole for the relief valve (arrow) with the vavle assembly at right. Other photo shows the valve retaining cap ready to be screwed into the block. This relief valve must be installed or there will be an enormous oil leak instead of pressurized oil to the rod and main bearings.

Hole for fuel-pump pushrod at the back of all flathead blocks (arrow) must be plugged if the stock fuel pump is not used. Otherwise there will be a massive oil leak and little oil pressure to the rods and mains. An expansion plug can be used to close the hole, or it can be tapped and plugged.

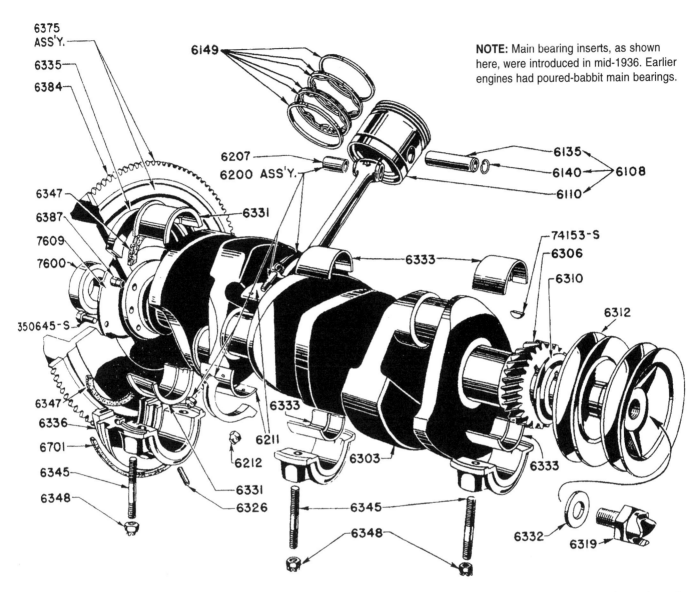

NOTE: Main bearing inserts, as shown here, were introduced in mid-1936. Earlier engines had poured-babbit main bearings.

The rotating and reciprocating parts of a 1932-48 crankshaft assembly. A wide rod bearing insert pair is used for every two rods, as shown in the photo below. This full-floating bearing insert is used with rods with no cutouts for bearing tangs as used on 1949-53 rods with individual rod bearings. If you cannot find these wide rod bearings at swap meets, Federal-Mogul still offers tin-plated copper-alloy wide rod bearings as 9800 for the Ford 1.999-inch journal diameter and 9805 for the 2.138-inch Mercury journal.

1950s crankshaft kit used full-floating rod bearings. One pair of rod inserts was used for two connecting rods. The connecting rod big-end bores were completely smooth inside because no bearing tangs were needed. Photo by Bill Fisher.

NOTE: Full-floating rod bearings can be used on all cranks from 1932-53. Individual insert rod bearings can only be used on 1949-53 cranks with two oil holes in each crankshaft rod journal.

Don Orosco - Benefactor

Once in a great moon, a sports participant shifts gears and become . . . well, for want of a better phrase, a patron of the sport. A patron, not in the sense of a customer, but rather of a benefactor. Don Orosco, an enthusiastic vintage race car shoe can legitimately lay claim to that title. He's taken the bull by the horns and accomplished a painstaking reproduction of not only the fabled Ardun OHV cylinder head conversion kit, but also makes the rare Smith and Eddie Meyer cylinder heads for the conventional valve-in-block flathead. All products are currently available, but the production runs are extremely limited. Interested buyers better not procrastinate.

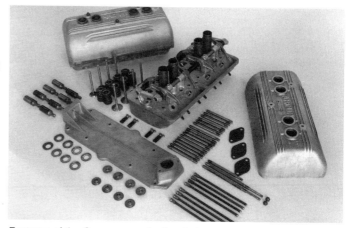

Features of the Orosco reproduction Ardun are too numerous to list here, but here are a few highlights: All aluminum parts are cast in premium Alcoa 356 alloy, then fully CNC-machined before being finally heat treated to T-6 specs. The rockers are investment-cast in 17-4 stainless steel, individually X-rayed and heat treated. The resulting product is undeniably superior to the original.

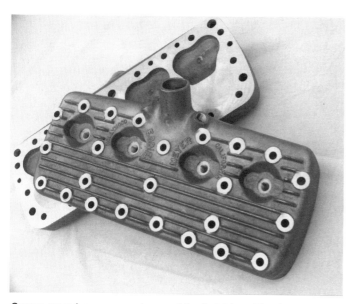

Orosco reproduces an exact copy of the first 24-stud head produced after WW II by Eddie Meyer for the 59AB and 8BA engines. Note the elliptical spark-plug wells that allow machining to install two spark plugs per cylinder.

Few, if any other flathead manifolds bring with them more nostalgia and mystique than the original Eddie Meyer two-carb model with exhaust heat. This underside view shows the high-quality material and machining of Orosco's reproduction.

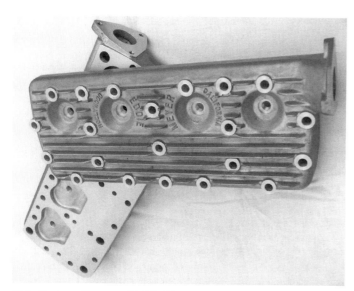

Only Cyclone, Evans and Eddie Meyer produced heads for 21-stud engines before World War II. The Eddie Meyer versions were very popular. Orosco's re-pops are for flat top or domed pistons.

Of all the aftermarket flathead lids manufactured prior to and following WW II, none are as mysterious as the original Smith. Who made them—and when were they made? At first blush, one might guess they came out of the fertile mind of the famed Clay Smith. Although primarily known for cam grinds, Clay Smith did make cylinder heads. Trouble is, all of the heads I have seen at swap meets are embossed "SMITH-JONES." However, Jack Underwood, a long-time flathead enthusiast and hot rod racing historian, believes the originals were cast in the mid-1950s by Don Smith in Bellflower, California. If true, his timing was off, because that's when the flathead lost favor. Well, Don Orosco's timing for a reproduction of the Smith head sure isn't off. These beautiful heads faithfully capture the art and essence of the originals with their larger-than-usual water jackets and the unique coolant-outlet log.

The Fluids
Modern Oil Filtering &
Traditional Cooling

The Oil Filtering System

Try as he might, Henry just never got around to putting an efficient oil-filtering system on the flathead. You may have suspected that when you took your own motor apart. It's a good bet that it was caked with sludge. If, like my own 1950 8RT truck motor, it still had the factory canister mounted on the head, you may have been curious enough to study that yellow-green decal with a magnifying glass. I did; it said something about a Fram® cartridge.

Now, Fram is a fine company, and I'm sure the 1950 cartridge was "state of the art." Unfortunately, what passed for the engine's oil-filtering *system* surely wasn't! Ford sales literature called it a "partial flow oil filtering system." Dunno what that *really* means, but I do know that the canister perched on the head was primarily for *looks* . . .an afterthought that Ford put on to sell cars.

Well, few people have studied the "system" with such intensity as Mark Kirby. "The flathead really never had a true oil filter. In the early days they used a hole to get into the main galley. In later years the canister was added. A little line went into the top, then out of the bottom. On the 59s it ran right back into a little fitting on the pan. It went into the bottom of the block on the 8BAs. At any rate, it was just a gravity-feed thing that really made a hole in the system. The company couldn't claim it was a full-flow oil filter.

"It used to be that you could not run detergent oil. You had to run

This is what all the flap is about, Motor City Flathead's Full-Flow Oil-Filter Kit (PN MCF-90-OFK). This cut-away display gives potential customers a clear idea of its form and function. The kit fits all flathead blocks and pans except the 1949-53 Ford center sump, <u>ribbed</u> passenger-car pan. In those cases, the engine builder will have to get the common smooth-sided pan. "What we've done is to modify the pump so when oil is picked up, it is redirected through our special ground and heat-treated bottom plate. One hundred percent of the oil is directed out of the bottom of the pump through a bulkhead fitting to a remote filter. The filter can be mounted anywhere you like. The filtered oil is then returned to the engine in a direct route to the rear main and the main oil galley. We still use the same pressure-relief valve in the pump; we just go in the back door. We now have a modern oiling system."

x

87

Figure 1

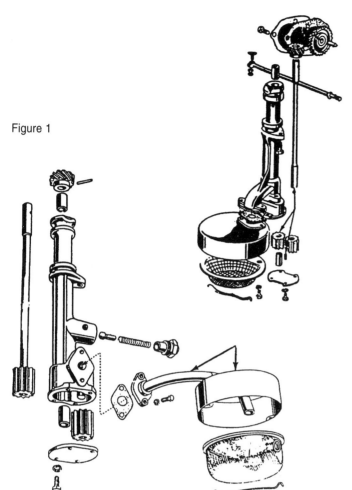

In 1949 the company came out with a redesigned pump with increased volume capacity. That pump (left) is known as—what else—a *short-body* pump. It still had spur gears, however. The *Motor's Manual* says that it could put out 57 psi at 40 MPH. Maybe yes, maybe no. Finally, in 1950, Ford switched from straight-tooth spur gears to *angle-tooth* helical gears. That one has been the hot rodder's pump of choice for more than 40 years. Chances are good that it and the correct pickup were installed in any flatmotor reconditioned since the 1950s. Nevertheless, if you do have the original pump in a pre-1949 motor, you must purchase a new short-body pickup in addition to the basic MCF full-flow oil-filter kit. Photo courtesy Speedway Motors.

Stock flathead oil pumps can be confusing, so a bit of clarification is in order here. If you are opening up a stock 1936 to 1948 flathead you may find the original "long-body" oil pump with spur gears used during those years. It was good for about 30-psi oil pressure at 30 MPH.

straight 30 or 40 weight. If you ran detergent oil the sludge would break loose and plug the oil pickup. Then you would really be in trouble. It was so bad that after many years of dealing with excessive sludge, Ford redesigned the truck oil pan in the late 1940s with a clean-out. The mechanic could drop it, reach up around the screen, and clean the sludge out of the bottom."

Kirby's fascination with the flathead's sludge problem eventually led him to design the filtering system depicted in cut-away form in the photo at the start of this chapter. He is obviously proud of it. "It isn't practical to attempt to install our kit on an engine in the car, but with the engine on the

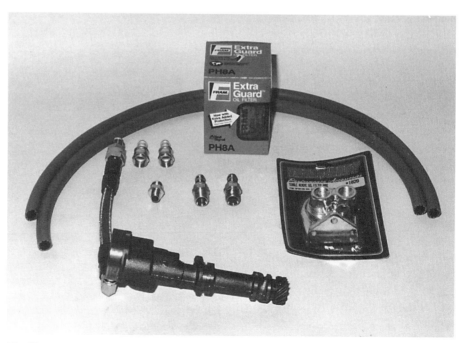

The kit comes with exact directions showing where to bore the 3/4-inch hole in the pan for the bulkhead fitting. A Melling short-body pump (no core exchange) is supplied along with 300-psi Goodyear hose. Literally hundreds of these oil-filter kits are in service with an enviable record of customer satisfaction.

Although the kit comes with full instructions, we'll let Mark walk us through the procedure to build up your confidence. The first step is to install the new pump. "Twist the pump all the way left (counterclockwise) and tighten it down. This gives us our best angle coming through the pan. The hose is already on the pump as it comes out of the kit, and the angle is preset for clearance. The installer has only one end to work with—the end that pokes through the pan. Don't loosen or twist any fittings. They are all tight and marked."

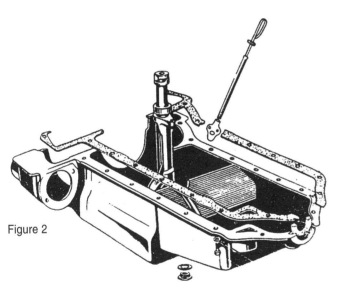

Figure 2

There are many types of flathead oil pans. This *Ford Chassis Parts and Accessories Catalog* line art shows the passenger-car pan used until 1948. Unfortunately, all Ford pans become leakers over time. One of the problems is that the dipstick housing is riveted to the pan. If you have been waiting for an opportunity to repair yours, this is it. Drill out the rivets, tap the rivet holes (there is enough metal for fine thread) and use bolts. Apply a liberal dose of silicone to the assembly and bolt it on.

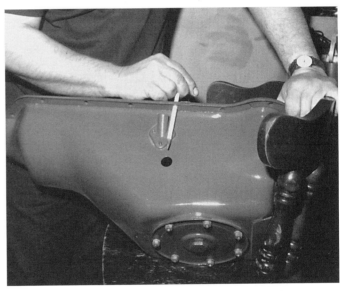

One of the more popular pans is the truck style with the clean-out on the bottom of the rear sump. The real point of this photo, however, is to show you where the hole for the oil-pump bulkhead fitting goes. It is 4-1/2-inches down from the bolt hole, just to the rear of the dipstick housing.

stand it is an easy, one-man job. Our oil-filtering system combined with superior modern oil means you can tighten up your engine clearances a little. And, you can run whatever oil you run in your everyday car. In the summer when it's hot, most of our engines run 20-50 weight, and of course we run detergent oil."

There have been other attempts to build external oil filtering systems for the flathead in the past. Mark has seen them, "But they were not full-flow oil-filtering systems. The oil to the rear main never got filtered. The oil return to the block was restricted through a 1/4-inch pipe fitting." The main oil galley requires a 3/8-inch passage "and

you have to maintain that to keep the volume up. So the fittings that go into the block in our kits are opened up. We designed our system to be 100 percent full flow."

The MCF oil-filtering system is sophisticated, but a home-shop retrofit is almost as simple as replacing a stock oil pump. The only significant modifi-

Next, install new packing seals in the channels at each end of the oil pan. Soak the seals in motor oil an hour or so beforehand. Mark recommends pinching both ends of the oil pan with a pair of pliers to tighten up the fit on the packing. Just another precaution against those pesky, almost inevitable oil leaks for which the flathead is famous. Of course, if you used the VEO aluminum ring with the neoprene lip oil seal, you don't need the rope seal on the front end of the pan. This VEO seal is shown on page 75.

Next install the pickup and screen. Remember that the pickup, which is not included in the kit, must be appropriate for the kit-supplied short-body pump. The redesigned pump that first appeared in late 1948 was further improved in 1950. It's helical gears moves more oil than previous versions.

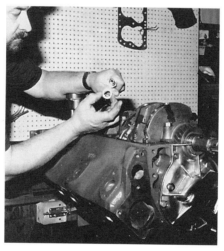

Don't forget the nylon washer that goes on the end of the male member of the bulkhead-fitting assembly.

cation the home builder has to make is boring a 3/4-inch hole in the pan for the bulkhead fitting that passes dirty oil from the engine into the external filter. MCF supplies all necessary hardware, a new Melling pump (no core exchange) and enough 300-psi Goodyear hose to allow placement of the filter where the car owner wants it. The home builder merely has to put the assembly together.

In fact, MCF cautions the home builder to refrain from making any further changes to the oil-circulation system other than deciding where the external filter will go. When it comes to an engine's oiling system, mistakes can be costly. The street rodder with a fresh flathead on the engine stand should stop what he's doing and pay close attention to the photos as Kirby demonstrates the right way to do the installation.

The Cooling System

Most experienced flathead engine swappers know that Ford manufactured several water-pumps styles over the years for the ever-evolving engines. In terms of efficiency and "swapability" (the pump casting also provides the foot of the motor mount) some are more desirable than others. The heavy-duty 1949-53 8RT truck pump is the one you want if you are planning to drop a 1949-53 engine in a 1948 or earlier car or pickup. It is a single-belt, wide-pulley design that gives you the correct motor mounting in an older chassis. Not only that, they are sealed-bearing units similar to more modern water pumps and provide greater insurance against leakage. The dual-belt truck water pump used on the 59AB engine also has sealed bearings, but you'll have a hard time finding any.

Engines, of course, use pulleys driven by the crankshaft to deliver a variety of goods. Well, some street rodders have decided that late-model stamped-steel pulleys, chromed or not, are too mundane for a modern rod. Enter billet-aluminum pulleys. Hey, are flathead rodders willing to take a back seat to the small-block crowd? No way, at least not if they know about the MCF billet-aluminum pulleys specially designed to fit the cast-iron flathead water pumps.

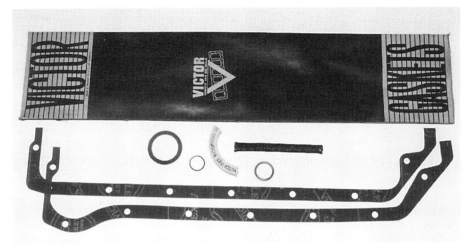

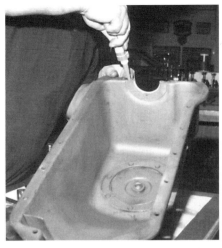

Every street rodder interested in flatheads surely is a loiterer around vintage auto parts emporiums in his off hours. He is well advised, therefore, to keep abreast of new finds by the proprietor. For example, I lucked into a set of NOS Victor pan gaskets that Harold Looney of C.W. Moss (402 W. Chapman Ave., Orange, CA 92666) acquired just weeks before we installed the pan on the 8RT. McCord still makes new gasket sets for the flathead.

Kirby is a big fan of silicone. He puts silicone on the rope packing and the front-cover area before the oil pan gasket is put in place. (Again, if you have used the VEO aluminum ring with the neoprene lip oil seal on the front end of the pan, this is not necessary.)

Coat the block gasket surface with stick'um (I use Gasgacinch®) and the mating side of the pan gasket. Let the Gasgacinch get tacky, then carefully lay the gasket in place. Make sure you do not cover the bolt holes. The ends of the gasket come up right close to the crank journal, but don't cut any more off than necessary to provide adequate clearance. If a little bit of the rope seal sticks up, don't trim it off. This is a judgement call because the ends of some seals may extend quite a bit. You want a little "squish" for good sealing, but not enough to leave a gap when you bolt the pan down. The pan gasket overlaps the rope seal.

They are particularly attractive on street rods where the traditional flat-head is *always* on display. Installation requires a little elbow grease and this is what Kirby had to say about that.

"Our aluminum pump pulleys come with a steel hub that has a flat. You have to grind a matching flat on your water-pump shaft so it will fit and lock. When you grind the flat, angle it in toward the engine just a little bit so the pulley won't come off.

We also have different pulley sizes for the guy who has a supercharged motor in his car. Maybe it's not relieved, and the compression is a little

Kirby also puts a dab of silicone in all four corners where the block/pan meet.

Okay, we did say that installing the full-flow oil-filter kit was an easy, one-man job. Well, yes and no. It is . . . up to the point of actually installing the oil-filter feed line on the bulkhead fitting just before dropping the pan on the block. Sure, Mark is able to do it by himself because he's done it so often. First time around, however, you really could use an extra pair of hands to support the pan.

higher. We can slow down the blower (with varying diameter pulleys) to where the engine only sees a few pounds of boost.

That brings us to a closing thought for this chapter, what computer software companies call *technical support*. With components such as the oil-filtering system and off-size pulleys, you can always count on technical support from Motor City Flathead. "When a man buys parts from us, we are happy to give him advice. We'll walk him through it. I spend a lot of time on the phone talking to customers."

What more can a guy ask for?

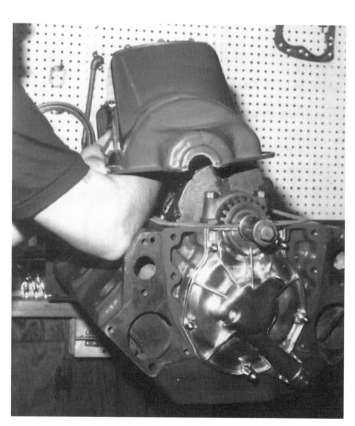

Now you're ready to put the pan on. Mark snugs up the pan bolts in three stages. The key word here is "snug." No need to squeeze the gasket out. "Just snug up the four corners. You don't want to tighten them. You just want to pull the rope seals down a little bit so you can get the other bolts in. Then go around and tighten all the bolts with a speed handle."

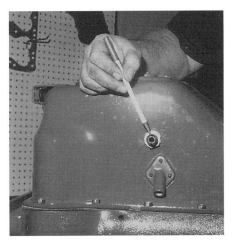

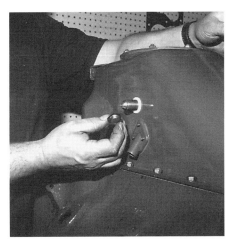

In this photo the bulkhead fitting was marked with a felt-tip pen for proper positioning. New fittings have a slot machined into the threads. Hold the slot vertical to the engine block. If the fitting is twisted off-vertical, it could kink the hose in the crankcase and cut off the oil supply. A kink could even push the hose into the crank.

Just as important as keeping the slot straight up and down is the correct tightening of the bulkhead locking nut and nylon washer. "There are two ways to tighten the fitting. You can put an Easy-Out® in the center of the fitting to hold it while you tighten the nut. But a better way is hold the flat (before the thread) with a pair of Channel-Lock® pliers while you tighten the nut with a wrench. If you gouge the flat a little, don't worry. It's not going to hurt anything because the sealing takes place on the cone. But if you are not comfortable with that, you can do just as well with the Easy-Out."

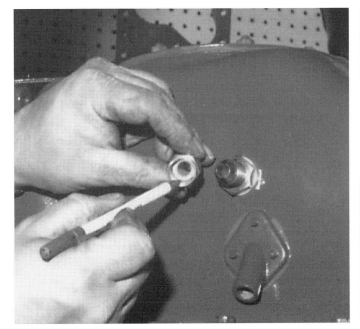

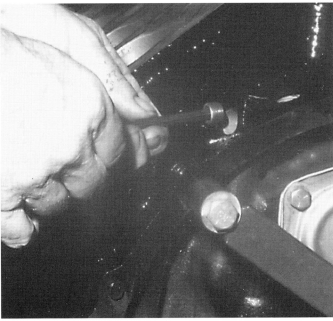

"Sealing takes place on this cone-shaped surface. The fittings are designed to seal easily. You don't have to get rough. We use a universal fitting that has a radius on it so it will fit a 45-degree or 33-1/3-degree aircraft or automotive application. The customer can add an oil cooler later as long as he does not change the indexing of the pan fitting. The correct positioning of the oil line inside the pan is critical." The last step is to plug the driver's side of a 1949-53 block where the old oil filter drained back. And there you have it.

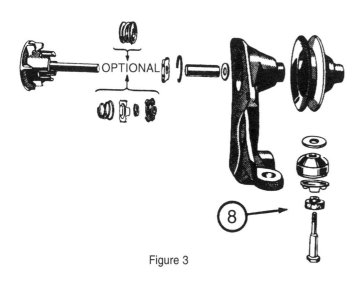

Figure 3

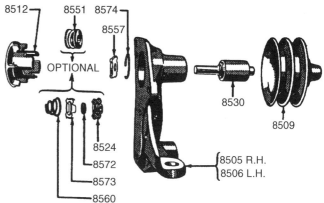

Figure 4

1937-41 8 CYL. 90 & 100 H.P. TRUCK WATER PUMP (79-8501-2)

Ford manufactured several slightly different water pumps over two decades of flathead production. The types most street rodders are likely to use are those for the 1937-48 90 and 100 HP passenger cars and trucks (Fig. 3), the 1937-41 90 and 100 HP truck pump (Fig. 4), and the 1949-53 pumps (Fig. 5).

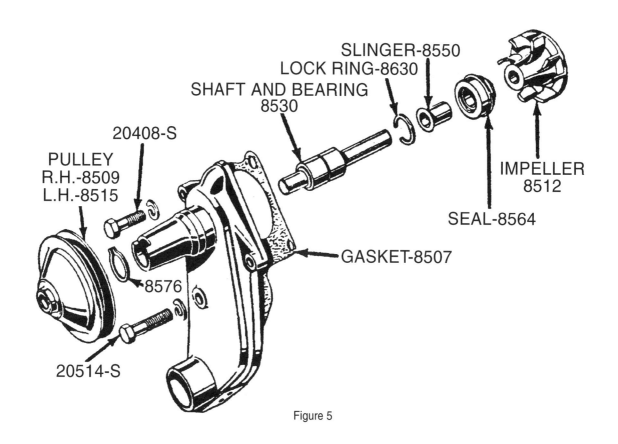

Figure 5

The preferred part for installing an 8BA block in a pre-49 chassis is the 8RT truck model pump with sealed bearings. Some later bus pumps are just as good, but their extra-long "snout" must be trimmed to fit most early passenger-car installations.

Another flathead dream shot: Cornhusker's adaptation of the 348-409 Chevrolet V-8 water pump with adapters. Matching machined aluminum crank and water-pump pulleys, machined motor mounts and steel mount for the A/C compressor and alternator. Fully machined timing cover adapts late-model distributor to earlier blocks. Use of Chevy pump slows water circulation for better cooling—an old race car trick. How can it get any prettier than this?

Timing Marks and Pointer

Before leaving your engine and before installing the cylinder heads, install the crankshaft pulley. Make sure it has a little bump or nib which is used for ignition timing. A pointer should extend from the timing cover and end almost at the edge of the crank pulley.

With No. 1 piston at top center and both valves closed, this pointer should align with the nib on the crank pulley. If not, bend the pointer until it does align.

If there is no nib on your pulley, file a small notch in it and fill it with white paint so it will show up when you use a timing light to check the ignition timing. If there is no pointer, create one and attach it under a timing-cover bolt. Position it so it points to the mark on the pulley at top center for No. 1 piston.

Ed Iskenderian once published a super-accurate method for finding top center: Bolt a strap across the top of No. 1 cylinder. Then carefully rotate the crank to bring the No. 1 piston up to touch the strap. Mark a spot on the crank pulley by the pointer. Then turn the crank one turn until the piston again contacts the strap. Again mark the pulley. Remove the strap.

Now a mark placed exactly between the two marks will be an accurate top-center mark on your pulley.

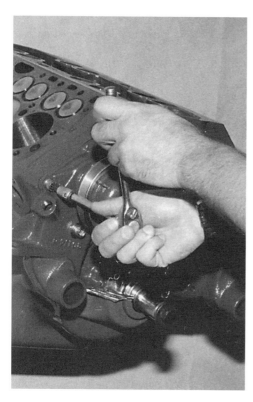

Install the pumps very carefully. Again, do not strike the shaft. Tighten the bolts using a crisscross pattern.

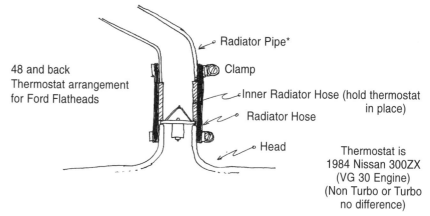

48 and back
Thermostat arrangement
for Ford Flatheads

Radiator Pipe*
Clamp
Inner Radiator Hose (hold thermostat in place)
Radiator Hose
Head

Thermostat is
1984 Nissan 300ZX
(VG 30 Engine)
(Non Turbo or Turbo
no difference)

* Note: This same arrangement will work with an all rubber hose. The inner hose will stay put just fine.

Allen Osborne came up with this slick trick. Use a Nissan 300ZX thermostat in the water neck of pre-1949 Ford and Mercury heads to regulate engine temperature.

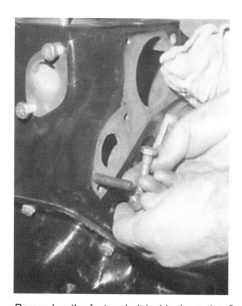
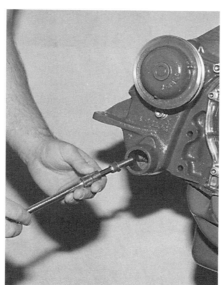
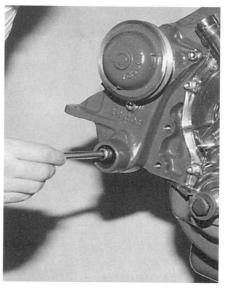

Remember the factory bolt inside the outlet. Some folks like to use a stud and a brass nut, some prefer stainless-steel socket-head bolts. Actually, I like stainless-steel bolts and washers all the way around. Use anti-seize compound on any stainless fasteners.

Handle new water pumps with care. Never strike the shaft, because this will damage the bearing. Position the new gasket on the pump with sealer on both sides. Chase the threads in the bolt holes. If they look damaged or rusted beyond use, install thread-repair inserts.

10 Capping Off The Block
Selecting & Installing Cylinder Heads

The cylinder head and its combustion chamber play a vital role in the efficiency of the normally aspirated engine. Theoretically, the cylinder is expected to draw in a volume of air/fuel mixture equal to its cubic-inch displacement. In reality, the true volume depends on the pressure and temperature of the mixture. In the case of the flathead, the valve arrangement and the configuration of the stock combustion chamber does not help matters. In fact, it works against volumetric efficiency by expanding the mixture and decreasing the weight per cubic inch. Consequently, the pressure rise during combustion is slower and less efficient in a flathead than that of the overhead valve combustion chamber.

Prior to World War II, most V-8 hot rodders were content with modified stock cylinder heads for the street and the lakes. Few had the money for such esoteric "lids" as the Bohnalite aluminum racing heads. The desired boost in compression could be achieved much more inexpensively by milling or machining material from the gasket surface of the head to decrease the combustion-chamber volume. A cut of 0.060 to 0.090 inch (depending on whether the engine was equipped with flat top or domed pistons) boosted the stock compression ratio from 6.15:1 to a street-safe 7.0:1. The more rambunctious rodders flycut and domed the stock heads for even deeper cuts. An alternate method, "filling" or brazing material into the combustion chamber was less effective and not often used.

Capping the block.

Shortly after the war, however, a variety of handsome, finned aluminum heads started to appear. By the end of 1947, a street rodder with a spare $75 could get a pair from Eddie Meyer who was one the first to cast a V-8 head for the hot rodder. Others, however, were soon to be come illustrious in their own right. Names such as (Vic) Edelbrock, (Earl) Evans, (Barney) Navarro, (Fred) Offenhauser, (Al) Sharp, (Tommy) Thickstun, (Bob)

Tattersfield and (Phil) Weiand graced most V-8 powered hot rods. A few lesser known marquees such as the Elco Twin with its two spark plugs per cylinder, Federal Mogul Thermo-Flow with its unusual spark plug spacing and the Kogel "Circular Turbulence" heads were available for those who wanted to step out and try something different.

Ford's own "on again/off again" use of aluminum alloy in stock cylinder heads during the 1930s led the 1940s

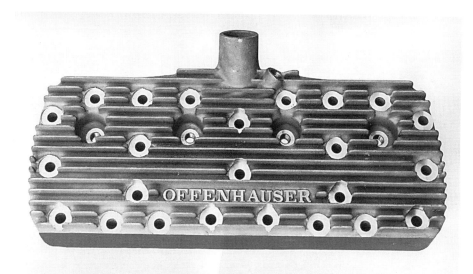

The ubiquitous finned-aluminum high-compression cylinder head has only one serious challenger for the all-time traditional piece of flathead speed equipment. Many brands made an appearance in the glory years following World War II, including the "Offy."

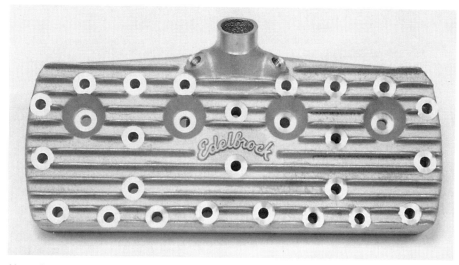

Not to be outdone, Vic Edelbrock, Jr. and Tony Baron have continued and advanced the equipment pioneered by their respective fathers.

speed equipment manufacturers to incorporate it as the preferred metal for high-compression heads. Aluminum conducts heat four times faster than cast iron, thus lowering the surface temperature of the combustion chamber. That in turn, increases volumetric efficiency and forestalls detonation. The hot rod heads also had larger water jackets for maximum cooling and combustion chambers designed for compression ratios from 7.5 to a whopping 10:1! Fins were another matter. Long assumed to aid in cooling by increasing surface area, the beneficial effect in a closed engine compartment (as opposed to open air cooling on early aircraft and motorcycles) was marginal at best. The only consensus is that fins really look good!

I've already talked about the pitfalls of swap-meet purchases regarding used cams and valve-train components. Here's some more thin ice. Used aluminum cylinder heads that may have lost much of their heat treatment potentially pose such a problem that experienced street rodders prefer not to install them. Mark Kirby of Motor City Flathead concurs. "It's just not a good idea to buy used cylinder heads at a swap meet. We've had too many problems with 'em. The buyer doesn't know how hot they may have been run or how many times they may have been milled.

"A customer once brought in a set of used heads, so I put them on. But they wouldn't seal. Eventually, I figured out that the heads were severely overheated sometime during their lifetime. Aluminum starts to lose its heat treat and will anneal at 500F to 600F. Those heads simply would not hold the (applied) torque. The motor was a "seeper." No matter what I did to it, it would work fine in the shop, but 20 miles down the road it would start getting hotter and hotter until it would boil over. Finally I installed a set of brand-new heads and that cured the problem!" (A "seeper" is what Mark calls an engine with minor combustion chamber/water jacket leakage that progressively worsens as the aluminum heads start moving with the heat.)

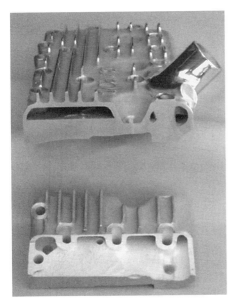

The Ford Motor Company's use of aluminum alloy during the 1930s for stock cylinder heads led aftermarket equipment manufacturers to take the ball and run. "hot rod" heads had larger water jackets for maximum cooling and combustion chambers designed for higher compression ratios, some of which would be incompatible with today's pump gasoline.

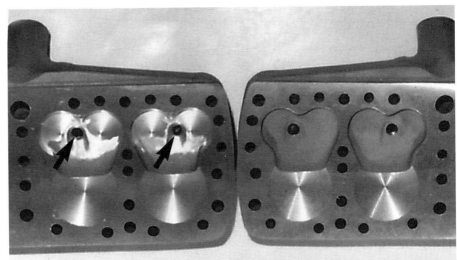

Are out-of-the-box heads ready for bolt-on? You be the judge. Run a spark plug into one hole of an untouched head. Notice that the plug bottoms out some two or three threads above a flush fit in the combustion chamber as it does in the head on the left. That isn't good. Spark-plug recession is a built-in spot for detonation and pre-ignition to start. One solution is Motor City Flathead's custom re-working.

There's more, however. The beleaguered street rodder can't simply rely on new heads to get him out of the overheating woods. "For instance, another customer whose motor I did four years ago, ran cool the first year he had it. The next year it ran 10 degrees warmer. The *next* year it ran *another* 10 degrees warmer, so he put a high-buck radiator in. But that really didn't help; it was progressively losing torque and was seeping. Once we realized that, the problem was solved."

Now there's a "hot" tip for you. To maintain the cooling efficiency you build into your motor, re-torque the cylinder heads every three- or four-thousand miles.

Now for some bad news . . . well, maybe not so bad, because the problem can be corrected. Kirby has noted that the quality control in the manufacture of some heads is not as stringent as it could be. I have to admit that during this conversation, I was a little uncomfortable with Mark's observations that brand-new heads weren't always top notch, so I pressed him further.

He told me of a motor he had built that ran very poorly, so he pulled the

plugs and did a compression check. "Water shot out of Number One! I knew there was porosity in there, on brand-new, out-of-the-box heads. It happens with all brands, but the street rodder has no way of knowing what's wrong. The porosity does not show up until after the engine has been run. If the heads have a bubble in the casting, it is all hollow under there." That's the bad news.

The good news is that a casting flaw can be detected if you know where to look for it. Study (with a magnifying glass, if need be) the entire surface of the cylinder head for pock marks before you lay your bucks on the counter. Usually, however, the

MCF re-domes or pockets the head (a milling operation) and unshrouds the spark plug by hand. The machinist does not go outside the gasket line for obvious reasons. Nevertheless, he uses every bit of space up to the gasket to unshroud the valve for better airflow. Also, this is a way of controlling combustion-chamber cc's (volume). Even if you have already installed your heads, you may want to talk to the boys in Michigan about the practicality of unshrouding and pocketing for your particular needs. Just unshrouding the spark plug holes alone is a worthy option whether you do it yourself or leave it to the pros. Even then, however, you're not done.

"Claying" may look crude at first glance, but it is a time-honored, effective method of determining piston-to-head clearance. Put a few pieces of modeling clay on two pistons in at least two directions, front and rear. You want check all different areas of the piston—the top of the dome and down at the bottom. Smear motor oil over the dome area of the head to prevent clay adhesion when the head is set in place. "Semi-torque" the head down over a new gasket to about 45 foot-pounds. That's enough to get a compressed thickness good enough for checking clearance, and you can still use the gasket. Gently turn the engine over a couple of times to compress the clay between the cylinder head and the piston. Carefully remove the head and cross section the clay in different areas to measure its thickness. Anywhere from 0.050- to 0.100-inch clearance is fine for a street motor, but there is a slight reduction in performance as the clearance exceeds 0.050 inch.

manufacturer's quality control inspector will detect the flaw and have it welded and re-machined. There's no significant problem with a factory repair. I just couldn't help thinking of the old racing axiom: Just because it's new doesn't mean it's right.

According to Kirby, that's not a bad philosophical approach, not only with aftermarket cylinder heads, but other flathead components made from decades-old patterns and tooling. Heads were on his mind, however, and he showed me brand-new pairs from two manufacturers. "Rub your hand across the gasket surfaces." They were rough; I could see and feel tooling marks. "Both need a little bit of attention. A good seal is critical. Stuff like this coupled with poor head bolts, and you have an overheating problem. Exhaust seepage into the water jacket may not be obvious; you may not see bubbles in the radiator. But if you go out and drive for 20 minutes, your engine starts to overheat.

"Another problem is that some guys think that a coarse deck holds the gasket better. So they go to their local machine shop and have the deck re-cut. If there is a tool dragging (and this happens quite often), there's going to be a coarse surface. That means it's going to be hard to seal. People put on a brand-new set of heads, and suddenly

Vic Edelbrock—enthusiast & manufacturer: The far-sighted vision of Vic Edelbrock, Jr. has grown Edelbrock Equipment into one of the largest performance aftermarket manufacturers. Although flathead equipment represents only a tiny part of Edelbrock production, that's where it all really started. Vic's pride and joy is this 1932 roadster.

they have heating problems. They blame the engine, but nobody really attacks the root causes of the problem. After we surface our block decks, we (hand) stone them to get a nice, smooth surface."

There's yet another problem with new aluminum cylinder heads—spark-plug recession. When most aftermarket heads were designed to deliver higher-than-stock compression, the spark plug stayed in the stock position while the combustion chamber was "filled." Although there is a subtle, cast-in unshrouding in aftermarket heads, there may be two or three exposed threads shrouding the plug electrode. This provides an excellent starting place for detonation and pre-ignition.

The fix for this problem is to hand grind away the excess material, further unshrouding the plug so a more efficient flame path is available. Perhaps hot rodders did this years ago, but I've never read of it. There's always something new to learn about old motors. Consider this . . .

Normally, piston-to-head clearance is not uppermost in the flathead rodder's consciousness. Maybe it should be. Kirby recommends "claying" whenever things "look spooky, but especially when you have installed the heads for your first time." That's understandable with regard to used heads. As noted above, one never knows for sure how much has been milled off over the years. But why do new heads need to be checked?

You can't simply install the early heads on a 1949-53 block. There are slight, but significant differences in block and head water passages. Before the early heads are installed, you have to plug a front water-passage hole in each cylinder bank of the 8BA block and one in the head. On the passenger side of the block, the water passage extends forward past the old-style head. Once tapped and plugged, it can be forgotten. Use a 1/8-inch pipe tap and a brass pipe plug. The hole does not need to be drilled larger, but chamfering it is a good idea.

Well, Mark has found a couple of areas that don't quite meet his high standards. "Sometimes, aftermarket cylinder heads are milled too much at the factory. We have to redome the head to provide more clearance. Rods stretch; an educated guess would be 0.015 to 0.020-inch at 4500 RPM. At 5500 to 5600 RPM, there's a minimum of 0.035 to 0.040-inch stretch. That's too risky. In time, you could have a problem with carbon build-up."

Mark recommends from 0.050 to 0.100-inch piston-to-head clearance for street rod engines. As with everything, however, there is a trade-off for the conservative builder who wants the safety of greater clearance. "You don't get any performance benefits with more than 50-thou clearance. You can't dissipate heat, and you can't get turbulence. It's got to be right down at about 50 thou for that." Valve clearance under the head with the gasket in place should be at least 0.040 inch with a gasket thickness of 0.055 inch. Again, use modeling clay to check your clearances because even new castings often vary considerably.

Kirby and airflow engineer Paul

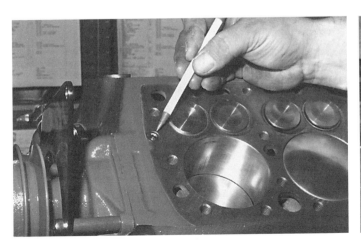

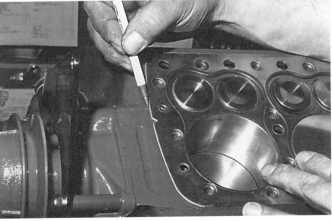

On the driver's side of the block, the hole to be plugged is under the gasket. Even though you might think it is covered, in service, coolant could leak past the gasket and out the front of the block. Install a 1/8-inch brass pipe plug here as well. Make sure it is a few thousandths of an inch below the deck surface.

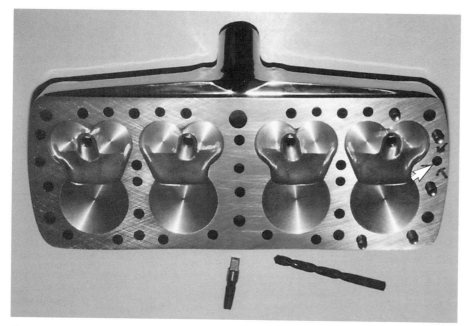

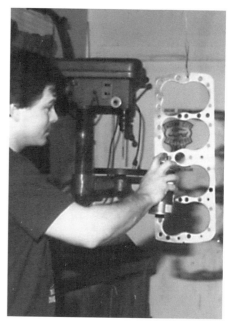

The early head used on the driver's side of the 8BA block must be tapped for a 1/4-inch pipe plug. Stuff a few bolts through the head, flip it over (top side up) and locate the proper hole. Here, it is a good idea to drill the head out to 7/16-inch before plugging it. (A finned aluminum head can get wiggly and catch the drill bit, so clamp it securely on your drill press table or mill.) And for goodness' sake, use the stop on the machine so that you don't go any deeper than necessary to seat the plug below the head surface.

Now you're ready to bolt those pretty new heads on the block. MCF recommends Victor 3036® copper "sandwich" gaskets, coated both sides twice with Permatex Gold Gasket Spray®. There is a bit of flathead lore that warns against copper gaskets, but Kirby has never found corrosion or erosion on any of his in-service motors.

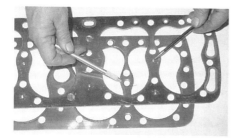

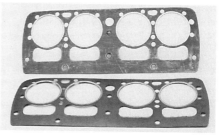

There are a variety of head gaskets. Some are NOS, some are new designs, and of course there is the 59AB and 8BA style. (To say nothing about a 21-studder that might show up!) Match your new gaskets to the block and head, and against whatever old gasket came off your engine. If in doubt, however, double check with your supplier. Photo at right courtesy of Speedway Motors.

Schalk have put a great deal of time into head re-working experiments for street performance. "We know that we pick up a significant amount of airflow around the valves (with our modifications to the head). In the old days we said 'Them valves ain't big enough, we gotta push 'em together!' Now we know we lost airflow because we shrouded this area. (In the modified head) we are picking up 360-degrees of airflow. In fact, on some of our research motors, valve diameters were *reduced* to pick up more air space. The reworked valve pocket combined with a good flowing valve really delivers

good performance. We also redo our flame travel (path)."

Kirby and his staff at Motor City Flathead modify a head somewhat differently for different applications. "If I do a blown motor, I'll pocket a little deeper so that I get about 69 or 70 cc's in the head. That's going to give me what I want. If I do a carbureted motor, I'll probably go a little less. The chamber design and relieving are the same for either one. We don't want to cut the deck too much.

"By keeping our valve sizes smaller, and opening the head up all the way around the valve (we have from 1/8- to

3/16-inch space between the valve and the gasket) we pick up a significant amount of smooth air around the valve. In the old days with big valves, you had an interruption of smooth airflow from 9 to 1 o'clock. This is the result of Paul's flow bench work, but Barney Navarro has found much the same thing. Barney has done an altogether different style head though—a hemi-head combustion chamber. We simply unshroud the valve to get more airflow. If we run a blown motor, we'll go a little deeper to get the volume where we want it.

"We use copper gaskets. I know

MCF offers a complete head-bolt kit including thick hardened washers. Much thought has gone into the whys and wherefores of common fasteners relative to the seasoned flathead. Head bolts can be part of a flathead's overheating problem if they allow seepage of hot combustion-chamber gases past the gasket into the water jacket. As long as the builder installs the proper bolt and washer, and pulls it down to the proper torque, the problem will disappear.

A bolt sealer is needed because all but two of the flatty's head bolts go into the water jackets. MCF recommends Fel Pro 217 Pli-A-Seal® on the threads about 3/4-inch up. "The block is about 5/8-inch thick where the head bolts thread in. A bolt or stud that is too long will bottom out on the top of the wrap-around exhaust ports on the very ends of the engine. This is not a problem on the 59AB. The pedestals for the head bolt on today's Offy or Edelbrock aluminum head are the same thickness throughout, and that takes a 2-3/4-inch bolt. On the 8BA head, the lower row of head bolts take a 2-inch bolt. There is a lot of variety on aftermarket heads, so be careful. Also, the torque reading on stepped 8BA heads is not as reliable as that on 59AB heads." Good words to the wise, check and re-check. Then, 500 miles down the road, re-torque.

some people don't like them, but we spray both sides of the gaskets with Permatex Gold® Gasket Spray. You can put them on immediately; you don't have to wait. With a coating between the two parent metals (aluminum and copper), they do not touch. Some say not to use copper with aluminum. When you look closely, however, you don't see erosion where the copper is touching the aluminum. The only place you see erosion is where the coolant is."

There's more to the head story than just heads, however. "Sometimes, when a rodder puts a set of high-compression heads on the block, the engine starts running hot." So what else is new? Isn't overheating the perennial complaint voiced by flathead rodders?

Besides, didn't we already say that removing the Original Sin—the core sand lodged in the water jackets since Day One—is the solution to overheating.

Well, a really clean block is critically important, but it is not conclusive. Mark continued, "The problem the rodder is now facing is that he doesn't have good head bolts. He's using a bolt that has been in the water jacket for 40 years, and the first few threads have been dissolved, eaten away. Sometimes they are completely gone." As far as Mark is concerned, the home builder should never use *old* original head bolts.

"There is minimum thread contact to begin with, only 5/8 of an inch. The flathead came with a Grade-5 bolt from

the factory, which was fine for a 6.5 or 7:1 compression ratio, and the motor didn't overheat. But the thread loss to corrosion is critical. If you must use stock head bolts, use new ones, and use thin stainless-steel washers. You

First you gotta put 'em on. Start by chasing the block threads. Use a clean 7/16-14 tap, and a little cutting lube. After each chase, clean the tap with a stiff bristle tooth brush and lacquer thinner. Yeah, there's 48 of 'em and you'll get bored, but it is necessary.

Blow out all the bolt holes, although admittedly most of whatever may have been in them will drop into the water jacket.

Next wipe down the deck and in the cylinder bore with a good quality paper towel and acetone. Make sure you check under lifted valves. Rotate the crank, and blow air around the circumference of the pistons.

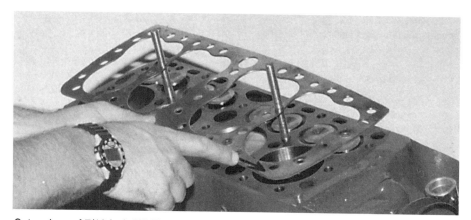

Get a piece of 7/16-inch "All-Thread" rod and cut off two 4-inch lengths for indexing pins. Install your gasket, noting the "Front" markings.

need as much thread as you can get. A thick washer would only worsen the condition."

Motor City Flathead's ready-made solution for the street rodder with 45-year-old head bolts is brand new Grade-8 head bolts and thick, hardened flat washers. Now, I have to admit that I use head studs rather than head bolts in most of my OHV engines, so I

couldn't resist asking Mark why he obviously preferred conventional bolts. "They are more convenient; studs can be a pain in the neck. When you have 24 studs sticking up, you have an alignment problem. A new Grade-8 stud is fine, however. The torque capability is not changed."

Okay, new bolts, but why is the MCF bolt kit so helpful in preventing

overheating? "You can see we are not only picking up good thread, but an extra thread. The original bolt with a low-compression iron head may not have been a problem, but with a high-compression head we are asking it to do more than it was designed to do, and under much worse conditions than when it was new. The (applied) torque is much better distributed with MCF bolts. Not only that, the thick, hardened washer pulls down more evenly on the (soft) pedestal on the aluminum head.

"The flathead really didn't have sufficient (head) torque to begin with. Now, we are making sure that we don't have a leaky head gasket. The bolt won't pull into the aluminum, and there won't be a loss of (applied) torque. With the combination of a clean block and a well-torqued head that is not leaking, the problem of inadequate cooling is gone. You will not have an overheater."

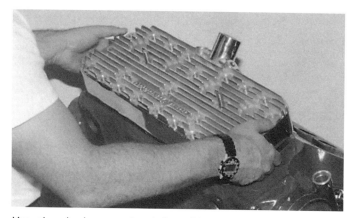
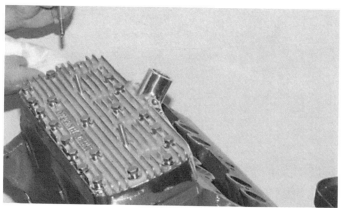

Very gingerly place your heads in position. Next apply your sealer to the bolts (careful not to drip anything on that nice new head) and start them in the block finger tight.

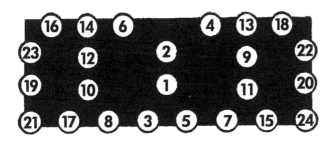

**Cylinder head tightening.
Ford and Mercury V8, 1938-48**

**Cylinder head tightening.
Ford and Mercury V8, 1949-53**

Cylinder-head tightening sequence for 1939-48 Ford and Mercury heads. No particular tightening sequence was recommended by Ford for 1932-38 engines. Nuts should be tightened from the center outward.

Torque the heads down in three 20 foot-pound increments to 60 foot pounds. Follow the torque sequence shown in the illustration.

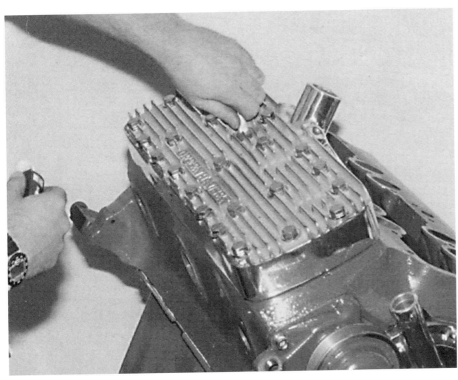

Finally, put a thin dab of aluminum anti-seize on the threads of your new spark plugs and install them finger tight (for now) just to keep anything from falling into the cylinder. (Don't laugh. When Angelo was 3 years old, he dropped a small lock washer into an open plug hole of an engine I was working on!)

Vintage stuff! Evans boat-racing heads with three water outlets. This particular set from the Bill Ewing collection is set up with domes to use pop-up pistons.

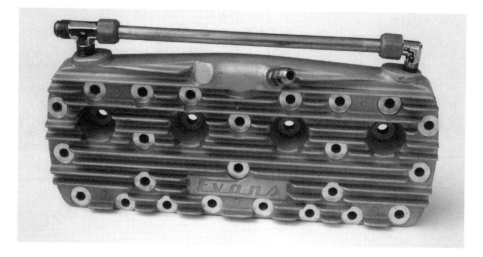

Roof head was made in two pieces that were bolted together. Note capscrews at each of the eight plugs. Dual plugs required using a Nash Twin-8 distributor to supply the sparks. From the Bill Ewing collection.

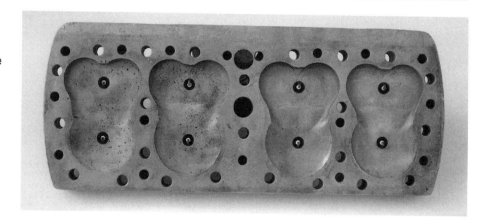

The Induction System Carburetors, Manifolds & Linkage

Did I throw a monkey wrench at you in the opening of the last chapter when I said that there was only one serious contender for the honored title of the all-time favorite piece of flathead speed equipment? Betcha I didn't. You knew I was talking about the multiple-carburetor manifold, the major component of the normally aspirated induction system.

Operational utility aside, the aluminum intake manifold with a couple of 97s or 94s atop it continues to occupy a very special place in the heart of every flathead enthusiast. After all, it was the first piece of speed equipment the "kid" purchased during the blossoming years of his hobby/sport so long ago. That's not all of the story, however.

No, it was the most complicated piece of speed equipment he believed he could properly install with his limited high school auto shop experience. Putting on a pair of heads was tricky; besides he didn't have a torque wrench. And a cam? Simply out of the question. But not a manifold. By the way, that's all it was ever called. Everyone knew you weren't referring to that 25-pound hunk of cast iron!

A visit to any major auto swap meet will find at least one blanket with a half-dozen aluminum intake manifolds of various configurations scattered about. And a glance at the price tags will soon remind you that it isn't 1953 anymore! Knowledgeable swap-meet merchants know that of all the automotive collectibles, the flathead intake manifold commands the greatest inter-

est. My old friend Bob Whitehead, who provided many photos for this chapter, has several score in his collection. He is not alone in his enthusiasm.

Fortunately, today's flathead builder has his choice of either a genuine 1953 production manifold, or a manifold that was cast and machined a few months ago! Best of all, either one will reliably meet his needs. That is, if he is aware of a few idiosyncrasies of speed equipment past.

* * *

"When Offenhauser designed their 3-carb manifold in the 1940s, they were engineered for the Stromberg 97. They never realized that there would be a problem with the later Holley 94. Today, because of the popularity of the 97s as the traditional carburetor of the 1940s, they got used up. They are virtually gone."

Mark Kirby laid down one of his manifolds and pointed to another. "Luckily, when Edelbrock designed his 3-carb manifold, he spaced the carb bases out a little farther. The 97 may be almost extinct, but 94s are still

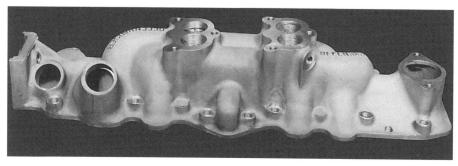

If you had the makings of a street rod in the 1940s or early 1950s, but it only had a stock flathead, the first piece of real speed equipment you saved up for was a dual-carb manifold. You had to make a decision, however, between the "Regular" and the "Super." The carburetors were close together and centered in the Regular manifold. This allowed the rodder to use his stock generator and fuel pump.

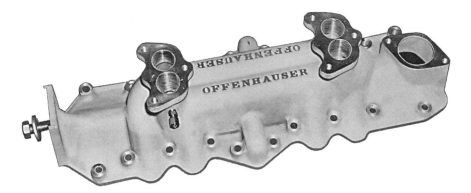

The carburetors were spaced farther apart in the Super manifold, one each over a set of ports with shorter flow paths that cut induction pressure losses. The Super could boast a 4-percent peak horsepower increase over the Regular, and with a few extra pieces of hardware, the generator could be bracketed over the cylinder head and the stock fuel pump used. Eventually it became the manifold of choice.

plentiful. If you are buying a (new or used) 3-carb intake manifold, you want to be aware of that. If you are purchasing an Offenhauser, you'll either have to run 97s or grind off the front bolt. You don't want to find that out after you get it home."

Mark retrieved a well-used carburetor from a box full. "Although there's a mystique surrounding the 97, the 94 is better because it flows a little bit more. That's why a guy shouldn't be afraid to run a 94 thinking that it is inferior to the 97. Besides, when the air cleaner, linkage and fuel lines are in place, most people can't tell the difference!"

* * *

The vagaries of ancient mini-carbs aside, the important thing to remember is that one needn't be afraid to buy a used intake manifold. If it looks good (no cracks or poor welds) chances are it is good. Just check around the bolt holes, ports and the other easy-to-damage places. Best of all, old manifolds will polish out just as purdy as new ones.

Now, some street rodders are not nearly so charmed by 50-year-old two-barrel carbs, remembering their propensity to leak. They have other favorites. Toward the end of the flat-

Today, street rodders want a smooth blending of the traditional and the high-tech, and what could be more in tune than a super dual-carb manifold with Motor City Flathead's beautiful custom-made packaging for a K & N air filter? All MCF induction assemblies are equipped with a Purolator fuel regulator and a Holley fuel-pressure gauge.

Before we go much further with modern flathead induction, I think you will get a kick out of looking over some of the more unusual pieces in Bob Whitehead's and Bill Ewing's manifold collections. I'm not about to stir up a raging controversy as to the precise date of manufacture of any given manifold, however. Some are pre-war, some are post-war. All are old, though, like this uncommon Alexander side saddle for two single-throat Winfield carburetors. Photo courtesy of Bob Whitehead.

head's street rod popularity, the four-barrel carb made its debut. That alone probably carried the valve-in-block engine along for another year or two. The 350 to 500 cubic feet per minute (CFM) four-barrel is a little big (in terms of maximum airflow) for small-displacement motors, but it is a good bolt-on for medium to larger displacements—those from about 258 cubic inches up.

I have to admit though, the three-deuce set-up with its adjustable (progressive) linkage customized to the driver's desires is still my favorite. It is the system I chose for the 8RT. It can accommodate the moderate 258 CID and mild cam with no trouble. Times change, today's *street* rodder is in hog heaven with a motor that most hot rodders of the early 1950s wouldn't have dared drive to work or school regularly. We owe a debt of gratitude to the inventive mind that dreamed up progressive linkage. But there's more.

At the early drags, the first thing our weekend warrior did was remove the popular chromed bonnet street air cleaners, and for good reason. The sexy, old-fashioned air cleaners did not pass enough air, and they automatically caused the carburetor to run rich. Today, the best bet is a K & N air filter; you can get plenty of clean air to the carbs with them. But there's more.

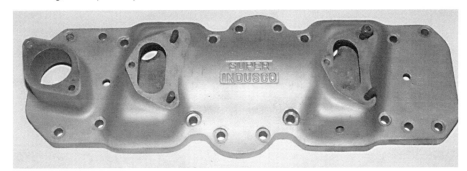

Early manufacturers tried various plenum-chamber and balance-tube designs, such as the Frieman (top), Sharp (center) and Battersby (bottom). In those days before airflow testing, did a design disappear because it did not perform or merely because it was not marketed well? Or did it die because the manufacturer/designer was under-capitalized? Top photos by Bill Ewing, lower photo by Bob Whitehead.

Equally curious is the wonderment about how big a factor cosmetics was in the mind of the designer. Was the Super Indusco (top) a "smoothie" for efficiency or looks? Did the engineer behind the Challenger (bottom) go for the pancake look because he thought it would work better, or simply to lessen production costs? Photos courtesy of Bob Whitehead.

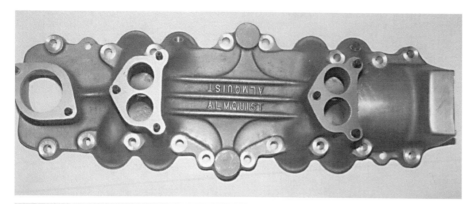

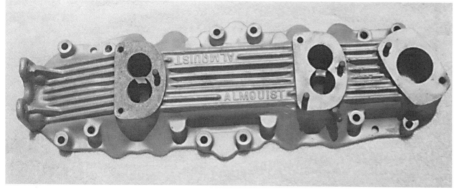

I have to think that the fins on the early Almquist (top) and the later Almquist (bottom), like fins on cylinder heads, were there more for looks than practicality. Photos courtesy of Bob Whitehead.

Most mid-Fifties hot rodders were committed to the electric fuel pump for flatheads, quickly realizing that the mechanical stocker just couldn't cut it. Trouble was, the carbs leaked badly. Only the truly sophisticated used a fuel pressure regulator in those days. Kirby's experience prevails. "You cannot run over two pounds fuel pressure with 94s or 97s, despite how many carbs are installed. Most 12-volt pumps are set for six or seven pounds. You have to use a regulator or you will blow the seats out and the carbs will leak all over the place. Many guys don't realize that, and that's why they foul plugs. They dump in raw fuel. That, and restrictive air cleaners create a lot of flathead problems."

Well, like I said earlier, installing the manifold is downright basic stuff, as is the rebuilding of old flathead two-barrel carbs. Nevertheless, we'll review those subjects. First, however, let's take a little walk down memory lane.

Some early "high-rise" manifolds did not catch on with the street and dry-lakes crowd, and the crude-looking Harrell (left) came and went sometime around 1940. The Eddie Meyer (right), however, has long been considered a class act. Who cares whether or not it really worked on the Lakes *or* the street? Especially when this newly manufactured, cast-from-the-original-molds, "vintage" piece can be purchased from Speedway Motors *today!* Photos courtesy of Bill Ewing (left), Speedway Motors (right).

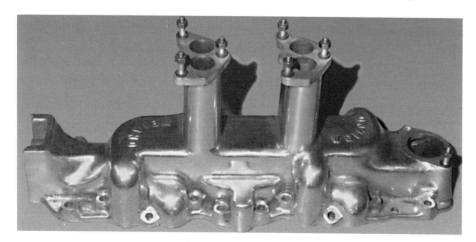

This beautifully polished high rise is the very first manifold cast by Phil Weiand. It was the forerunner of what today is a major line of late-model intake manifolds manufactured by Weiand Industries.

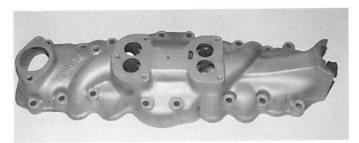 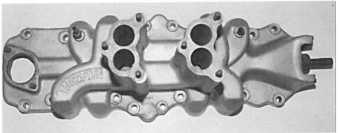

Finally, compare the "Art-deco" Burns manifold (left) to the early Thickstun (right) which just emphasizes efficiency. The early street rodder wanting a pair of carbs for that much touted 10-12 percent boost in horsepower above 2500 RPM had a full plate! Photos courtesy of Bob Whitehead.

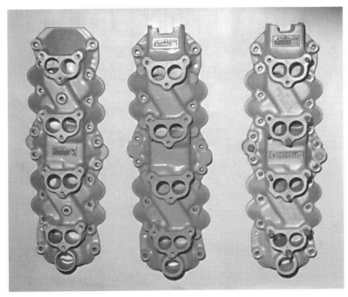

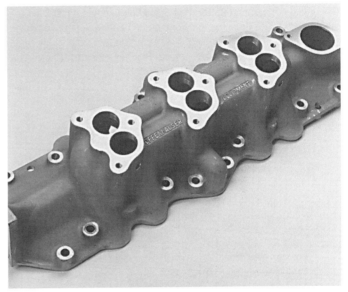

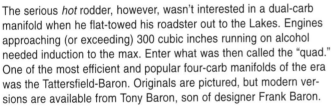

The serious *hot* rodder, however, wasn't interested in a dual-carb manifold when he flat-towed his roadster out to the Lakes. Engines approaching (or exceeding) 300 cubic inches running on alcohol needed induction to the max. Enter what was then called the "quad." One of the most efficient and popular four-carb manifolds of the era was the Tattersfield-Baron. Originals are pictured, but modern versions are available from Tony Baron, son of designer Frank Baron.

What's this, *three* deuces for a street flathead? True, in the early days, a triple manifold was far better suited for racing than cruising. Not anymore. With properly jetted, progressively linked carbs in a regulated fuel pressure induction system, you can keep your cake and eat it too. Just remember, Edelbrock manifolds can mount either Stromberg 97s or Holley 94s. Offenhauser manifolds only accept three 97s.

I chose the Offy manifold for the 8RT. By the way, in years past, racers paid great attention to the match of cylinder-block ports to intake-manifold ports. A quick inspection (using a new gasket as a pattern) satisfied me that my out-of-the-box Offenhauser was close enough for street work. (The 8RT is the designated hitter for that roadster I told you about in the Foreword.) Significant port mismatches, of course, should be rectified by carefully filing or grinding the *manifold* ports. My manifold was soon dropped off at Charlie Sihilling's for one of his magnificent metal-polishing jobs.

When it was returned, it was shipped to Motor City Flathead along with three fresh 97s that I convinced Patrick Dykes to part with. The Stromberg designs first appeared around 1937, and grew in popularity throughout the flathead years. As long as only 2-psi maximum fuel pressure is maintained, they are as trouble-free as one can expect for a 60-year-old design.

The choice of carburetors for the hot rod flathead has never been a particularly difficult task, as only one brand name at a time dominated the scene. "In the beginning" it was the Winfield. Four single-throat Winfields are mounted on this pre-war Frieman manifold. Photo courtesy Bob Whitehead.

Davies manifold with two Winfield carburetors is one of the first true high-rise manifolds. That this was the right idea was proven in later years: get the mixture straightened out over a distance and it should be more evenly distributed when it enters the engine. Bill Ewing collection.

More old manifolds from Bill Ewing's collection. Robert R. Roof manifold from Anderson, Indiana had two external (copper) balance tubes. While this was one of the first four-carb flathead manifolds, the first was probably made by Schnell in Washington.

KEN-RICH of Los Angeles made this boat-racing manifold with tilted and twisted carburetor mounting flanges to help make the fuel go where it should under g forces in turns. Bill Ewing collection.

There were three early fuel injections: Hilborn, Algon and Howard. This is the Algon. Fuel lines from barrel-valve/distribution block to injectors have not been installed. Hilborn's current flathead offering is shown in the suppliers chapter. Bill Ewing collection.

Finally, there is Motor City Flathead's latest foray into the arena of modern high-tech for the old girl: a street fuel injection. Kirby and Phil Sievers have been working on it intermittently for several years, and if that were all either of them had to do, you could order one now. As of 1997, they weren't quite ready to offer it to the public.

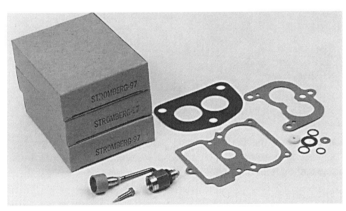

Rebuilding the 97 and 94 is a lot easier than rebuilding your engine, so don't hesitate. The kit comes with all gaskets, needles, seats and a new accelerator pump. Normally, full instructions are also included, so I won't re-invent the wheel. Jets are plentiful, and easy to change once a performance baseline is established. Photo courtesy of Speedway Motors.

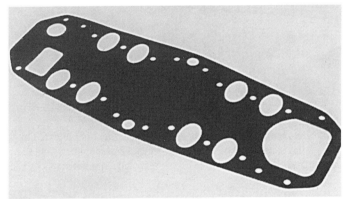

There's never a problem with gaskets. All vintage parts dealers carry an ample supply. Some are universal fits; others are model-specific. New old stock gaskets designed for late blocks may not have all the holes needed for the older blocks, however. Photo courtesy of Speedway Motors.

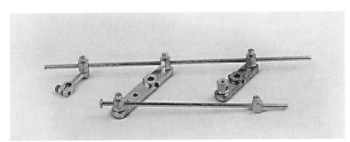
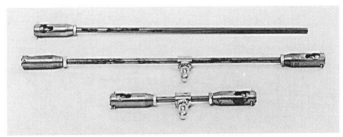

Carburetor linkage for duals or triples is not a problem . . . as long as you are dealing with a supplier who deals with vintage flathead hardware. Often, linkage kits for late-model carb/manifold applications won't fit just right, and the rodder has to cobble something together. Photos courtesy of Speedway Motors.

Portside or starboard, I have to admit, MCF's approach to setting up a triple-carbed manifold turns me on! This was the way my manifold and carbs came back home, ready for immediate installation on the 8RT.

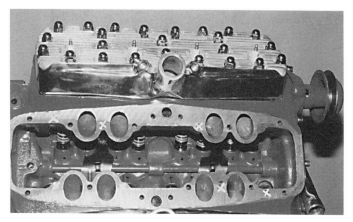

One could hardly ask for a simpler installation than that afforded by the flathead. 'Cept, maybe that it would have been nice (and less confusing!) if the factory had continued the original 20-bolt pattern and the use of indexing dowels on the later blocks. No problem, though. Just run a couple of standard-thread 5/16 x 2-inch studs into the manifold bolt holes finger-tight for alignment.

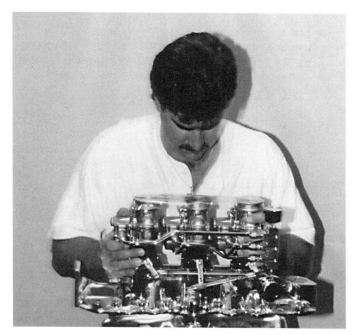

Pay attention to the "right side up and forward" configuration of the gasket (most aren't marked), smear a light film of white grease on both gasket surfaces, index it and gently lower the manifold (assembly) into place.

Snug the manifold bolts down and verify an uninterrupted fit. Use a torque wrench with precise low-end calibrations, and following the pattern in Fig. 1, torque aluminum manifold capscrews to 25 ft. lb. Remember that later blocks are not drilled for as many bolts as are the early blocks.

A freshly polished three-carb manifold atop a sparkling new flathead is an impressive sight. Coupled with polished, finned aluminum cylinder heads, it practically shouts "traditional hot rod" and "horsepower" in the same breath.

In the late 1940s, the Holley/Chandler Grove 94, which flowed a bit more than the Stromberg 97, came into vogue. Photo courtesy of Speedway Motors.

Figure 1

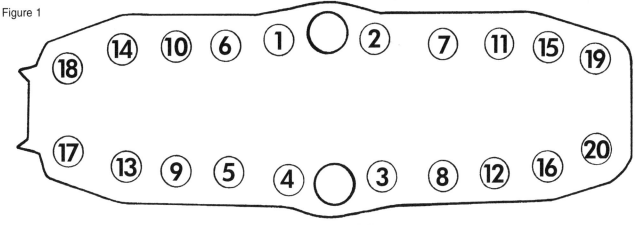

Bolt tightening sequence for a flathead intake manifold, torque bolts to 25 ft. lb.

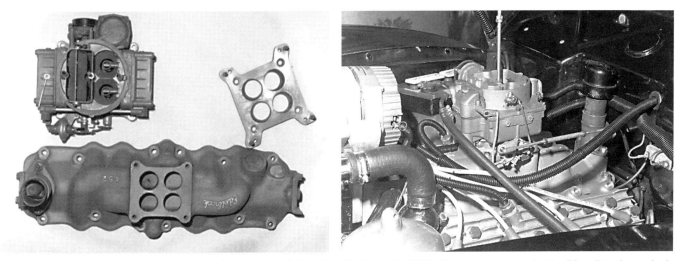

The final link in the evolutionary chain was the four-barrel carb introduced in the early 1950s. To some card-carrying traditionalists, it may look a little out of place on a flathead, but in reality, a four-barrel is probably the most practical choice of all. Take care, however, to choose the right carb for a mild engine; one and a half times the piston displacement is just about the right cubic feet per minute (CFM) rating.

Huff & Puff Stuff

B & M Supercharger, Edelbrock 4-barrel carburetor, Edelbrock cylinder heads, tubing headers.

Paul Anderson of Taylor, Michigan had Motor City Flathead create this engine for his 1946 1/2-ton panel truck. Three two-barrel carburetors, B & M Supercharger, Edelbrock heads and Fenton headers.

Excitement! Those zoomies will create exhaust music that's hard to beat!. B & M Supercharger, Offenhauser heads, early style ignition. Photos courtesy Motor City Flathead.

Supercharging: Forced Induction For The Flathead

n 1937 William Lawrence made headlines when he drove a brand-new car across the United States in a record-setting 57-1/2 hours with an average speed of 50.9 MPH. It was the first successful use of an aftermarket supercharger on an American automobile. The automobile was a Ford flathead-powered street rod.

Well, maybe I'm stretching a point, but only a little. Wild Bill Lawrence was a well-known stock-car racer of the day, and the cross-country run was sponsored by the McCulloch Engineering Corporation of Milwaukee to promote their newly introduced centrifugal supercharger. Still, a production car reworked for performance and then driven 3000 miles or so down the highway is a street rod. Right?

The McCulloch supercharger Wild Bill had on his flathead when he drove to victory back in '37 was a "centrifugal" type. Such a blower consists of a single rotor with radial blades on one side. The air/fuel mixture is taken in at the base of the hub and spun around by the blades. The mixture is pulled toward the outside edge of the rotor by centrifugal force and pushed through the outlet into the intake manifold at high velocity. The rotor, spinning from 20,000 to 30,000 RPM when the engine is buzzing along, delivers a fuel-mixture exit velocity of approximately 800 feet per second. That results in a "boost" of about six pounds per square inch (psi) in the manifold over normal atmospheric pressure (14.7 psi at sea level). Unfortunately, the heat generated by all the mechanical commotion in a

Awright, OK! So Bob Whitehead's S.Co.T-blown, Ardun isn't really a flathead! Nevertheless, the Arkansas-based beauty is the epitome of early hot rod forced induction.

centrifugal supercharger causes the pressure output (and net efficiency) to drop.

Enter the Roots type blower, invented by Mr. Roots. (No kidding.) In this design, the air/fuel mixture is caught up on the inlet side by interlocking rotors, carried around the outer edges and simply discharged into the intake manifold. Each complete revolution of

the blower produces four pressure pulses as the rotor tips pass the blower outlet port edge. Don't be confused, it is just an air pump. As such it's really quite simple, and it works very efficiently.

So, without belaboring the merits and shortcomings of the Centrifugal vs. Roots blower, let's just get down to brass tacks. The Roots type is the

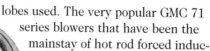

MODEL-39M

MODEL-39F

The McCulloch was the pioneer flathead supercharger. Installation kits were manufactured for the V-8 from 1937 through 1940; they were a pricey $124.50 complete with a dual-exhaust system.

lobes used. The very popular GMC 71 series blowers that have been the mainstay of hot rod forced induction since the early 1950s have three lobes. This characteristic quiets the pulses, but makes it more expensive to manufacture.

GMC superchargers, usually the 3-71 or the 4-71 have been used on flatheads, but mostly for competition purposes. They are large relative to the intake manifold that mounts them, and somehow just don't look "right" on flathead-powered street rods.

What did look right to postwar hot rodders was a small Italian-made Roots-type positive-displacement supercharger built by Italmeccanica. The little blower was a good performer; unfortunately, it was poorly constructed and unreliable. Italmeccanica went out of business in the early 1950s, but an American concern took over the manufacturing facility, redesigned the unit and re-named it the S.Co.T.

It was immediately accepted by hot rodders far more familiar with names such as Edelbrock and Offenhauser than the strange looking acronym or the tongue-twisting "Italmeccanica." The hot rodders re-named it again, calling it the *Scot*. Unfortunately, the cost of the S.Co.T. (about $500 in 1953) dampened their enthusiasm.

The McCulloch was a centrifugal-type blower with water jackets around the impeller housing to help vaporize the fuel. Its major problem was weak bevel gearing that couldn't handle violent acceleration. Nevertheless, Wild Bill Lawrence successfully used it on the V-8 that he drove (carefully!) to a cross-country record in 1937.

Consequently, normally aspirated induction systems continued to reign supreme on the typical flathead-powered street rod.

The "typical" street rodder of today, however, is a bit older and a tad more affluent than the young man of the 1950s. If he likes, he can outfit his flathead with a modern blower, the B & M Roots-type Powercharger that is perfectly suited for today's flathead.

The B & M is not designed to be used as a competition blower; it is efficient at speeds and pressures normally at home on the street. The B & M handsomely helps the small displacement flathead in "breathing" like a much bigger *normally aspirated*

supercharger of choice for most hot rod applications. It has stood the test of time and is considered the more efficient of the two.

Although all Roots blowers function the same way, there are minor differences in the shape and number of

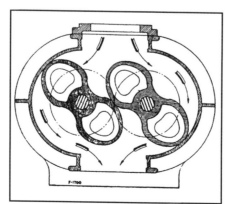

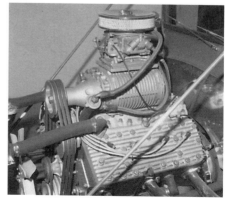

No doubt about it, the Italmeccanica/S.Co.T. huffer, so much desired in the late 1940s and early 1950s, is the one that flathead rodders think of first. The cross sectional view of the two-lobe Roots-type supercharger depicts its inner workings.

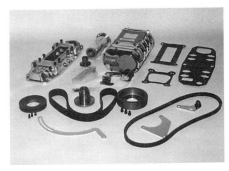

The modern B & M Powercharger is quite similar to the old S.Co.T. and is exclusively distributed by Motor City Flathead. The kit is complete with blower, manifold, belts, pulleys and gaskets. If you want to empower a flathead and to overcome the drawbacks of that engine's basic design, do it this way!

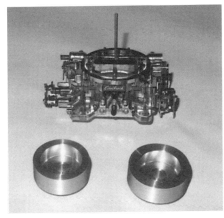

MCF provides a properly set-up Edelbrock 500-CFM carb and all the necessary drive pulleys. The carb will work as is out of the box.

One last pitch for the MCF modified valve-relief job. A supercharged engine is the most appropriate venue for this cylinder block rework. And, don't forget, forged pistons are essential in a blown engine.

overhead valve V-8. Best of all, the compact unit easily installs on a flathead and looks just right.

The street rod powered by a supercharged flathead will have more torque available at all engine speeds and will be very "throttle-responsive." Yet, with installation of the highly recommended manifold vacuum/boost gauge, the driver will note that the pointer remains in the vacuum range most of the time. It will only show a manifold boost from about half throttle upwards. When you do get on it, the manifold boost will rise with engine RPM enough to remind you that your flattie is blown. There may be a millisecond of hesitation if you tromp the throttle suddenly, but I guarantee you won't notice it. A four- to five-psi boost at 3,000 RPM is downright dramatic!

Beyond demonstrable performance, street rodders love the sounds they have come to associate with traditional speed equipment. After all, whoever heard of stock mufflers on a rod? The same goes for the howl of the straight-cut spur gears in a Halibrand Quick Change . . . and the shrill whine of a supercharger.

Except that a little bit goes a long way. I'm sure that the Better Half who accompanies you on your boulevard cruises will appreciate the relatively quiet Powercharger. Although it is a little noisy at wide-open throttle, the Poly-V drive belt system is surprisingly well behaved and quiet.

The B & M supercharger is primarily designed to use a four-barrel carburetor. If, however, you want the traditional look of the early Lakes and

Bonneville racers with a brace of 2-barrels atop a S.Co.T blower, you can have it. A pair of Holley 94s or Stromberg 97s is just as at home on a Power-charger as on an "Edelhauser."

There is a downside, however.

If you *think* you might have eyes for a supercharged flathead, firm up your decision early in the game. Plan on building your engine with a low static compression ratio, custom forged pistons and a tough bottom end. The increase in performance with a B & M flathead supercharger brings with it the potential problem of detonation or knock. The installation of a blower increases the effective compression ratio of the engine about two points at 6 pounds boost. That means if your static compression ratio is 8:1, you're gonna bump it to about *10:1* with a supercharger.

That much compression is incompatible with the low-octane fuels available nowadays. Even a very limited amount of detonation can damage the engine. Not only that, a supercharged engine is *less* tolerant of detonation than is a normally aspirated engine.

The typical street rodder of today is not going to hammer his engine regularly. Therefore, with the boost pressure in the three- to four-psi range, he can get away with a compression ratio of up to 8.5:1. Consider that figure an absolute maximum, and some spark retard may still be needed. My personal favorite static compression ratio is 7.5:1. This opinion is based on the compression ratios of the highly successful turbocharged Porsche road engines.

It is not necessary to build a bullet-proof engine to handle boosts in the three- to five-psi range, just a tough one. Not only do flathead cranks meet that requirement, high loading on crank journals comes from high engine speeds, not high cylinder pressures. The beauty of a blower is that it produces extra power in the mid-RPM range; the motor doesn't have to be spun to the "red line." Besides forged pistons, polished and shot-peened stock connecting rods are adequate with prudent driving. You do, however, need good oil pressure, and excellent

Installation begins with the drive pulley and the steel crank hub and any spacers supplied with the kit. Use thread sealer on these bolts and tighten the bolts evenly. Tighten the intake manifold bolts in the sequence specified in the last chapter to 30 lb-ft. It is important to follow the tightening sequence and torque readings accurately to ensure that the manifold is not distorted. Then install the blower-to-manifold gasket. Make sure that nothing falls inside while everything is opened up!

valves and rings for proper cylinder sealing and oil control.

Traditional street rodders were reared on the "need" for a hot cam. They might find it difficult to accept the fact that the mildest of grinds is darn close to right on when a blower is installed. Cams with too much overlap are detrimental to a supercharged street engine's performance. Usable air/fuel mixture is lost through the tailpipe the longer the exhaust and intake valves are open simultaneously. There is one caveat, however. Supercharger boost pressure acts on the back side of the intake valve, trying to push it open. A blown engine needs stronger valve springs.

The combustion chamber in any engine, much less a supercharged flathead, is important. Not only is there the basic need for piston strength and a low static compression ratio, there is the need to be ever wary of pre-ignition and detonation hot spots. At the very least the builder must smooth off the sharp edges and corners surrounding the valves in the stock block. As discussed earlier, the full traditional relieving is questionable at best—and

best not done at all.

The Motor City Flathead relief, however, which does not weaken the integrity of the cylinder bore really shines here, as do their cylinder-head modifications. If you are seriously considering supercharging your flathead, MCF has head modification down to a science. Don't even consider bolting on a box-new pair of heads until you talk with them.

By the way, standard head gaskets work very well in a typical street rod application.

Carburetion

The installation of a supercharger obviously increases the distance from the carburetor to the combustion chamber, but modifications to the carburetor are usually minimal. My best advice to someone buying a blower kit is to get the recommended carb along with it. That way, you solve all your potential problems before they arise.

If you want to experiment, however, just remember that a richer mixture is usually needed on a supercharged engine to better control detonation. Naturally you want to run an electric

fuel pump. If you decide to run 97s or 94s, you will also need a fuel regulator and a fuel-pressure gauge. Mount the regulator in the line between the pump and the carburetors, and the gauge between the regulator and the carbs. Adjust the regulator to deliver about two psi at idle. Do not install the fuel-pressure gauge in the driver's compartment unless it is electric or unless it has an isolator that keeps fuel in the engine compartment.

A blown engine requires airflow in direct proportion to the engine's displacement. For a five-psi boost in the typical flathead, a total of 500 cubic feet per minute (CFM) is recommended. Vacuum secondaries in four-barrel carburetors are also recommended for street use.

It is always desirable to use the best fuel available with an extra shot of an octane enhancer. Then to be as safe as practical, run the wide-open throttle mixture a little fat (rich).

A water-injection unit (available from Edelbrock and Holley) is often the best way to cure detonation when a blower is installed on an engine not originally built for supercharging.

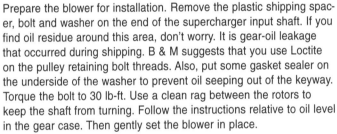

Prepare the blower for installation. Remove the plastic shipping spacer, bolt and washer on the end of the supercharger input shaft. If you find oil residue around this area, don't worry. It is gear-oil leakage that occurred during shipping. B & M suggests that you use Loctite on the pulley retaining bolt threads. Also, put some gasket sealer on the underside of the washer to prevent oil seeping out of the keyway. Torque the bolt to 30 lb-ft. Use a clean rag between the rotors to keep the shaft from turning. Follow the instructions relative to oil level in the gear case. Then gently set the blower in place.

Check the flatness of the intake manifold by placing the supercharger on the manifold and rocking it. If the manifold is flat, the supercharger will not rock. If there is more than 0.010-inch rocking, the supercharger housing may become distorted when it is bolted down. Check this by placing a feeler gauge between the bottom of the rotor housing and the intake manifold. Put white grease on both sides of the blower-to-intake manifold gasket. Tighten these bolts to 5 lb-ft. with a precise torque wrench, and then to 10 lb-ft. Turn the input shaft of the blower as you tighten the bolts. If the manifold is not completely flat there will be an increase in the torque required to turn the blower. If the torque to turn the input shaft is not over 25 in-lb at these tight spots, the Teflon seals will wear in during the first few miles of driving. If the turning torque is over 25 in-lb, then loosen one hold-down bolt at a time to see which one is causing the blower to bind up. Leave this one bolt at a lower torque level, but at least 5 lb-ft while the blower is being run in. Tighten it later when the Teflon has seated. Do not tighten the bolts to over 10 lb-ft or the threads in the intake manifold may strip. Two holes in the idler bracket are used for the mounting bolts for the spring loaded tensioner. The idler assembly should be bolted to the support bracket. Mount the idlers and tighten the screws, but do not use the thread sealer at this time. Be sure the bolts securing the support bracket to the drive housing are also tight. The nut on the threaded rod extending from the end of the idler assembly should be fully tightened to pull the idler all the way in.

The water injection must be carefully tailored to your driving needs because too much can hurt performance. B & M also recommends using a 50-50 mixture, by volume, of water and denatured alcohol. They have found that this eliminates knock without hurting power, as the alcohol will burn, adding power back into the engine while suppressing knock. (One-hundred percent alcohol injection has not been shown to make any significant power difference over a 50-50 mixture, so don't get carried away!) The biggest problem with water injection is that unless you monitor the reservoir frequently, it will run dry when you can least afford it. In cold climates there is a freezing problem, but the 50/50 water/alcohol mixture takes care of that.

Octane enhancers or boosters are a mixed blessing. A few years ago experiments were performed with octane booster additives at San Diego State University. Different brands of additives were added to 92-octane unleaded gasoline burned in a supercharged engine. The octane number of the fuel was measured and in some cases a substantial increase was found. The best was Moroso Two® mixed 16 ounces to 22 gallons of gasoline. A gain of 12.5 octane numbers was found. That's significant, but there's no gain with no pain. Super juice can add more than 50 cents per gallon to your fuel bill!

I've personally tried the El Cheapo brands found in discount auto-parts stores and in general have been disappointed with their performance. I guess it all depends on how much you drive your street rod. If weekend events adequately satisfy your urge to merge

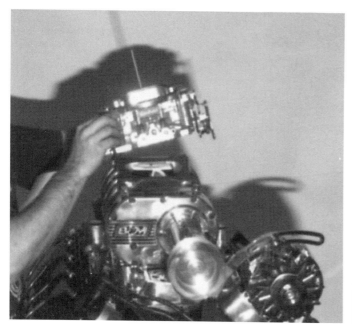

Install the carburetor on the supercharger. Some gaskets have a channel at the back that can cause a vacuum leak. Check the carburetor gasket and spacers that you are using. Be sure that they fully seal both the bottom of the carb and the top of the blower. If there is an air leak between the carburetor and the blower the engine will not run correctly and it will probably run lean. It's a good idea to use a non-metallic spacer between the carb and blower as a heat insulator. Made by several manufacturers, these are available from speed shops and auto-parts houses.

If you were concerned that the blower installation might poke out of your cherry early Ford hood, forget it. As you can see, ol' Henry designed in enough room.

in traffic, high-quality octane-booster additives can be just the ticket. If however, you are a daily wheeler dealer, the cost quickly adds up.

The Ignition System

A vacuum advance unit should be used for all street driven supercharged flatheads for an improvement in both derivability and fuel economy. Getting the right vacuum-advance operation is something of a trial-and-error procedure, however. It can be connected either to the ported vacuum connection on the carburetor or to the intake manifold. Try connecting the vacuum advance to the carburetor first. If you do not experience ping or knock, leave it alone. If, however, you detect part-throttle detonation, switch the connection to the intake manifold; this will reduce the amount of advance at part throttle. If detonation persists, reduce the initial advance.

Spark retard will reduce detonation, but the spark should only be retarded

under boost. More advance is needed at part throttle for mid-range performance and fuel economy. B & M offers an electronic boost-retard unit (#91070) that will retard the timing from 1 to 3 degrees per pound of boost. The manufacturer states that it will work with any electronic trigger ignition system. There are others on the market, but determine their compatibility with your ignition system before you buy.

B & M also reports their in-house tests have shown that dropping the total spark advance back to 25 degrees results in a loss of only 2 percent of power and torque up to 4,000 RPM, and a 4 percent of power and torque at 5,500 RPM. It's a good tradeoff, because there is a considerable reduction in detonation for the small loss in power.

Spark plugs are always a consideration when performance gains are wanted. A blower installation is no exception. A plug that is too hot can lead to pre-ignition under boost condi-

tions, but usually a one-or-two step colder plug is all that is necessary. Here again, making sure there are no exposed threads in the spark-plug holes is critical for the blown engine.

The Exhaust System

Of all the engines ever designed in Detroit, the stock flathead exhaust manifold has to win some kind of prize for inefficiency. Nobody but a 1000-point restorer would ever put one back on. Naturally then, a free-breathing exhaust system is critical when supercharging the flathead, although they do not provide the performance increase that they do on a normally aspirated engine. (That's why "zoomies" are used on supercharged race cars instead of tuned tubes.)

Well, zoomies aren't a good idea on a street rod, but aftermarket or custom-built headers are essential. The traditionalist will no doubt be thinking of the Fenton cast-iron header and fortunately he won't have to go back in

George Chilberg - keeping the old flames alive

George Chilberg has six antique race cars. This champ car has a flathead Ford V-8 with Birner heads and Birner injectors modified with Hilborn nozzles, barrel valve and pump. Car turned 136 mph at El Mirage dry lake and has competed in vintage road race events around the country. Engine is 3-5/16 X 4-1/8, Crower camshaft, Ross pistons on stock rods. Lean back and imagine sticking your foot in the throttle. Feel the noise and acceleration! Chilberg resides in Bonsall, California. The car was completely restored by Bill Ewing. Photos courtesy of George Chilberg.

Birner-equipped engine after being Ewing-ized.

136 mph at El Mirage dry lake!

Before restoration, car in Bruce Johnston's garage in Burbank, California.

time to get a pair; he just has to give Patrick's Antique Cars and Trucks a call!

Instrumentation

There are a few more things to remember when installing a blower on a flathead. One is that you need a boost gauge so that you will know your engine vacuum or boost pressure at a glance. The B & M gauge is designed to be used with their system, and reads 0-30 inches of vacuum and 0-15 psi boost.

Speaking of gauges, a mechanical oil pressure gauge is essential for a supercharged engine. Your engine *must* maintain a minimum of 30-psi oil pressure at idle, and significantly more as engine RPM increases. It may even be preferable to switch from 30-weight to 40-weight oil.

Maintenance

What can you expect in the way of maintenance when you finally get that blown flathead-powered rod on the road? Well, the B & M Powerchargers that MCF sells for flathead use are designed for trouble-free service. About the only thing you have to do is check the oil level in the gear case every 5,000 miles and add SAE 80-90 gear oil when needed. While you're at it, visually inspect the Poly-V belt. It should last at least 30,000 miles in normal use, but replace it if it shows signs of excessive wear on the inside surface or if it is slipping too much. Excessive slippage can be detected by rubber dust collecting on top of the idler assembly.

Bill Ewing - Collector & Restorer

Building a T-V8 roadster when he was in high school in Tucson, Arizona, started Bill Ewing's life-long interest in building and racing hot cars and motorcycles. In 1973 as he was selling some scrap copper, he spotted a Weiand triple in the scrapyard office as he was about to be paid. After a brief negotiation, that manifold was acquired and it began one of the world's premier Ford flathead V-8 paraphernalia collections.

His collection includes one each of every known name manifold and several others not found in any list of equipment manufacturers. And, he has one of every high-compression head for both 21- and 24-stud engines. Then there are at least 20 kinds of ignitions hanging on the wall. V-8 60 equipment is also well represented. When you start talking overhead-valve conversions for the flathead, Bill has owned three sets of Arduns, one set of the rare Dixons and one of only three sets of Arnold Birner heads ever made.

As a restorer/constructor, Bill is famous for his new "old" racecar creations (10 as of 1997), many of which started as small fragments of an original car. Running in vintage events all over the country and at dry lakes and Bonneville speed trials, some are flathead-powered, most are Offy-engined and several have modern engines. He has also built numerous roadsters and coupes for the street rodding scene.

Then there is the reproduction side. Together with Mike Russell over in Southern California, Bill and Mike repopped the FGS manifold and the Davies manifold, an original of which is pictured on page 112. Bill does the machining and Mike handles the marketing side. Because of their reputations for high quality, word-of-mouth through interested collectors sell the small runs before they are completed.

All photos courtesy of Bill Ewing.

Arnold Birner made three sets of these 24-stud heads. This very first set ran on Birner's belly-tank racer at the dry lakes. He made his own fuel injectors, this 4-carb intake manifold, and sandcast pistons with offset pins. Valves are Model A, actuated by Buick rockers. As with the other non-hemi overhead-valve conversions, valve size was severely limited by the flathead's small bore size. Water is taken out at four places along the top of the heads through an aluminum manifold. Exhaust is through 4 squarish ports. Bumps at each end of the rocker cover are for head-bolt clearance.

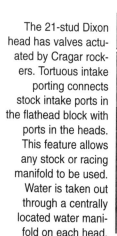

The 21-stud Dixon head has valves actuated by Cragar rockers. Tortuous intake porting connects stock intake ports in the flathead block with ports in the heads. This feature allows any stock or racing manifold to be used. Water is taken out through a centrally located water manifold on each head.

Ewing-built Ardun with highly polished everything. He made his own manifold with alternator mount and a single Holley 4-barrel carburetor.

This 1948 engine resided in Ewing's 1929 real-steel roadster for many years. How many other toothed belt drives with idler and tensioner pulleys have you ever seen on a flathead? Blower is S.Co.T. with two Weber sidedrafts on a Ewing adapter. Heads are Osikei with reversed water manifolds. Engine is 3-5/16 X 4, Jahns pistons, Isky 400 Jr. camshaft, Vertex magneto and Weber flywheel.

13

Modern Flathead Ignitions and The Rest of the Electrical Story

When it comes to flathead distributors, some enthusiasts find themselves between a rock and a hard place. Many (including myself) find the "two-cap" distributor that was used during the early 1940s most attractive. Mounted way down low in an almost-secret place with the plug wires coming up from the nose of the engine, it has a streamlined, "no-nonsense" look about it. Today, the early distributor is as good as any as a starting place for modern electronic technology. However, its location out of vision and accessibility does prevent a quick glance at its innards for troubleshooting.

The later-model distributor is often more appealing to the street rodder accustomed to an accessible unit he can readily service. Not only that, the front and top mount conventional distributor is wide open with regard to all sorts of upgrades. He can install a dual-point conversion in the stock housing, or he can install the fine aftermarket dual-point Mallory distributor. He can also have a breakerless (no points) Mallory outfitted with either the magnetic-impulse triggered or the Unilite, the Stinger or the Multiple Spark Discharge (MSD).

The flathead rodder indeed has a full plate. He can also install an early distributor on a late block, or a late distributor on an early block by swapping and modifying timing-gear covers. He simply has to weigh the pros and cons of each style within the framework of what he is most comfortable with. In the case of the 8RT, I ultimately chose

A superior ignition system is demanded by today's street rodder. That means modern electronics for the traditional flathead.

function over form and stuck with the late-model "post-hole" distributor.

I surely didn't have to waste any psychic energy on chosing the *means* of creating the spark of life for the 8RT. I knew what I wanted going in—electronics. But let's not get ahead of the game.

At this point, I would be remiss if I did not at least mention yet another alternative—the magneto. It is true though, that most street rodders won't have any trouble choosing between a battery ignition and a magneto. The battery will win hands down. Still,

there are some who will put up with the shortfalls of the flathead mag (hard starting, for one) just to say they have a mag on the end of their flathead. More power to 'em, and that's just what they will say in defense of a mag!

Another of the problems with a mag, however, is that it uses ignition contact points. And you don't have to visit every dealership in town to know that breaker points have gone the way of the generator . . . into the relic pile.

Hold on now, I know there are those who would lift an eyebrow at that seemingly contradictory statement.

Pictured here is the long-gone Harman & Collins mag. There was a time when the self-contained magneto was considered the ultimate ignition. Unlike a battery-powered system, the voltage output curve closely followed the engine's horsepower curve. That is, the voltage increased as RPM rose. Unfortunately, some magnetos did not have a built-in advance mechanism. Others, particularly the Swiss-made Vertex, used a cam-actuated advance mechanism. The Vertex mag is available from Speedway Motors. Photo courtesy Bob Whitehead.

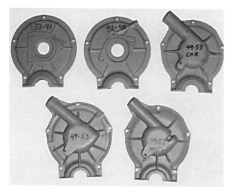

Several timing-gear covers were produced through the years for all the many flathead applications, but you are most likely to run across one of these. The top three, 1932-41, 1942-48 and the 1949-53 passenger car covers are cast-iron. The bottom two are die-cast aluminum. The 1932-41 cover was a 3-bolt design, and the distributor used two parallel caps. The 1942-48 was a 2-bolt design and used the well known "pancake" or "crab" distributor. Unfortunately, the bundled plug wires in the early models sometimes create crossfire. The 1932-48 distributor is driven directly off the nose of the cam, and the 1949-53 distributor is gear-driven from a gear on the nose of the cam.

No, it's not the invasion of the body snatchers, or even the flathead snatchers, it's just a pair of Echlin coils mounted on the cylinder head. Dual coils were extremely popular when battery ignitions were used during the heyday of the flatmotor. Distributor is a Harmon-Collins, photo courtesy Bob Whitehead.

After all, doesn't the whole darn flathead engine belong in the relic pile? Well, yes and no, but you don't have to throw the baby out with the dirty bath water. The flathead is the traditional hot rodder's baby, but contact points are the bath waters of modern ignition systems.

Coils for the flathead battery ignition, just as in any OHV ignition, are available in many high-performance guises. But there are differences. The street rodder is best advised not to experiment. Use the coil the distributor manufacturer recommends for compatibility and best results.

The same is true of primary ignition leads—the plug wires. The thicker 8mm wire has been the choice of high-performance enthusiasts for several years now, and that is what I chose. Be advised, however, that a compatible wire loom and distributor cap is necessary. Many manufacturers offer these, just be sure to verify compatibility before you buy anything. And don't be concerned if you favorite old ignition is still in working order, but limited to 7mm wire. The thinner wire is fine for normal street use.

The final consideration in the ignition system is the lowly, but critical spark plug. Spark and flame travel is the essence of lively performance. Unfortunately, the flathead is prone to detonation, that is, self-ignition or

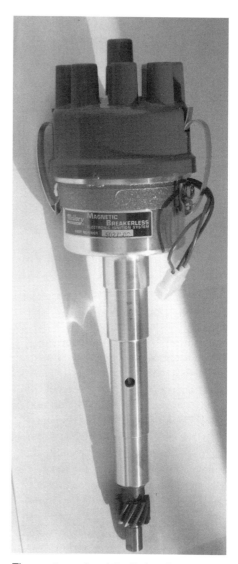

The most popular of the flathead post-type distributors was, and still is, the Mallory. This is their "Magnetic Breakerless" model for the 1949-53 engine. Patrick's Antique Cars and Trucks includes the drive gear (shown here) at no additional cost. He also has all of the Mallory tune-up and service parts as well as matching Mallory coils for their electronic and dual-point distributors.

spontaneous combustion. During normal combustion, the spark plug ignites the fuel/air mixture and the flame races out from the point of ignition across the combustion chamber, building pressure and temperature as it goes. In the flathead, the spark has to climb out of a hole into a poorly designed combustion chamber. These are real problems for any plug including the traditional street choice for decades, Champion's H-10. Well, step aside,

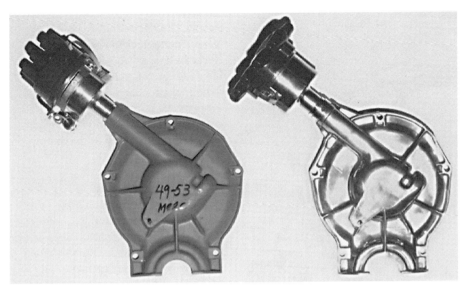

The 1949-53 distributor hold-down is on the 1949-53 cylinder head. The guy who wants to put 1948 and earlier style heads on his block to max out the traditional look loses this feature. Motor City Flathead modifies the late-model die-cast timing gear cover (usually found on Mercury engines). That cover has an extra distributor-shaft-stabilizing boss at the bottom of the cover. MCF machines the top of the cover where the distributor goes in and press-fits a collar around the outside of the housing. The collar locates and secures the distributor in the correct position. A set screw holds the distributor secure after the engine has been timed. The reworked gear cover can be installed with the factory gasket and seals. MCF will, *on an exchange basis,* rework a customer's cover.

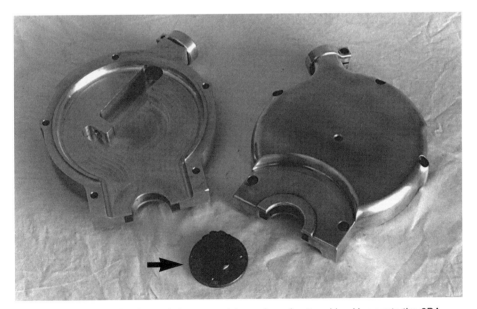

Cornhusker's milled-aluminum timing cover (shown here front and back) mounts the 8BA distributor to the earlier 59AB blocks and provides a collar to secure the distributor. An adapter gear is available to add a distributor drive gear (arrow) to the four-bolt camshafts.

Patrick Dykes invested a great deal of time and effort working with Mallory to develop a new 12-volt magnetically triggered distributor. Except for the coil, they are completely self-contained, requiring no power module. The early style is available for 2- or 3-bolt mounting. Note slotted holes for adjusting ignition timing. Bill Fisher photos.

If your ignition has a vacuum advance, make sure it is working. Vacuum advance provides a big advantage for the street-driven engine, especially for economy and cooling. Always use a timing light to check whether your ignition is set correctly. A lot of flathead overheating is strictly due to running with a retarded spark.

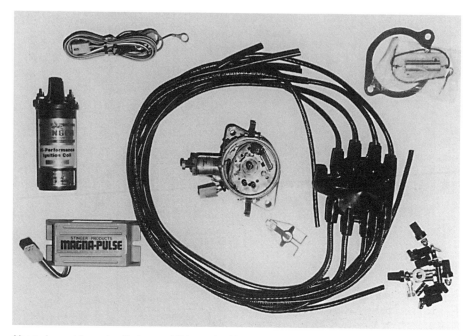

Not to be outdone, Leslie Long of Stinger Ignitions developed his own version of an electronic spark-maker for both early- and late-model flatheads. Indeed, the flatmotor enthusiast's cup runneth over with modern upgrades!

Arnold. The Motorcraft® AL-7 is a worthy contender to the throne. Nevertheless, as with many aspects of hot rodding, the practicing street rodder should document his trial-and-error forays into the world of high-performance ignition. His efforts will eventually pay off in maximum efficiency.

Producing The Energy

Okay, I've already denigrated the stock flathead generator. Yet, I know there are die-hard traditionalists who will want to stay with Henry's dynamo. Perhaps, just so they can wrap one of those good-looking stainless-steel or chromed covers around it. If that's your bag, at least consider a conversion to 12 volts, negative ground. You can buy a 12-volt generator, or get the stock 6-volt unit converted by installing 12-volt field coils in the case.

The rodder with a taste for the modern, however, will choose an alternator without hesitation. Most popular is the 70-ampere, one-wire (no-voltage-regulator-required) G.M. unit. Most flathead engine builders and parts resources have just the right ticket, another reason to build an extensive library of catalogs.

The Fuel Pump

This brief discussion of the need for an electric fuel pump could have just as easily been fitted into the chapter on induction; but after all, it is one of the electricals. No matter. Any of the name brands, Carter, Holley, etc. will do the trick. Just don't forget that their normal output of about six pounds of line pressure is far too high for early two-barrel carbs. A fuel-pressure regulator set at two pounds is mandatory. If you are using a small four-barrel carburetor you can experiment with higher pressures.

Turning It On and Over

Unlike the stock generator, there's no viable alternative to the stock starting motor. No problem though, every city of consequence has a starter/generator rebuilding shop. Visit the one nearest you with your starter in hand. New brushes and

A row of ignitions. Left to right we see a VECO Dynamag with Wico magneto, a pair of Lucas 4-cylinder distributors with linked advance, a Pounden Wico magneto, an aircraft mag adapted by Pounden, a no-name dual-coil distributor, Mallory distributor and finally a Roof distributor/tachometer drive with a Nash Twin-8 distributor for the Roof dual-plug heads. Ewing collection.

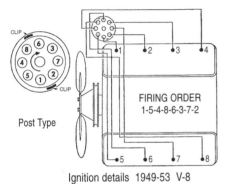

Post Type

FIRING ORDER
1-5-4-8-6-3-7-2

Ignition details 1949-53 V-8

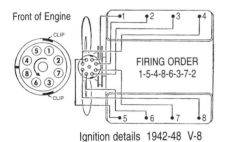

Front of Engine

FIRING ORDER
1-5-4-8-6-3-7-2

Ignition details 1942-48 V-8

Mallory housing with Stinger Conversion. Sinking the distributor and approximating the timing on the late-model flathead is simple enough. Align the rotor with No. 1 spark plug wire terminal in the cap, and drop it in with No. 1 piston on the compression stroke. Use a hex wrench to tighten the set screw (Arrow 1) on a modified timing cover. Later, when the engine is in the car and the accessories have been installed, recheck. The timing pointer (Arrow 2) must be aligned with the mark on the crankshaft pulley in addition to the above before attempting to fire the engine. Then start the engine and precision set the timing with a light.

bearings will put you in business, and don't worry about the 6-volt/12-volt conflict. When it comes to starters, either is fine, but of course a 12-volt, negative-ground system is preferable in any but a restored car.

And that about winds it up, folks.

Construction of the 1932-48 direct-drive distributor is such that the advance is pre-set by the manufacturer. However, there are aftermarket parts that allow adjusting the timing on the 1932-48 distributor. The Offenhauser Quick-Set Ignition Lead Plate is shown in the Flathead Buyers Guide Chapter 15.

Here is a fine example of where a picture is worth a thousand words. This full-dress Edelbrock-equipped MCF flathead highlights the quintessential nostalgic engine with a modern flair. It also shows off several pieces of ordinarily nondescript, but critical hardware—their wire looms and coil bracket for starters. The bracket is a polished stainless-steel number that tidies up the front of the intake manifold. Another type is used with a blower installation where space is at a premium.

By virtue of the spark plug location, wire looms are critical to the engine's performance. Traditional wire looms mount on top of the intake manifold and interfere with multiple carburetion, progressive linkage and the necessary fuel lines. Beyond that, they simply can't be used on a supercharged engine. The universal MCF 8mm loom comfortably fits both early and late series engines with all the accessories. Note Patrick's Mallory distributor between the polished pulleys at the front of the engine. Finally, speaking of accessories, the alternator is the popular GM one-wire type mounted on beautiful polished-aluminum bracketry. Photo courtesy Motor City Flathead.

It has been said that only the most diehard traditionalists still use a generator. I think that's true, but there's still a place for the old dynamo. And that's right up in your face mounted off to the side of an engine with multiple carburetion! The only real problem with the old generator is that it only produces 6 volts. New 12-volt generators can still be purchased, or the existing 6-volt unit can be converted by installing 12-volt coils in the existing generator case. This is a Patrick Dykes specialty. Pat also reminds us that unlike an alternator, a generator will charge a *dead* battery!

Installation and Fire-Up

For all practical purposes, you have now built your flathead; I hope the book has fulfilled its promise. The goal of your endeavor, however, was not to sculpt a visual piece of mechanical art destined to languish under plastic in the corner of your garage. Your engine is a street rod *power plant*. As such, it is time to consider its installation in a chassis, an appropriate drive train and the initial fire-up.

There are street rodders who love the flathead and the cars in which they came. Nevertheless, they have not-so-fond memories of replacing early Ford transmissions, U-joints, axles and drive shafts. In the early days of street rodding, a mildly "suped" engine rarely gave up the ghost, but boy, everything connected to it did! There are modern replacements that are far more durable. Not only that, because they are discretely out of sight, they do not interrupt the traditional flavor of early street rodding.

Yet, there are many who profess a willingness to take their chances with the 1939 floor-shift transmission or the 1940-48 side-shift transmission and 1940-48 running gear. With that in mind, I will limit my discussion of engine swapping to stock-bodied cars on original or close-to-original reproduction chassis with an early-Ford drive train.

Admittedly, a flatmotor installation is not an engine swap in its truest sense. The typical Ford-based street rod came in with a flathead. If it exits your garage with a rebuilt flathead

Dropping a flathead back into an early Ford should be a no-brainer, right? Not always. There are a few things the street rodder should be aware of. Jim Bremner's Forty swallowed an 8BA nice 'n' easy, but only after he modified the radiator and installed 1948 truck water pumps.

from the same series, you haven't *technically* swapped engines. However, install any engine other than a series engine, and you are swappin'! If so, here are a few things you should be aware of.

The 1928-31 Model A: First off, because the four-banger used completely different motor mounts, new front motor-mount supports must be fabricated and welded to the frame rails. Next, it is impractical to try to

First things first. Although all bolt holes should be "chased" early in the game, if you forgot those at the exhaust ports, run a clean-up tap through them now before putting the engine in the chassis. When you are buying studs and brass nuts, remember that the exhaust mounts with two different sizes.

use the Model A transmission (the bolt pattern is different), so install the V-8 engine and transmission as a package. That means rear mounts also have to be fabricated.

A universal tubular cross member (available from street rod chassis shops) can be welded into the frame, or bolted to mounts welded or bolted to the frame. A second tubular cross member can be similarly installed mid-ships for the transmission. A platform can be welded onto the cross member to provide a support for 1946-48 Ford type rubber-insulated transmission mounts. A better method, however, is to use an aftermarket X-member because it adds rigidity to the frame and body assembly, and still permits easy removal of the transmission.

You'll have to make a recess approximately 3 inches deep by 11 inches wide at the lower edge of the firewall to accommodate the engine bellhousing.

Trial-fitting the headers now is easier when you can get at the nuts. Dykes' rejuvenation of the traditional and beautiful (and quiet!) Fentons will fit with no problem. But no matter how carefully constructed, tubing headers with multiple flanges usually have to be tweaked slightly to get them on.

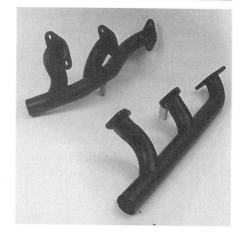

O.K., I'm not going to tap-dance here. *I do not recommend the use of the original early Ford 3-speed transmission in a street rod with even the mildest flathead.* If you want to shift for yourself, get a 1964-1973 Ford 4-speed "top-loader" tranny. This transmission is different from most modern passenger car 4-speeds in that it is serviced through a large removable access cover on the top of the case. Thanks to the fact that the transmission was later retrofitted with a top-side gear selector for use in Jeep utility vehicles, older units can be converted with a selector assembly available from Jeep dealers. (See *Street Rodder Magazine*, December 1990 for conversion details.)
For the gearheads among you, the ratios are as follows:

	1st	2nd	3rd	4th
Wide Ratio:	2.78	1.93	1.36	1.00
Close Ratio:	2.32	1.69	1.29	1.00

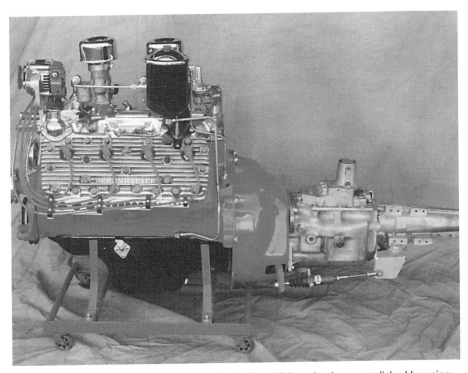

Mounting the 4-speed transmission on the back of an 8BA engine is accomplished by using the 1949-53 cast-iron bellhousing or the full-coverage stamped-steel bellhousing. Starter plates are not interchangeable, so whatever you use, get all matching parts. Photo courtesy of Steve French.

You'll also find that the left cylinder head interferes with the steering box, so a new setup is in order. Street rodding is like that—modification never ends. Change one thing, and you'll have to change something else. You might thumb through HPBooks' *Street Rodder's Handbook* for a few ideas.

Flatheads need plenty of cooling capacity, and even a repro Model A radiator can't be expected to get the job done. Besides, you need two inlets and two outlets; so a heavy-duty, pressurized custom radiator is in order. So is one of the slim aftermarket electric fans, as you suddenly find out you filled the engine hold!

The Early V-8 (1932-34): Obviously, flathead swapping gets much easier when you're dealing with a frame originally fitted with one of Henry's green V-8s. The big problem in the 1933-34 is the limited room between the engine and the front crossmember.

There are several different accessory-drive arrangements, but some are impractical to try to use in the early V-8 chassis. The 1932-41 engines used

The third possibility is the abbreviated stamped-steel bellhousing and an Offenhauser aluminum adapter plate. Offy adapters are numerous, you could even install a Chevy transmission if you like!

No shortage of aftermarket flywheels, either. Speedway Motors and Centerforce undoubtedly have what you need. Make sure you get the right pressure-plate bolt pattern, however.

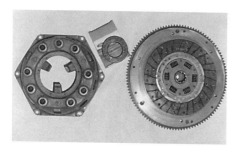

Why? 'Cause there's more than one pressure-plate bolt pattern, that's why. FoMoCo still has original clutches, too. Some of you may recall that the 1949-53 Merc used the same 10-inch Borg and Beck pressure plate and bolt pattern as the early 1950s Chevy. The "big-spline" clutch disc is a Ford dealer item as it was used on pickups through the early 1960s (PN B7C7550A). Beyond that, aftermarket concerns such as Centerforce can make up custom applications. Check 'em out.

a single 5/8-inch belt to drive the water pumps and the generator-mounted fan. The 1942-48 Ford and Merc, and 1949 Ford engines used a double 5/8-inch pulley and an idler. Engines in 1949-53 Mercs and 1950-53 Fords used a 3/8-inch and a 1/2-inch belt arrangement with an idler pulley for the generator and fan.

If a 1949-53 engine is installed in the 1933-34 frame, use the 1948 truck water pumps and the 1949 Ford double pulley. However, the front pulley has to be cut off to clear the early-chassis spring U-bolts.

The Early V-8 (1935-38, 1939 Standard and 1939 Pickup): The only real headache confronting you here is the slanted radiator, but a radiator-mounted electric fan normally covers that base. Again, 1948 truck water pumps take care of the front motor-mount problem on the 1949-53 block.

The Pre-war V-8 (1939 DeLuxe, 1940 Passenger Car and 1940-41 Pickup): Installing the 1946-48 engine in this chassis is a snap. If you want to use the original 1939-40 generator, crankshaft-mounted fan and pulley, just exchange them for the double-belt crank pulley and idler. Otherwise, use the two-belt setup.

If you are going to use the 1949-53 Ford/Merc engine, again bolt on the 1948 truck water pumps and the 1949 Ford dual wide-belt pulley. Occasionally the stock fan must be trimmed to clear the upper radiator hoses. The radiator, of course, has to be modified for the smaller hoses.

You're pretty much home free in the remaining models of passenger car and pickup. Make no mistake about it, though, in all cases, you can't beat the electric fan. There's plenty enough room to mount it on the leading side of the radiator in all models from 1939 DeLuxe on. Alternators, of course, will require custom bracketry for any installation, but don't forget the special generator brackets Offenhauser still manufactures for multiple carb installations.

Big-spline trannys use this clutch-release bearing (PN COTZ-7580-A). The smaller-spline top-loader uses a standard Ford Long-style clutch-throwout bearing. And always use new clutch bolts.

The Last Holdout for the 1939-48 Ford Transmission

If questioned closely, the tradition-bound street rodder will admit that his affinity for this transmission, either the stick or the side shift, is primarily because Lincoln Zephyr gears can be installed in the case. Well, Zephyr gears are occasionally available from one or another antique-parts emporiums . . . if you are willing to pay the price. Most who are interested in a cog swap, how-ever, already have the gears.

The larger question is not where you can get them, but what is this mystic within a mystic based on? That is, what is the true effect of Zephyr or 1942-48 Lincoln gears in the early Ford transmission?

To hear some old timers talk, you'd think the gears alone were worth addi-tional horsepower. Not so! No trans-mission gear has any effect other than changing the ratio between engine RPM and road mph in first or second in the three-speed gear box, or first, second and third in a four-speed box. First and second gears in the standard pre-1949 Ford-Merc transmission were 2.82:1 and 1.60:1 respectively; corresponding ratios for the type "26H" (1942-48) Lincoln 25-tooth gear cluster are 2.12:1 and 1.44:1. Because the parts

are interchangeable, the Lincoln clus-ter can be installed in the Ford case to give the latter set of ratios.

The real advantage of these gears is that they let the street rodder wind his flathead out further in first and second. He gets higher usable road speeds in the gears and a more gradual wind-out. A flathead-powered street rod capable of 5000 RPM with large rear tires and 3.78 rear-end gears can hit 40 MPH in first and 70 MPH in second with a stock transmission. But man, he can go better than 50 and 80 MPH with a 25-tooth Lincoln cluster! Don't forget though, his true rate of acceleration is *less* at any given road speed with the Lincoln gears because the torque mul-tiplication is less. They don't do a thing for acceleration times unless there is a traction problem and less torque multi-plication gives a better bite.

For practical street work, however, Lincoln gears do offer a subtle advan-tage. They are "close-ratio" gears—that is, the ratio spread between any two speeds is in the range from 1.20:1 to 1.50:1. Such a low gear ratio is useful coming out of slow corners at 30 MPH or so, while a quick down-shift to sec-ond adds a bit of punch in the 50-70 MPH range.

The big *disadvantage* of any early

Clutch linkage is a problem unique to your own engine/trans/chassis combination. As such it may require a unique approach. Some folks like mechanical linkage, others find hydraulic slave units more accommo-dating.

Ford Motor Company gears (beyond the lack of synchromesh on low gear) is that they are old. Very old! Use them at your own risk. At the very mini-mum, have all steel transmission parts Magnafluxed before the box is built. Eliminate as many potential problems as you can as soon as you can.

Still, I just can't forget that the last time I ran an early Ford transmission behind a torquey flathead. I could push the cluster right through the bottom of the case any time I wanted . . . if I did-n't twist a drive shaft or rupture an axle keyway first! That's why I think a thoughtful, modern street rodder should give some serious consideration

I'm here to tell ya, nothing is quite as simple as an automatic transmission adaptation! Sure, you could bolt up the Mercury Liquamatic Drive introduced in the 1942 models. Yeah, sure. I'm not even going to buy into any of the 1949-53 automatic offerings. If you're hell-bent on a restoration, fine. Just don't saddle a street rod with one. The Ford C4 automatic transmission from 1971 or later with the 26-spline shaft is the way to go for flatheaders who want to give that left leg a rest, particularly in the cramped quarters of 1937 and earlier cars. Gene Benson of Automatic Transmission Specialties in Salem, Oregon has done all the hard work for you. Gene has a Flat-O-Matic conversion for any of the 1932-53 engines, the V-8 60 and even the Lincoln V-12. However, the abbreviated stamped-steel bellhousing sure works well with the 8-BA engine. All conversion kits include the flex plate, torque converter, aluminum adapter, hardware and complete installation instructions.

to an optional drive train from the crankshaft rearward. I've covered the best choices in the accompanying photographs.

The Moment of Truth: The Start-up

Most of us will fire the engine for the first time within the confines of the car that it will power. That means the starting and ignition system must be properly wired at the very least. It is not absolutely necessary to have the cooling system functional, though. A garden hose connected to makeshift plumbing can get water into the engine, but usually this is more messy than it is worth. Most rodders are well aware that anything can go wrong, so why install and then have to remove the radiator? Once the engine makes smoke and fire for a few minutes, it can be shut down and the radiator put in place.

Installing the flathead power package in a modern street rod frame is a whole new ball game compared to the days when more-or-less stock suspension was used in a more-or-less stock chassis. For instance, when a 1949-53 engine is installed in a stock 1933-34 frame, 1948 truck water pumps are used along with a 1949 Ford double pulley. Then, the front pulley has to be cut off to clear the early chassis spring U-bolts. However, install something like a Mustang II independent front suspension in any of 'em (as Jim Bremner did in his '40), and you may well have to do some independent front line thinking! But that's another story for another book.

In most cases some sort of electric fan is going to make life easier. Aftermarket types abound, but Bremner uses a homemade adaptation incorporating a belt-driven aftermarket fan, early generator mount and stock pulleys.

Would that we all had the luxury of a mobile engine test stand! However, few of us build or swap motors with such regularity that the time, effort and expense of building one could be justified. Still . . .

I can't say the same for the exhaust system. Because muffler shops don't make home calls, the car has to be trailered to the worksite, or driven there with open exhausts. I would be a liar if I said that I had never done the latter, but don't. No need to re-live every phase of our youth; borrow or rent a trailer. You definitely want quietness for the first time you listen to your engine run.

When you are sufficiently certain you can fire the engine, i.e., the battery is fresh, there are 5 quarts of 30-weight oil in the pan, and there is fuel delivery . . . stop. Remove the distributor cap and wires, then the spark plugs. You want to check out two systems simultaneously—the starting circuit and the oiling. You can do this by yourself; but a friend standing ready to lend a hand is more than worthwhile.

With the transmission in neutral, spin the unencumbered engine over, all the time keeping an eye on the oil-pressure gauge. Don't grind on the starter more than 10 seconds at a time, and allow 30 seconds between spins. Have your buddy check for fuel and oil leaks. As long as everything seems okay, continue until you see an oil-pressure reading in the 30-psi range. At

that point, stop and replace the plugs and ignition wiring.

If your ignition timing is on or even close, and everything else is functioning properly, the next few spins should fire the motor. If not, verify ignition and fuel delivery just the way you were taught in your high school auto shop class. The flathead, even a hopped up one, is still a very basic and simple engine. Trouble-shooting is a straightforward matter.

If, however, the engine fires, but makes some Gawd-awful noises, localize their origin as quickly as possible. This is the best reason to complete the exhaust system before you get down to the nitty gritty of firing a fresh engine. You need to be able to listen for any unusual problems.

Now, I don't want to borrow trouble, or build a mind-set for failure. So I'm not going to make a laundry list of all the things that could possibly go wrong. Every nut, bolt and component could conceivably fail. (Thirty-three of the best and most affluent racing teams in the world are on the starting line the morning of the Indy 500. Rarely do all 33 fire-up immediately upon Mrs. Hulman's command!)

We're going to assume, then, that

your engine fires without hesitation. Great. Shut it down and complete the assembly of the cooling system before you go any further.

That done, you can do the initial break-in. You want about 20 minutes running time right there in the garage. Hopefully the car is in an area where water spillage won't be a big problem. If not, move it. Put a garden hose in the radiator fill neck with the lower petcock open. You want a trickle of cool water going in and a trickle of warm water coming out. You want the engine to "normalize," that is, reach about 180F running temperature and stay there.

Fire up the engine again, and this time (as best as you can) check for water leaks.

Let the engine fast idle for five minutes, then goose the RPM up to 2000. Let it settle down for five minutes, then goose it again. When you have repeated this procedure for about 20 minutes with no apparent problems, shut it down and retorque the heads and manifold. Now you can finish the engine installation, charging system, etc., and the car if necessary. The next time you fire it up, you want to drive out of your garage.

Most of us will fire the engine for the first time within the confines of the car that it will power. After an initial break in at home and final tuning for roadworthiness, the real break-in takes place on the street. Put several hundred miles on the engine, varying the RPM as you do. That is, accelerate, then decelerate as traffic permits. Getting on and off the freeway at one mile intervals is a great way to do this. Prudence dictates that you stay in your own neighborhood, however. After about 200 miles of this, your rings should be seated and the engine broken in. Change the oil and filter, and start enjoying your labor of love.

The Flathead Buyers' Guide

The years 1946 through 1954 were the undisputed heyday of the street rod flathead, but as you have seen in this book, the old girl is alive, well, and getting better! Nevertheless, the high-performance equipment manufacturers and vintage-parts purveyors who cater to the flat-head market have dwindled down to a precious few.

This is not a baleful lament for the good ol' days; it is just the opposite. It is a tribute to the precious few who have hung in there through the lean years when flatheads were, to put it mildly, on the back burner. Guys like Edelbrock, Iskenderian, and Offenhauser, never forgot that Henry Ford's brain child started them down the road to financial success.

It is also a recognition of manufacturers who are newer on the scene, those who have taken up the mantle to nurture the flathead into the next century. Guys like Tony DiCosta, Patrick Dykes, Mark Kirby, Tony Baron, *et al*, also risked capital in the start-up of businesses catering to a market that many would charitably call *small*.

Without them, the resurrection and restoration of the Ford flathead V-8 would be a moot, futile pursuit.

* * * * *

Andersen's Race and Restoration
3027 Jefferson Street
San Diego, CA 92110
619/295-1106

New and used flathead parts and equipment and hard-to-find driveline components.

Antique Auto Parts, Inc.
9113 East Garvey Ave.
Rosemead, CA 91770
818/288-2121
Catalog

Gene Scott, the opinionated but lovable Grand Master of Street Rodding, started the chassis components industry in the late 1950s. His present-day shop dominates a block or more in Rosemead, and he usually has some of everything. If you need a flathead or just a part or two, do yourself a favor and give him or Jim Gordon a call early in your search. They manufacture Sharp intake manifolds.

Antique Auto Parts' engine stand adapters for 60 and 85 HP Ford & Mercury engines attach to exhaust port bolt holes.

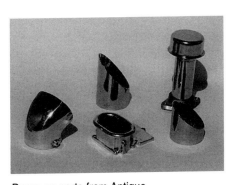

Dress-up parts from Antique.

K & W engine lifter from Antique Auto Parts locks into block after removing manifold, adjusts to balance engine with or without transmission.

Automatic Transmission Specialties
2195 Commercial St. NE
Salem, OR 97303
503/364-6194

Proprietor Gene Benson has perfected the adaptation of the Ford C4 automatic tranny to the flathead block. His Flat-O-Matic is a unique and extremely popular product.

Ford C4 transmission adapted from automatic transmission specifications.

Baron Racing Equipment
19935 Redwing Street
Woodland Hills, CA 91364
818/702-0043
Catalog available

Tony Baron's dad Frank designed and built a 4-carb intake manifold for flathead racers back in 1948. Tony now precision machines his own version of an eight holer with the choice of Weber carburetion, throttle bodies for nitro, or electronic fuel injection. With appropriate induction, it is ideally suited for the street rodder or the nostalgia racer. Tony also offers ignition systems, cylinder heads, and racing main caps and girdles.

Baron manifold with fuel injection.

Cylinder heads are 3-1/2 inches thick!

Cross-bolted girdle and heavy-duty main caps.

BC & Sons Fabrication
361-D Oak Place
Brea, CA 92621
714/529-0907

Specialized machine work for street rod projects including flathead adaptations.

BC & Sons Fabrication

Centerforce Clutches
2266 Crosswind Drive
Prescott, AZ 86301
520/771-842?
Catalog available

Bill Hays originally made his mark in the hot rod world building clutches and flywheels, as his Centerforce Company does today.

Cornhusker transmission adapter.

Classic Motorbooks
P.O. Box 1
Osceola, WI 54020
800/826-6600
Catalog

Here's where you can find every imaginable auto book that is currently in print, including the one you hold in your hands. All of the Fisher Books, Flat Out Press, Don Montgomery's, and Ron Hollearn's books are available from Classic Motorbooks. Dean Batchelor's American Hot Rod is the classic book describing the early days of hotrodding. It is a must-read for any hotrodder worthy of the name.

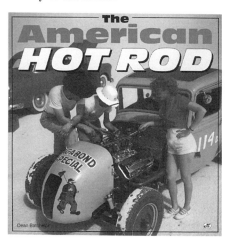

Cornhusker Rod & Custom, Inc.
R. R. 1, Box 47
Alexandria, NE 68303
402/749-1932

Gary Mussman makes beautiful flathead pieces, including custom mounts for A/C compressor and alternator, 348-409 Chevrolet V-8 water-pump adapters, and a milled aluminum timing-gear cover to adapt the 8BA top-mount distributor to the earlier 59AB engines. His adapter to put the T-5 GM 5-speed overdrive transmission behind the flathead is shown below. This converts the drive train to open drive. These transmissions come in some Camaros and Firebirds and in the S10 and S15 pickups and Blazers.

Dan's Garage
38805 E. Benton Road
Temecula, CA 92592
909/699-9039

An early Ford restoration buff, Dan Krehbiel has been on the street rod scene for many years. He has accumulated (and sells) flathead engines and parts.

* * *

The Eastwood Company
P. O. Box 3014
Malvern, PA 19355
800/345-1178
Catalog

Eastwood's great catalog is a dream book for car enthusiasts. Whether it is a special tool, heatproof paint or whatever, they're sure to have something you need. Get their catalog!

* * *

Edelbrock Corporation
2700 California Street
Torrance, CA 90503
310/781-2222
Catalog available

The street rodder with a feeling for tradition would be hard pressed to come up with a name with a longer continuous history in his hobby/sport than Edelbrock. The company goes back to the late 1930s, is still family-owned, and has not forgotten its roots.

Super Dual Manifold for 1938-48 includes a generator bracket (not shown).

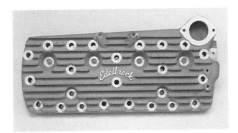

Heads have rugged internal and external ribbing. Available for both versions of the 24-stud engine.

Edelbrock heads are made of T-6 tempered 356 aluminum alloy and are extremely rugged with both internal and external ribbing. They are available for both versions of the 24-stud engine. A compression ratio of 8:1 assumes the block has a 3/16-inch base relief and a stock bore and stroke. The ratio increases approximately three tenths of a point with each additional 1/8-inch over the stock stroke.

Edelbrock's Super Dual Manifold for the 1938-48 flathead includes a generator bracket. Brackets are also available for the 1940-41 engine and the 1942-48 engine.

* * *

Egge Machine
11707 Slauson Avenue
Santa Fe Springs, CA 90670
800/866-3443
Catalog

Egge is a leading supplier of pistons and rings, especially for older vehicles. They offer 4-ring replacement pistons up to 0.125-inch oversize. 3-ring pistons are available in 0.125 and 0.250 oversize for stock 3-3/4 stroke and 4 and 4-1/8-inch strokes. These are permanent-mold T-6 alloy, solution heat-treated pistons. They also offer all of the other internal parts for the flathead: valves, lifters, springs, gaskets and complete rebuild kits.

Elgin Cams
53 Perry Street
Redwood City, CA
415/364-2187
Spec sheet available

If you need an authentic Harman & Collins or Winfield cam grind, Dema Elgin has all of the H & C masters and the Winfield masters. His flathead cams have durations from 248 through 280+ degrees and lifts from 0.302-0.364 inch. Higher lifts and longer durations are available. To make sure you get the best-possible grind for your application, he asks for an information sheet on your engine. Then he may be able to suggest something that will work even better. Dema also grinds stock cams.

* * *

Fisher Books
4239 W. Ina Road, Suite 101
Tucson, AZ 85741
520/744-6110

In addition to this book, the Fishers (Bill and Howard) have produced several other dandy automotive books, including a repop of *California Bill's Ford Speed Manual* from 1952, and repops of Roger Huntington's *Souping the Stock Engine* and *How to Hop Up Ford & Mercury Engines* from 1950 and 1951, respectively. Their *Automotive Upholstery Handbook* is essential for the person wanting to do upholstery. You can buy these books at bookstores, speed-equipment dealers and Classic Motorbooks.

See Fisher Books on previous page.

Flathead Jack
P.O. Box 31175
Walnut Creek, CA 94598
510/932-2233
Catalog available

Jack Schafer manufacturers hard parts and appearance accessories for the flathead. Photo below shows some of his polished-aluminum pulleys.

Flat Out Press
P.O. Box 66874
Portland. OR 97290-6874

Al Drake has written the finest historical book ever on dry lakes time trials from 1930 through 1950. *Flat Out* allows you to relive and understand what our early hero-enthusiasts were doing: the equipment they used, how they overcame problems and how they got results. All of the famous names and their cars are in this book, especially the early makers of speed equipment.

Another book from the same author and press is *Hot Rodder! From Lakes to Street* (an oral history). This is the first history of hotrodding from the '20s to the '90s as told in the participants' own words. Interviewees included Bill Kenz, Eldon Snapp, Burke LeSage, Bill Edwards, Karl and Veda Orr, John Riley, Vern Houle, Jack Henry, Ken Jones, Rolla Vollstedt, Len Sutton, Joe Bailon, Bob Kaiser, Roger Huntington, Peter Sukalac, Henry Gregor Felsen, Keith Peters, Larry Purcell, Dee Wescott, Dave Juhl and Stan Ochs. There's a whole chapter on Bonneville.

I guarantee that when you pick up these books you won't put them down until you have read the whole thing. They are that good!

Fuel Injection Engineering Co.
25892 Glenwood Drive
Aliso Viejo, CA 92656-1520
714/360-0909
Catalog available

The first and foremost mechanical fuel injection for a flathead racer—the Hilborn—is still available from the source.

Garage Art
P.O. Box 9902
Brea, CA 92622
Catalog available

Poster-size reproductions of flathead line art, early street rod and dry lakes photographs.

* * *

Hail's Automotive Machine Shop
648 W. Williamson Ave.
Fullerton, CA 92632
714/871-2054

Allen Hail's shop specializes in antique and classic engines as well as providing all other machine-shop services.

Hail's Automotive

Ron Holleran
P.O. Box 241
Chester, VT 05143

Ron's book *Nostalgia: Rebuilding and Modifying the Ford V-8*, covers many of the points in the book you are holding. He also he offers unique insights into carburetors, porting and relieving and special exhaust-port modifications which have never been published anywhere else that I know of. He emphasizes correct parts combinations for street rods and circle-track racing.

Hot Rod and Custom Supply
1304 SE 10th Street
Cape Coral, FL 33990
941/574-7744
Catalog available

Tony DiCosta's establishment has been building flatheads and supplying a full line of parts since 1982. His alternator bracket to mount the GM alternator to a flathead and other parts are shown here. A completely HC&RS equipped engine is on page 55. Tony also has special engine tools to help the flathead builder.

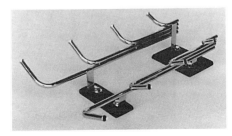

HR&CVS stainless wire looms.

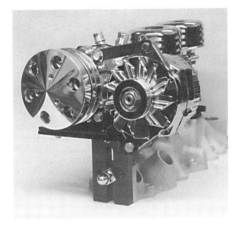

A/C compressor mount for Sankyo or Sanden is available in three versions to fit any flathead. HC&RS.

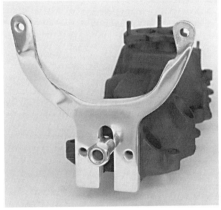

Alternator mount for use with three deuces for 49-53 engines. HC&RS.

Iskenderian Cams
16020 S. Broadway
Gardena, CA 90248
213/770-0930
Catalog available

Ed Iskenderian's love affair with the flathead camshaft is a well documented story. The starting roster may have slimmed down a little since the late 1940s, but there's still plenty of choices for both the street rodder and nostalgia racer. See table of current camshafts on page 56.

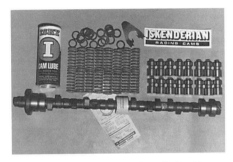

Iskenderian camshaft with installation kit.

The venerable Camfather and a devoted fan (the author) back when the fan's waistline was a tad slimmer.

Jahn's Pistons
1360 N. Jefferson St.
Anaheim, CA 92807
714/579-3795

This is the oldest west coast piston company still stocking pistons for the flathead. Their 3-ring racing pistons are available in bore sizes from 3-3/16 through 3-1/2 inches for strokes from 3-3/4 through 4-1/4 inches. Their 4-ring replacement pistons (shown below) are available in overbores and strokes as shown in their catalog sheet.

Mallory Ignition
550 Mallory Way
Carson City, NV 89701
702/882-6600

Everyone knows the Mallory name because it has been synonomous with top-quality ignition products for over 60 years. Their machined aluminum 1949-53 flathead distributors are available with conventional points, UNILITE phot-optic infrared L.E.D. and magnetic-breakerless self-contained electronic ignition. All are for 12-volt systems.

Don Montgomery's Hot Rod Books
636 Morro Hills Drive
Fallbrook, CA
619/728-5557

A serious hotrodder from 'way back when, Don's hotrod history books capture the essence of the way it was. Two of his books that are of most interest to flatheaders are shown here: *Authentic Hotrods* and *Hotrod Memories*.

No. 5 Of The Series

C.W. Moss
402 W. Chapman Ave.
Orange, CA 92866
714/639-3083
Catalog available

"C.W. Moss" is a retail store that displays Vintique Reproductions to the public. Harold Looney, a major player in the rehabilitation of early Fords, owns both enterprises. Upon the many shelves of original and reproduction parts, sits the most unusual hot rod dress-up items ever. And they weren't even originally designed for cars! The tear-drop shaped aluminum Thickstun dual carb and cylinder head covers were marine items, but you know how those roadster jockeys were in the old days. If you want to add some real finned flash to your flathead, the Thickstuns are just the ticket.

(Hey, it's your cake, you baked it. Put on the icing you find most tasty!)

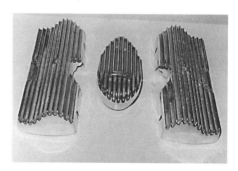

Motor Arts
P.O. Box 9902
Brea, CA 92822
Catalog available

Take it from me, there are two things that are difficult to do with a flathead. One is to move it around your garage (the stocker weighs more than 600 pounds). The other is to hoist it up with those delicate finned aluminum heads bolted on. Motor Arts' solution is the Motor Roller and the Flat-Lift. The Roller bolts to the exhaust flanges; the Flat-Lift bolts to the intake manifold deck and can be adjusted for the semi-complete engine, or the engine with transmission. Motor Arts also sells ring-squeezer sleeves for a tidy installation of the piston assembly. Photo below.

Motor City Flathead
13624 Stowell Road
Dundee, MI 48131
313/529-3363
Catalog available

MCF hardly needs any further introduction than the preceding pages, a work in which the company played a major role.

Custom *avant-garde* machine work is just one of their specialties.

* * *

Navarro Engineering Company
4212 Chevy Chase Dr.
Los Angeles, CA 90039
818/241-6644
(Spec sheet available)

Barney Navarro is, without a doubt, a true legend in Bonneville and Dry Lakes flathead racing. If you're looking for heads or manifolds, drop him a line.

* * *

Offenhauser Sales Corporation
P.O. Box 32218
Los Angeles, CA 90032
213/225-1307
(Catalog available)

Even those only remotely interested in motorsports know that the company's motto "The Greatest Name In Racing" is well deserved. Most street rodders are aware that the low-key, present-day Offenhauser Corporation is related to the famed Indianapolis 500 engine, but they're not quite sure how. The traditionalist street rodder does know, however, that the Offy outfit manufactures today's most prolific line of flathead armament. Think I'm putting you on? Just look at the catalog. You'll find scads of intake manifolds and heads for the 1939-48 engine, the 1949-53 engine, *and* the V8-60. To say nothing of critical accessories such as linkages, fuel blocks, generator brackets, gaskets and transmission adapter plates. I'm gonna show you some of their wares, but I don't want to tease you any further about the Offenhauser family tree.

Harry Miller, a man of great imagination, designed a racing engine in the mid-1920s. He was helped by two fellows who kept Miller's imagination within practical limits. Miller's able assistants were his shop foreman Fred Offenhauser and draftsman Leo Goossen. Miller went bankrupt in 1933 and two years later, Fred Offenhauser started to build the four cylinder, twin cam engines on his own for oval track racing. That's when and why the Miller engine came to be known as *the Offy*. The business took off like Gangbusters, and Fred soon brought in his young nephew, a machinist, to work for him. That's where it gets a little confusing—the nephew's name was also Fred Offenhauser!

After World War II, Uncle Fred became interested in the Novi V-8 engine and sold the Offy four-cylinder engine to Louis Meyer and Dale Drake. Nephew Fred, well aware of the burgeoning hot rod movement, started his own company (Offenhauser Equipment Corp.) on National Boulevard in Los Angeles. His first advertisement appeared in the October 1948 issue of *Hot Rod Magazine*. Today, Nephew Fred's son, Fred "Tay" Offenhauser, Jr. is the hands-on president of the company. Okay, 'nuff history. The Offy manifold flathead line-up includes Super Dual and Triples for the 1932-41 engine, the 1942-48 engine, and the 1949-53 engine. All are available with generator brackets. On "Super" manifolds, carbs are spaced farther apart than on "regular" manifolds. However, there is a regular Dual for the 1949-53 engine. Offy also has a Single Four Throat manifold for the 1932-48 and 1949-53 series.

Three-carb manifold

As if that isn't enough, Offy has aluminum high-compression heads for 1939-48 and 1949-53 engines.

Offenhauser's Quick Set Ignition Lead Plate was originally designed for the 1932-48 competition engine. The Lead Plate makes ignition lead changing simple, quick and easy. There is no

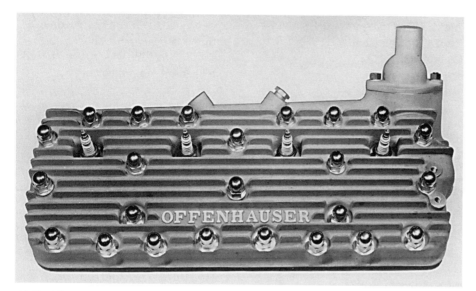

1949-53 head

Racecars in Retrospect
P. O. Box 3116
Alliance, Ohio 44601
330/823-6167

Jeff Martin specializes in rebuilding Chandler-Groves and Stromberg carburetors, What more do I need to say? He also offers complete 2- and 3-carb setups with stainless-steel fuel lines, oval air cleaners, alternator brackets and main-bearing-support kits. One of his set ups is shown below.

possibility of upsetting the synchronization of the magneto or distributor, yet the lead can be advanced or retarded in a matter of seconds. They are available for the 1942-48 2-bolt-style distributor and the Harmon & Collins magneto.

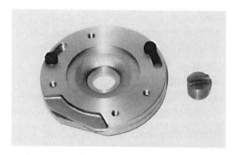

Quick set ignition lead plate

Don Orosco
10 Harris Court, Suite C-2
Monterey, CA 93940
408/649-0220
Catalog available

Photos of Ardun conversion kit, Eddie-Meyer manifolds and Smith heads are on page 86.

* * *

Patrick's Antique Cars & Trucks
P.O. Box 10648
Casa Grand, AZ 85230
520/836-1117
Catalog available

If a guy had to depart this veil of tears with only one legacy, I'll bet that Patrick H. Dykes would be hard pressed to come up with something better than his resurrection of the classic Fenton cast-iron header . Just look at how gracefully they adorn the flatheads pictured throughout this book. Patrick's is more than just headers, he distributes nearly everything flathead from acorn nut covers to Zephyr transmission gears. Not only that, he imagineers a new product every few months.

Another of his outstanding creations is the 1932-48 crab-type distributor made exclusively for him by Mallory Ignitions. It is available in both points and electronic types and is completely self-contained, requiring only an external coil. Patrick also has Mallory distributors for the 49-53 models and matching coils for both dual-point and electronic distributors.

* * *

Patrick's 1932-48 distributor.

Red's Headers
5832 Gibbons
Carmichael, CA 95608
916/488-4532

Red Hamilton has been bending header tubes to fit Henry's flathead for more than 20 years. He also has a full machine shop specializing in vintage engines, and is a distributor of all major brands of flathead equipment.

Ross Racing Pistons
625 S. Douglas
El Segundo, CA 90245
310/536-0100
(Catalog available)

The latest production item from this company is a faithful reproduction of Art Sparks' original forged flathead racing piston. Offering maximum strength and minimum weight, they are machined for all stock size rings. The top ring land is 0.280-inch from the crown to accommodate relieved blocks. They are stocked in 3.312, 3.42 and 3.375-inch bore sizes, but custom pistons can be made in two to three weeks.

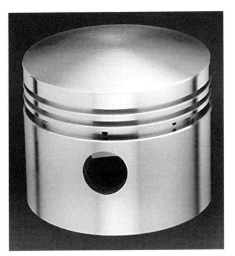

Roto-Faze Ignitions and Equipment
23136 Mariposa Avenue
Torrance, CA 90502
310/325-8844

Joe Panek is a busy fellow. He not only has a 1949-53 flathead distributor in his line of high-performance ignitions; he turns out precision steel-billet camshaft blanks in his custom machine shop. Serious nostalgia racers and inventive street rodders now have the opportunity to try out some of those exotic grinds they have been thinking about.

Roto-Faze distributor

Schneider Racing Cams
1235 Cushman Ave. #14
San Diego, CA 92110
619/297-0227
(Catalog available)

Schneider has been one of those low-profile purveyors of critical parts that those of you not on the West Coast may have overlooked. If so, you missed out. The company has more than 30 different grinds available for the flathead. If you give them a call, they'll send you a descriptive sheet.

* * *

Sihilling Metal Polishing
1018 E. Chestnut St.
Santa Ana, California
714/543-7051

Charlie Sihilling has continued the family tradition, metal polishing, *par excellence.* All aluminum components on my own 8 RT, as well as its cast-iron Fenton headers were polished by Sihilling. Nowhere is meticulous as well as superb metal polishing so critical as it is on delicate flathead components.

* * *

Speed-O-Motive Products
12061 E. Slausen Road
Santa Fe Springs, CA 90670
310/945-2758

A long time source for flathead stroker cranks and engine balancing. Call for current availability.

* * *

Speedway Motors
300 Speedway Circle
P.O. Box 81906
Lincoln, NE 68501
402/474-4411
Toll Free Fax 800/736-3733
(Catalog available)

Bill Smith's Speedway Motors is the nation's largest distributor of all manner of flathead equipment: cams, pistons, manifolds, headers, dress-up items, you name it. He's been putting the good stuff into the hands of street rodders and racers for more than 40 years. Not only does the company offer proprietary cams, valve springs and wire looms Helmsman Smith is currently reproducing Eddie Meyer manifolds.

Stinger Ignitions
2266 Crosswind Drive
Prescott, AZ 86301
520/771-842?
Catalog available

Bill Hays and Leslie Long have a racing association that goes back to the 1950s, so it wasn't surprising when they joined forces in the early 1970s to design and produce electronic ignitions. Originally called Hays Ignitions, it became Stinger Ignitions as operations expanded. Now Leslie and Bill have put their heads together again, this time to bring modern technology to the old spark makers. The crab-type ignition is built on a stock base; the 1949-53 model uses a Mallory foundation.

VEO Products
1000 Piner Road, Ste. G
Santa Rosa, CA 95403
707/576-0218

Just say "nope" to rope. That's what the folks at VEO Products say about their new 360-degree front pan oil seal. It fits all 4-cylinder and 8-cylinder 1928-53 Fords, and promises no friction, no leaks and no wear. See photo on page 75.

* * *

Bob Whitehead's
Vintage Acquisitions
7 Robin Lane
Bella Vista, AK 72715

Publisher of the *Flathead Dream Book,* a compilation of early flathead advertising.

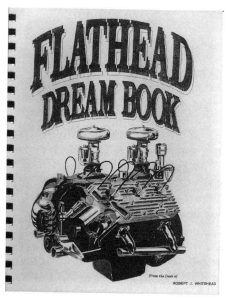

Stinger distributor

Kenny Kloth - Bonneville Record Setter

Nine years at Bonneville, plus intensive hard work with diligent study and experimentation has enabled Kenny Kloth to set several records. His 1949 Mercury coupe currently holds "X" Class (old engines) records in Production Coupe & Sedan at 140.551 mph and Unblown Altered at 145.360 mph. Best one-way time in 1994 was 148 mph. Lots of flathead-powered roadsters can't get close to these speeds.

Never content to let others do the work, Kenny used his Superflow flow bench to prove that the best flow was obtained with a mere 5.8:1 compression ratio. The cylinder heads started out as unmachined castings. He designed the masters for his roller camshaft and constructed his own roller lifters. He machined his block and built special tools to allow installing 1.550-inch-diameter Crower Chevrolet V-8 style springs with 100 lb. seat pressure and 400 lb. at maximum lift. Valves are set the old-fashioned way by grinding the valve stems to the desired clearance.

Car uses Goodyear Frontrunner tires pumped to 70 psi on all four corners. Moon discs are standard wear on Bonneville cars. This is the dress for Production Class (XF/PRO), complete with bumpers, seats and horn! Kenny uses a Jericho transmission after seizing up two highly modified Muncie transmissions. Rear end is a 9-inch Ford.

Engine in the car, ready to roll. Large air cleaner has flexible hose connected to a cool-air inlet at front of car.

267-cubic-inch engine on dynamometer. A large exhaust balance tube connects the two collectors on the 1-5/8-inch headers. Offenhauser head castings were extensively modified to work with Ross flat-top pistons flush with the block deck. Kloth-designed roller camshaft has 0.510-inch lift on the intake and 0.410 inch lift on the exhaust. Ignition shown here is an HEI GM distributor, but an Electromotive crank-triggered ignition is also used. Ignition advance is 35 degrees. An Offenhauser four-barrel manifold has an added 1-1/2 inch height at the center. Carburetor is a 650-cfm Holley 4150 double-pumper.

All of the Mobil 1 5-30 oil is routed from the engine to an Oberg oil filter fitted with an adjustable pressure relief valve (with gauge) to set the pressure. The relief valve in the pump is removed and blocked. Oil returns to the engine through the fuel-pump-pushrod hole. Adapter plates on end ports are used with special porting for better exhaust flow.

Motor City Flathead - Flatheads to go!

A visual feast! Note that all of the two- and three-carburetor engines have fuel pressure regulators, and many have a fuel-pressure gauge on the fuel block. Many thanks to Mike Kirby for taking the time and spending spending the money to make these MCF-built engines photo-ready and have them professionally photographed. Photos courtesy Motor City Flathead.

1949-53 dressed with pre-49 heads. Edelbrock dual manifold and heads, full-flow oil filter, tubing headers.

Offenhauser-equipped, Edelbrock four-barrel carburetor, full-flow oil filter, tubing headers, power-steering pump.

Dual-carbureted late engine with Offenhauser equipment, full-flow oil filter, Fenton headers.

1949-53 engine with early heads, Edelbrock heads and manifold, three carburetors, full-flow oil filter, tubing headers.

Index

A

adjustable tappets 53, 55, 74
airflow 45-49
    engine's CFM requirement 120
    tests 48
    related to valve size 54
Alexander, Colonel 6
    manifold 108
align-honing cylinder block 36
alternator 128, 130
aluminum alloys 33
AmPro block cleaner 26
Anaheim Balance Shop 37
Anderson, Alan 37
Anderson, David 5
Anderson, Paul 116
Andersen's Race & Restoration 139
Antique Auto PArts 16, 139
Atkinson, Wayne 7
ARDUN cylinder head 68, 86, 117
assembly bench 77
Athans, John 4
author biography vi
automatic transmission 135, 139
Automatic Transmission Specialties 139
A/V-8 6, 131

B

balancing rotating and reciprocating
    mass 37
Baron Racing Equipment 36, 58, 98,
    139, 140
Baron, Tony 5, 36, 58, 98, 139-140
Batchelor, Dean 10
BC & Sons Fabrication 140
bearings, camshaft 43, 72
bearings, connecting-rod
    measuring clearance 82
    full-floating 3, 81, 85
    installation 80
    side clearance 82
bearings, main 43, 63
belly tank 4
bellhousing removal 15
Bertrand, Pierre "Pete" 7
Birner overhead-valve conversions 123,
    124
block, see cylinder block
block cleaning methods
    alkaline electrolytic immersion 23, 25

    mild hydrochloric acid dip 23, 25
    thermal 23
    AmPro 26
B & M 11, 44, 116, 119, 124, 129-132
Bohn Aluminum Co. 5
bolts, cylinder head 103-104
bolt sealer 103
Bonneville Salt Flats 7, 45
Bradley, John 70
breather tube 15
breathing, see airflow
Bremner, Jim v, 8, 17, 62, 137
Bruce, Earle 44
Bug, The 5
Burke, Bill 4
Burns, Dave 7
bushing, see valve guide
buyers guide 139
buying a block 13

C

Cagle, Clark 13, 23, 24, 39
California Bill's
    Hotrod Manual 32
    Ford Speed Manual 141
Charles, Casey 9
camshaft
    bearings 22, 37, 62
    degreeing 73
    duration 56
    gear removal 20
    gear 54, 72, 75
    installing 72
    Iskenderian 52, 56
    lift 56
    lobe size 47
    long-nose 71
    Motor City Flathead 52, 56
    removal 20
    selection 45, 51
    short-nose 71
    specifications 56
    "walk" 76
carbureting supercharged engine 120
carburetor linkage 113
caustic soda hot tank 24, 26
Centerforce Clutches 140
center main girdle 36
Chandler-Grove carburetor 107, 115
channel relief 49

Chilberg, George 123
Childs & Albert gapper 78
circlip, piston-pin 80
Classic Motorbooks 140
clearance measuring
    main bearing 82
    piston-to-head 101
    rod-bearing 82
    rod side 82
    with clay 100
    with Plastigage 82
clutch 134
clutch linkage 135
collectors 14
combustion 46
combustion-chamber volume 47, 97
compression ratios 48, 50, 103
connecting rods 33
    alignment 35
    assembly and installation 77, 80-82
    cleaning 79
    measuring clearance 82
    rebuilding 35, 79
    removing 18
    torque 82
cooling system 90
cope-and-drag casting method 30
core-sand residue 25
"core-shift" block 29
Cornhusker Rod & Custom 95, 127, 140
corrosion, internal 17
cost-effectiveness 29
crank pin protectors 81
crankshaft
    balance
        factory 37
        internal 38
    chamfer oil holes 28
    cleaning 30, 60
    cradle 60
    end play 43, 65
    final assembly 66-67
    gear 63
    grinding 34, 35
    identification 31
    installation 63
    kit 33, 85
    Motor City Flathead 31
    offset in block 3
    oil slinger 63, 75

parting lines 29
plugs 28
pulley 17
reconditioning 34, 35
selection
sleeve 63, 75
stroking 29, 30, 32, 33
trial assembly 63-65
cross-bolted center-main girdle 36, 140
cylinder block
align-honing 36, 63
boring 29, 36
buying 13
center-main support 36, 64
cleaning 59
"core-shift" 29
corrosion, internal 17
cracks in 13, 24
decking 34
deck surface angles 33
derusting 33
designations 20, 21
girdle, center main 36
history 2
honing 36
identification 20, 21
inspection 23
military 20
pressure testing 27, 28
reconditioning 29
selecting 13
surfacing 34
washing 59
cylinder-bore distortion 29
cylinder-bore taper 32
cylinder head
aftermarket 50, 97-90
bolts 103-105
bolt pedestals 103
compression ratios 48, 50
doming 99
early on late block 101
gaskets 102-104
hardened washers
installation 97-105
milling 97, 101
pocketing 99
porosity 99
removal 17
sealer 103
studs 104
torquing 104-105
used 98

D
Dan's Garage 141
DeSaxe Principle 3, 77
Detroit News 4
DiCosta, Tony 55, 139, 142

displacement 29, 32
distributor types 16
Dixon overhead-valve conversion 124
drilling lifter bores 37
Drake, Albert ii, 142
Dykes, Patrick 123, 127, 132, 139, 146

E
Eastwood Co., The 141
Edelbrock 7, 97-98, 103, 107, 119, 141, 149-150
Egge Machine 141
electric fan 137
Emley, Scott 35
engine
assembly bench 77
fire up 136
installation 131
stand adapters 16
types and designation
assembly
engines used in book 21
Evans, Earl 97, 106
evolution of flathead V-8 1
Ewing, Bill ii, 109, 112, 124
Excelsweld USA 27
exhaust
header 4, 123, 132
manifold 14
expansion rates 32
exploded views
camshaft and valve train 21, 71
crankshaft with associated parts 85
oil pumps 88
valve assembly 71
water pumps 94

F
factory crankshaft balance 37
fan, electric 138
Federal Mogul Thermo-Flow heads 97
feeler gauge 76
Fenton headers 8, 69, 116, 122, 123, 125, 132, 150
firing order 129
flame travel 31
Flathead Jack 140
Flat Lift, Motor Arts 15
Flat Out Press 142
flywheel 15, 134
Fisher Books 141-142
Ford Engines
Bearing Data 42
Configurations 10
General Specifications 10, 41
Service Bulletin 12
Valve Specifications 41
Forties Limited Club 14
Frame, Fred 6

fuel injection
Algon 112
Hilborn 3, 123, 142
Motor City Flathead 113
Holley 69
fuel, low-octane 119
fuel octane increasers 121
fuel-pressure 110, 120, 128
gauge 120, 149-150
regulator 110, 120, 128, 149
fuel pump 128
pushrod hole 84
full-floating bearings, see bearings, full-floating
flywheel removal 15

G
gapping piston rings 78
Garage Art 142
gasket surface renew 34
gear timing 20-21, 54, 71-72, 75
generator 128, 130
girdle, center-main 36
grinding crankshaft 34. 35
Grubbs, Jim 26

H
Hail, Allen v, 19, 23, 33
Hail's Automotive Machne 19, 23, 33, 142
Harmon & Collins
cams 141
magneto 70, 126
header, exhaust
Heli-Coil 23
Herbert, Bill ii, 69
Hilborn, Stuart 3
history of flathead 1-12
Holleran, Ron 143
Holley
Chandler-Grove carburetor 115
fuel injection 69
Homrich, Jim 30
Hot Rod & Custom Supply 55, 143
Hotrodding, early 6
hot tank, caustic soda

I
ignition system
designer 3
distributor swapping 125
Hayes Stinger 128
magnetic-impulse 125
Mallory 125-126
Patrick's Mallory 127, 130
points 125
Indianapolis 500 6
induction system 107
installed height, valve spring 74

intake manifold, see manifold, intake
introduction iii
Irontite Products 40
Iskenderian Cams 51, 52, 56, 143
Iskenderian, Ed 51, 52, 56, 143

J

Jackson, Kong 69
Jahn's Pistons 144
Johnson adjustable tappets 53, 55
Jordan, Greg 7

K

K & N 108, 109
Kirby, Mike v, 8, 23, 31, 45, 77, 87-90,
    98, 107
Kloth, Kenneth 149
Kong cylinder heads 69
Kraft, Dick 5
Kurten, Jim 7

L

Lawrence, Bill 117
LeJuerrne, Richard 149
lifters 53
    adjustable 53, 55, 72
    bores, drilling 37
    bores, grinding tops of 38
    chamfering edge 54
    installing 73
    removal 20
lifting tool 15, 139, 145
Lincoln Zephyr gears 135
lock ring 20, 72
Loctite 60, 79, 82
Looney, Harold 91

M

machine work 33
Magnafluxing 14, 17, 23, 27, 35
measuring thrust clearance 65
main-cap
    bolts 65
    studs 64
    support 36, 64, 83
Mallory Ignition 125-127, 144
manifold, exhaust 14
manifold, intake
    Alexander 108
    Almquist 108
    Battersby 108
    Burns 111
    Challenger 109
    Dixon 112
    Eddie Meyer 86, 110
    four-barrel 115, 132
    Freiman 109, 112
    Harrell 110
    Hexagon Tool 6

installation 114
    Ken-Rich 112
    Miller 3, 6
    Offenhauser 108, 111
    Roof 112
    Sharp 109
    Super Indusco 109
    Thickstun 11
    torque sequence 115
    Weiand 110
McAfee, Jack 7
McCloskey, Mike 7
Melling oil pumps 88
Mercury Engines
    Bearing Data 42
    Configurations 10
    General Specifications 10, 41
    Valve Specifications 41
    4-inch crank 30
Meyer, Eddie 7
Miller, Ak 45
Miller, Eddie 3
Miron, Andy 37
monobloc design 2
Montgomery, Don 144
    Hot Rod Books 144
Morrison, Ed 7
Motor Arts 16, 79, 145
Motor City Flathead 31, 87, 116, 129-
    132, 145, 149-150
Motor Roller 15
Moss, C.W. 91, 144
Mushroom-tipped valves 21
Mussman, Gary 95, 127, 140

N

Navarro, Barney 97, 145
Navarro Engineering Co. 97, 145

O

Offenhauser, Fred 97-98, 103, 107. 108
Offenhauser Sales Corp. 32, 145
oil baffle removal 20
oil filter
    full-flow system 87-92
    stock 16
oil-gallery plug 72
oil pan
    clean-out 88
    gaskets 91
    install 84
    seals 75, 91
    truck 88
oil passage cleaning, crank 30
oil-pressure relief valve 84
oil-pump
    idler gear 84
    install 84,
    long-body 88

pickup 88
    removal
    screen 90
    short-body 88
oil relief-valve assembly 15
Ord, Mal 7
Orosco, Don 86, 146
Orr, Karl 7
Osborne, Allen 11, 96
overbore 29
    limits 29
overhead valve conversions 6

P

painting engine 61
Patrick's Antique Cars 126, 127, 146
parts, see Buyers Guide 139
performance 29
Permatex 61, 102
pickle fork 71
piston
    aftermarket 29, 32
    assembly 80
    head clearance 101
    replacement 33
    sizes
    speed 31
    types
piston pins (wrist pins) 32, 80
    bushings 35
    offset 32, 33
    weight 33
piston rings
    compression 77
    end gaps 78
    expander tool 80
    installing 80-82
    oil-control 77
    sealing 29
    sleeve 82
    thickness 77
Plastigage 59, 79, 82
plug, oil-gallery 61
porting 45, 51
port size 50
Potvin, Chuck 7
pressure plate, clutch 134
pressure relief valve, oil 84
pressure rise, during combustion 97
pressure testing cylinder block 27, 28
private collectors 14
pump, water, see water pump
pushrods 53
pushrod, fuel pump 84

R

Racecars in Retrospect 146
reaming cylinder ridges 18
Redi-Strip Derusting 17, 23

Red's Headers 147
reliability 29
relief 45, 50
relief valve, oil 15
reinforcement, main bearing 64
removing
    cam bearings 22
    connecting rods 18
    core sand 25
    oil pan 18
    oil-pump idler gear 19
    oil pump idler-gear shaft 19
    pistons 18
relieving 45, 50-51
    factory relief 55
Ricardo, Harry 46, 49
ridge reamer 18
Riley, George 6
ring compressor 79
Roof, Robert 106
rope seals 65, 91-92
Ross Racing Pistons 147
Roto-Faze Ignitions 147
Russell, Mike 11, 124

S
"safety checks" 82
Schalk, Paul 45
Schmidt, Bill 8
Schneider Racing Cams 147
Scott, Gene ii, 72, 139
seal
    rope 65
    neoprene 75
    VEO Products 75
seeper 98
Sharp, Al 97
Sheldrick, Laurence 4
side-valve design 2
Sihilling Metal Polishing 147
Silv-O-Lite 29
sleeve, piston-ring installing 81
Smith, Dewey 14, 21
Smith, Terry 27
Sorenson, Charlie 2
Southern California Timing Association
    (SCTA) 6
    Racing News 7
Spalding, Tom 7
spark advance 50
spark plug
    shrouding 101
    threads 99
Sparks, Art 7
speed equipment 6, 9
Speed-O-Motive Products 147
Speedway Motors 102, 110, 113, 115,
    148
stackable-core casting method 30

stainless-steel, types 53
starter removal 15
STP 61
streetrodding, modern day 8
Stinger Ignitions 148
stroking, see crankshaft, stroking
Stromberg carburetor 107-108, 110,
    111, 113, 115
stud puller 17
studs, cylinder head 104
superchargers
    B & M Powercharger 11, 72, 116,
    118-120, 124
    centrifugal 117
    Ford T-Bird 69
    Frenzel 11
    GMC 118
    installation 121
    Italmeccanica 118
    McCulloch 117-118
    Roots type 117-118
    S.Co.T 117, 118
supercharging 117
support, main-bearing cap 83

T
tappet, see lifters
tappet adjustment 74
Tattersfield-Baron 4
Tattersfield, Bob 97
Thacker, Tony 10, 97
thermostat 96
Thickstun, Tommy 7
TRW 29
telescope gage 32
tetraethyl lead 55
thermal cleaning 26
timing gear 75
timing cover 19, 91, 126, 127
top center, finding 95
top-loader transmission 133
torque 29
torque output table 32
torque cylinder heads
    sequence 105
    values 105
turbulence 50
thrust bearing flange clearance 65
thermostat, 96
timing cover
    pointer, timing 95
    seal 75
timing light 95
timing marks 95
tools 59

U
unleaded gas 54
Usrey, Ron 25

Utah Salt Flat Racers Association
    (SFRA) 7

V
vacuum advance, with supercharger 122
valve-guide retainers 19, 71
valve, oil-pressure relief 84
valve seats 39
    grinding 39
    replacement 39
    and unleaded gas 54
valve springs 53
    closed-coil ends
    heavy-duty 53
    installation height 73-74
    pressure
    seats 74
    shims 73
valves
    adjustment 76
    big 54
    Chevrolet V-8 52
    clearance under head 101
    composition 53
    lift 48
    removal 19
    size 50
valve train
    component selection 45, 71
V-block 35
VEO Products seal 75
Victor Gaskets 91
vintage parts dealers 14
Vogele, Tom v
volumetric efficiency 45, 47, 97

W
washers, cylinder-head-bolt 103
water injection 120-121
water pumps
    Chevrolet 95
    exploded views 94
    installation 96
    removal 17
    types 90, 94-95
Weiand, Phil 7, 97
Whitehead, Bob 68, 107-110, 117
Williams, Ron ii, 57
Winfield, Ed 7
Winfield
    carburetors 112
    cams 141
wrecking yards 14
wrist pin, see piston pin

Z
Zoerlein, Emil 3